DIAGNOSIS FOR ORGANIZATIONAL CHANGE

THE PROFESSIONAL PRACTICE SERIES

Working with Organizations and Their People:
A Guide to Human Resources Practice
Douglas W. Bray and Associates

Diversity in the Workplace:
Human Resources Initiatives
Susan E. Jackson and Associates

Human Dilemmas in Work Organizations:
Strategies for Resolution
Abraham K. Korman and Associates

Diagnosis for Organizational Change:
Methods and Models
Ann Howard and Associates

Diagnosis for Organizational Change

METHODS AND MODELS

Ann Howard and Associates

THE GUILFORD PRESS
New York   London

A Pulication Sponsored by
the Society for Industrial and Organizational Psychology, Inc.
a Division of the American Psychological Association

© The Guilford Press
A Division of Guilford Publications, Inc.
72 Spring Street, New York, NY 10012

Printed in the United States of America

This book is printed on acid-free paper.

Last digit is print number: 9   8   7   6   5   4   3   2   1

Library of Congress Cataloging-in-Publication Data
Diagnosis for organizational change : methods and models /
Ann Howard and associates
    p.   cm.—(The Professional practice series)
    "Sponsored by the Society for Industrial
    and Organizational Psychology"—Pref.
    Includes bibliographical references and index.
    ISBN 0-89862-480-0
    1. Organizational change. 2. Manpower planning. 3. Employee
empowerment. I. Howard, Ann, 1939– . II. Society for Industrial and
Organizational Psychology (U.S.) III. Series.
HD58.8.D5   1994
658.4'063—dc20
                                                    93-40424
                                                       CIP

The Authors

ANN HOWARD is president of the Leadership Research Institute, a not-for-profit organization dedicated to research on the selection and development of leaders and managers. Before cofounding the institute in 1987, she was for 12 years associate director and then director of two longitudinal studies of the lives and careers of managers at AT&T. Her prior experience includes 9 years with a management consulting firm and 6 years in human resources functions in financial organizations. In addition to numerous journal articles and book chapters, she is the senior author (with Douglas W. Bray) of the award-winning book *Managerial Lives in Transition: Advancing Age and Changing Times*, which summarizes 20 years of the longitudinal research. She is a recent president (1988–1989) and a Fellow of the Society for Industrial and Organizational Psychology (SIOP) and a past editor of *The Industrial-Organizational Psychologist*. Her PhD in psychology is from the University of Maryland, and she has an honorary Doctor of Science degree from Goucher College.

THOMAS P. BECHET is a partner in The Walker Group, consulting in human resource strategies, executive succession and development planning, human resource information management, and related areas. Before joining Walker, he spent 8 years with the management consulting firm of Towers Perrin. He is chair of the Professional Development Committee of the Human Resource Planning Society. His MBA is from Columbia University.

DOUGLAS W. BRAY is chairman of the board of Development Dimensions International. Previously, he spent 28 years in human resources research and practice with AT&T, retiring as director of Basic Human Resources Research. Early in that period he designed and implemented the first management assessment center. He has received many awards for his work, including the Gold Medal for Life Achievement in the Application of Psychology from the American Psychological Foundation and the first Professional Practice Award from SIOP. His PhD in psychology is from Yale University, and he has an honorary Doctor of Science degree from his alma mater, American International College.

W. WARNER BURKE is professor of psychology and education at Teachers College, Columbia University, and director of the graduate program in social-organizational psychology there. He is also chairman of W. Warner Burke Associates, an organizational consulting firm. Previously, he was with the National Training Laboratories' (NTL) Institute for Applied Behavioral Science, was executive director of the Organization Development Network, and chaired the Department of Management at Clark University. In 1989 he received the Public Service Medal from NASA, and in 1990 he earned the American Society for Training and Development's (ASTD) Distinguished Contribution to Human Resources Development Award. His PhD in psychology is from the University of Texas, Austin.

WILLIAM C. BYHAM is president and chief executive officer of Development Dimensions International, a leading human resources programs and services firm, which he established in 1970. He is active worldwide in the application of assessment center and behavior modeling techniques and in helping organizations in empowerment, work-teaming, and other efforts. Among his many writings are the recent *Zapp! The Lightning of Empowerment* and *Shogun Management.* His awards include the Professional Practice Award from SIOP and the Distinguished Contribution to Human Resources Development Award from ASTD. His PhD in psychology is from Purdue University.

KIMBALL FISHER is a cofounder of Belgard•Fisher•Rayner, Inc., a high-performance work team consulting and training firm. He was formerly an organizational development consultant with Procter & Gamble and Tektronix. He is a frequent speaker at conferences on teams and organizational redesign. He has published widely on these subjects, including his recent *Leading Self-Directed Work Teams: A Guide to Developing New Team Leadership Skills.* His master's degree in organizational behavior is from the Brigham Young University Marriott School of Management.

EDWARD E. LAWLER III is professor of management and organization in the School of Business of the University of Southern California. He is also the founding director of the Center for Effective Organizations there. He has consulted worldwide on organizational development, organizational behavior, compensation, and related matters. His prolific writings include the recent *High-Involvement Management* and *The Ultimate Advantage.* His PhD in psychology is from the University of California at Berkeley.

HARRY LEVINSON is chairman of The Levinson Institute, which he founded in 1968. He is now clinical professor emeritus of the Harvard University Medical School, where he served on the faculty from 1972. His prolific writings include *Organizational Diagnosis* and *The Great Jackass Fallacy.* He has received many honors and awards, most recently the American Psychological Association's Award for Distinguished Professional Contributions to Knowledge. His PhD in psychology is from the University of Kansas.

DAVID A. NADLER is president and chief executive officer of the Delta Consulting Group. Earlier he was a faculty member of the Graduate School of Business at Columbia University. His specialties include large-scale organizational change, executive leadership, organization design, and senior team development. Among his numerous writings is the recent *Organizational Architecture: Designs for Changing Organizations*. His MBA is from the Harvard Business School, and his PhD in psychology is from the University of Michigan.

ROBERT W. ROGERS is chief operating officer of Development Dimensions International (DDI), a firm he has served for more than 16 years. Previously he was an officer in the U.S. Air Force, where he pioneered the use of the assessment center for officer development. In addition to leadership responsibilities at DDI for sales, marketing, human resources, and other key functions, he actively consults with senior executives in outside industry on value-driven organizational change, total quality, empowerment, selection and assessment, and performance management. He has addressed human resources conferences around the world. His master's in education is from Troy State College.

JAMES W. WALKER is a partner in The Walker Group, which he established in 1986. Earlier, he was vice president with the consulting firm of Towers Perrin and served on the business faculties of Indiana University, San Diego State University, and Arizona State University. His consulting activities include developing strategies for improved staffing, management succession and development, and management practices. He is the founder of the Human Resource Planning Society and author of several books, including the award-winning *Human Resource Planning*. His PhD in business administration is from the University of Iowa.

ELISE WALTON is a director at the Delta Consulting Group and also teaches in the Graduate School of Business at Columbia University. Earlier, she was an independent consultant. She specializes in change management, global strategy, organizational design, and quality improvement. In 1987 she coauthored "Organization Change and Development" in the *Annual Review of Psychology*. Her PhD in organizational behavior is from the Harvard Business School.

RONALD E. ZEMKE is president of Performance Research Associates, a firm he founded in 1972. He specializes in organizational and productivity improvement through needs analysis, service quality audits, and service management programs. He is senior editor of *TRAINING* magazine and editor of *The Service Edge* newsletter. He is the author of *Computer Literacy Needs Assessment* and coauthor of a number of other books, including *Figuring Things Out* and *Stressless Selling*. His master's degree in psychology is from the University of Minnesota.

Preface

This is the fourth volume in The Professional Practice Series sponsored by the Society for Industrial and Organizational Psychology (SIOP). The series was initiated by the society to illuminate human resources practice in organizations. Although such activities are ubiquitous, they have received little systematic attention in the professional literature. By deciding, in 1988, to launch this endeavor SIOP moved to correct to some extent the imbalance between reports of academic research and those of applied psychology.

The first book to result from this initiative was *Working with Organizations and Their People*, of which I was senior author. This was a foundation volume focusing on the process of practice in major practice areas and in major practice settings.

The next two volumes were devoted for the most part to case studies detailing approaches in a number of business and governmental organizations to human resources challenges. The first of these, *Diversity in the Workplace*, authored by Susan E. Jackson and associates, provided instructive reports of programs and procedures instituted by a variety of organizations in responding to an increasingly diverse workforce and new conditions of work. The second took a similar approach to the human problems of organizations. Abraham K. Korman was senior author of this book, entitled *Human Dilemmas in Work Organizations*.

The current volume breaks new ground. Management and human resources practitioners are often suspicious that all is not well in an organization. However, an ever-present difficulty is that of problem identification and causal analysis. Perplexity has increased in this era of dramatic organizational change. And there is always the danger that, on the one hand, management may misidentify the causes of problems and that, on the other, interventions may be recommended by practitioners without sufficient problem analysis.

This book is devoted to methods of organizational diagnosis, illustrated by real-life examples. The contributors are noted practitioners who approach such analysis in different ways and who have different emphases, depending on their theoretical orientations. The aim of the volume is not merely to present such variety but to attempt an integration of these approaches.

The senior author of this book is Ann Howard, a member of the editorial board of the series. When the board was exchanging ideas for the subject of our fourth volume, she suggested that it be integrated organizational diagnosis and developed an outline with proposed chapter authors. The board quickly and enthusiastically approved.

Ann is both an excellent writer, a creative editor, and a serious student of social trends as they affect the practice of industrial/organizational psychology. We are most fortunate that she undertook the task of producing this intriguing volume. It is the latest of her many contributions to SIOP over the past 20 years.

DOUGLAS BRAY
Series Editor
Tenafly, New Jersey

Acknowledgements

The authors of this volume are accomplished writers who, for the most part, did not particularly need another feather in their well-decorated professional hats. This makes me especially grateful for their willingness to contribute. I owe special thanks to Warner Burke, who helped me plan the book and plot a straight path through the organizational side of industrial/organizational (I/O) psychology. Also sincerely appreciated are the considerable efforts of series editor Doug Bray, who faithfully read and commented on each chapter and provided advice and moral support every step of the way.

Contents

DIAGNOSIS FOR ORGANIZATIONAL CHANGE

INTRODUCTION

CHAPTER 1

Diagnostic Perspectives in an Era of Organizational Change

ANN HOWARD

A short time ago some colleagues and I were summoned by a transportation company to install a developmental assessment center for their struggling area managers. The company, here called Translines, had recently eliminated the job immediately above the area managers, leaving them unprepared for the managerial responsibilities that fell on their shoulders. Of particular concern, they seemed unable to delegate.

Our first task, like that of most consultants, was diagnostic. What kinds of developmental needs should the assessment center illuminate? Or, in assessment center terminology, what dimensions should be evaluated and how should they be defined? Once this task was completed, we could proceed with the rest of the process: building exercises to bring out the behaviors represented in the dimensions, preparing exercise materials, developing software to speed the assessors' work, and training the assessors. Our contract thus embraced two layers of diagnosis: a job analysis (diagnosis of the requirements of a job family) that would be used to develop a procedure for a training needs analysis (diagnosis of training needs).

The job analysis quickly catapulted us into the organizational thicket in which the job was embedded. The area managers were expected to work as a team, but no formal mechanism brought them together. Our questions about structure were disregarded by the client, despite our protests that they were essential for the job analysis. Influencing skills, for example, would assume greater importance if the area managers had little authority.

Translines was a progressive company with a clear recognition of the need for change, and we eventually learned that another consultant was working with the top executives on organization development (OD). But the client declined to identify the OD consultant, insisting that we stick to the developmental needs of the area managers and ignore the broader or-ganization and where it might be headed. It soon became clear that we would be consulting blind.

The overriding theme of this book is that to best facilitate change, be-havioral science practitioners need a clear, unobstructed vision of an orga-nization and its direction, one that manifests the confluence of all relevant systems. Rapid and radical organizational change, increasingly attempted at the end of the 20th century, cannot be piecemeal. A planned, compre-hensive strategy, though energy depleting and painful, is the only reliable road to sustainable change. And that requires an integrated organization-al diagnosis.

Let me illustrate by returning to Translines, whose symptoms are fair-ly typical of companies courageous enough to confront major organiza-tional change.

DIAGNOSTIC PERSPECTIVES ON TRANSLINES

After prying some background information from our client, we conducted interviews to inform our job analysis. We questioned incumbent area managers about the nature of their current job and managerial responsi-bilities; asked their department manager bosses to relate critical incidents of good and poor area manager performance; and interviewed depart-ment vice presidents, one level higher, about the job and where they saw it headed in the future. The organization's traditions and culture stalked through these interviews. We began to question whether our efforts to identify developmental needs for this group of area managers, however accurate, would have even a small chance of leading to organizational im-provement. What follows is a sampler of what we learned and the dilem-mas posed.

Structure

There were three primary departments in the company: Shipping, which handled movement of freight; Carrier, responsible for vehicle mainte-nance and repair; and Sales. Shipping, the heart of the business, was the dominant department, leading the others in head count, budget, and pow-er. Translines had a centralized, functional structure, and the area man-agers reported up the department line. Within each geographical region, the area managers of Shipping, Carrier, and Sales had once reported to a regional manager. This was the job that had been eliminated. The area managers' job, once purely technical, now included all aspects of manage-ment as well.

There was no structure or process to bring the area managers together within the region. As one reported, "We have to go more places with less authority to get things done." Departments myopically pursued their own priorities, yet the area managers obviously depended on each other's functions. Relating to other departments was described as "rough as sandpaper."

Leadership

The president of Translines was an astute leader who recognized that the company needed to sharpen its competitive edge to attract and keep increasingly discerning customers. But like many leaders today, he wrestled with how best to bring a traditional organization into the modern age. He was refreshingly open to experimentation, and Translines was known as an industry leader. Yet the experiments did not flow from one guiding philosophy and frequently caused the company to change direction, which confused those lower down in the organization. He was still evaluating whether the latest reorganization would propel the company toward the level of customer service to which he aspired.

The department vice presidents differed markedly in their approach to management. The Carrier vice president was promoting worker empowerment, while the Sales vice president believed a laissez-faire approach encouraged creativity. The Shipping vice president thought the organization ran better in a top-down fashion, without the extra layer imposed by the defunct regional managers, because of the urgency for action posed by almost daily crises. Not surprisingly, the area managers received mixed signals and felt that they had to be everything to everyone.

Yet all of the vice presidents had success stories, which they felt justified their own approach. The sales group was breaking into new markets, and Carrier department teams had made notable progress toward quality goals. The Shipping department had recently realized significant cost savings by innovative centralized scheduling.

Job Climate

The area managers could hardly be accused of not trying to stay on top of their jobs. They worked 16-hour days. They were constantly on call and drove thousands of miles a month from one office to another to oversee their staffs or see their clients. The Carrier and Shipping area managers lived in fear of accidents and injuries; the company's goal was to reduce the number of accidents 20% from the previous year, and the area managers were ultimately accountable. Another major goal was reducing costs. Customer contracts imposed penalties if shipments were late, but overtime in the heavily unionized company dramatically escalated expenses. It was a delicate balancing act.

Job stress was high. "It's easy to become unraveled," said one area manager. "It's like being in charge of a complaint department, especially with labor. If you don't have the full story, they come at you with both guns blazing."

Training Systems

There was no formal training program for area managers; it was strictly on-the-job training. The department managers and vice presidents felt that the area managers lacked knowledge about budgets and other aspects of management, and that they lacked confidence. This was impressionistic, however; there were no comprehensive methods, such as assessment centers, for evaluating individuals, which was why our help was requested. Budgeting was difficult because the corporate staff held financial information close to the vest. Thus, it was impossible for the area managers to run their operations like business units, even if they knew how.

Developing subordinates was a responsibility the area managers took seriously. Those in Carrier and Sales, where more worker responsibility was encouraged, were consciously involved in coaching subordinates. This frequently took the form of modeling appropriate behavior on visits to maintenance facilities or customer sites.

Groups and Teams

Neither Shipping nor Sales put much emphasis on teamwork. The Carrier area managers, however, nurtured teams with some self-management responsibilities, in line with their department vice president's conviction that worker empowerment would boost the company's performance. Said the vice president, "You can't *up* quality and *down* costs unless you get every man and woman involved." Teams were responsible for finding ways to improve both safety and quality, and employees directed these functions on different days of the week.

Management Practices

From the top, Translines was run in a traditional military fashion. "Each level chews out the next," said one interviewee. "It's motivation by intimidation." Micromanagement had escalated with advanced information technology, which broke down performance indicators into fine details. "We find out you're most likely to get injured if you're 44 and it's Tuesday morning," commented one area manager.

Particularly noxious to many of the area managers were the system-wide conference calls initiated at the corporate level. These daily sessions, dubbed the "gong show," were a rehash of everything that had gone wrong the previous day. Although instituted with the admirable intent of enhancing responsiveness to customers, the calls had unfortunately come to be viewed as a ritual dance of "What happened, you idiot?" The corporate calls spawned lower-level conference calls, often before dawn, to prepare for the grilling. The area managers were personally accountable for explanations in the gong show. One Carrier area manager, consistent with the emerging philosophy of empowerment in his department, proposed having subordinates represent his region's activities on the calls, perhaps on alternating weekends, as an opportunity for coaching and development. He was quickly dissuaded by higher-ups who cautioned that others would fault him for not doing his job.

Culture

Historically, Translines excelled in a crisis. "We can always get the ox out of the ditch," said one interviewee. The company's heroes triumphed in the crucible of crisis management. "We often confuse activity with progress," admitted a department manager. The area managers complained that they were always reactive and lacked time to be proactive. The byword was "Ready, fire, aim."

Working ceaselessly was another corporate value. "I work more hours than you work" was a major assertion of one's "macho image." Although excessive hours were clearly an imposition on the area managers' home lives, some saw this as progress. "It used to be that the guy who screamed the most got promoted," said one. "Now it's the one who works the most."

Dilemmas

Like so many other companies today, Translines was battling the reverberations of an authoritarian past but unsure how to proceed into the uncertain yet demanding future. A key feature of the organization was its lack of alignment. The vice presidents ran their departments in their own idiosyncratic ways despite the centralized control that tried to bring the total operation together. To score more runs the company needed a team, but its leaders operated more like toddlers in parallel play.

There were certainly reasons to suspect that the area managers lacked management skills, though perhaps not as many as some believed, and our assessment center would uncover these. The corporate staff was highly motivated to shore up any weaknesses revealed by the assessment center with targeted training and development. But given the nature of the organization, would any of this hard work and good intention enhance the bottom line?

Let us suppose that the assessment and development efforts fully succeed in preparing the area managers for their managerial responsibilities but the present environment does not change. The area managers learn how to delegate, but the system holds them personally accountable for the gong show. They learn how to build teams, but there is little business information to guide or motivate their teams toward true self-direction. Moreover, there is no mechanism for an area manager team. The area managers learn how to reward achievements, but the system metes out punishments. They learn to support their subordinates' self-esteem, but higher management is obsessed with errors and offers mostly negative feedback about those subordinates. They learn time management but still must drop everything to deal with and account for minute details of crises. I could go on, but the point should be clear.

The company's desire to strengthen its area managers and its willingness to invest in their development were certainly laudable. Our assessment center was, in fact, highly touted by management; we delivered what they wanted. Although we could cultivate this island in the company sea, we could not subdue our anxiety that a big wave would wash it away.

Management would have been better served if they had positioned this improvement effort within a larger framework—a diagnostic model that could focus and integrate the company's efforts. Translines needed a vision of organizational change.

A VISION FOR THIS VOLUME

This volume describes how to develop road maps that will guide and direct organizational change. This process involves organizational diagnosis, a systematic method for gathering data about how organizations function as social systems and an analysis of the meaning of those data. Whether it is called problem identification (Bray, 1991), organizational analysis (Mills, Pace, & Peterson, 1988), or organizational assessment (Lawler, Nadler, & Cammann, 1980), organizational diagnosis is a problem-solving activity that searches for causes and consequences. It identifies gaps between what is and what ought to be (Weisbord, 1978). Interventions are then designed to close those gaps and bring about positive organizational change. Diagnosis is thus forward-looking, a "process of using concepts and methods from the behavioral sciences to assess an organization's current state and find ways to increase its effectiveness" (Harrison, 1987).

Organizational diagnosis is a critical step in the change process and an essential part of a competent practitioner's role. A recent membership survey of the Society for Industrial and Organizational Psychology (SIOP) showed that practitioners spent 32% of their time in problem identification (Howard, 1991a). Launching ambitious interventions without adequate organizational diagnosis is akin to, as related by Doug Bray (personal communication, June 1, 1993), "venturing into a strange country with no map and no facility in the language. Failure is not always inevitable, but diagnosis would make success more likely and more complete."

A proper diagnosis should correctly identify core problems. All too often, "with the several layers of other, less fundamental changes obscuring the truly core issues the system needs to change, organizations wind up attacking problems that are symptoms and find that the problems keep popping back up, often in slightly different forms" (Porras, 1987, p. 13). In managing fundamental change, a diagnostic approach surpasses an action approach: "The vision is used as a guide to determining what should change, rather than today's presenting symptoms being triggers for action" (Beckhard & Pritchard, 1992, p. 8).

To generate better understanding and appreciation of organizational diagnosis, this volume has three primary objectives:

1. *Practice*—To illustrate how various practitioners approach organizational diagnosis.
2. *Scope*—To demonstrate the breadth and complexity of organizational diagnosis.
3. *Integration*—To explore a more integrated approach to diagnosis, suited to an era of organizational change.

Each of these objectives warrants more explication.

The Practice of Organizational Diagnosis

Journal articles and academic studies can further knowledge in their own way, but they don't necessarily reflect what is happening in applied settings. Because this volume is part of the SIOP Professional Practice Series, an important criterion was that it provide insights into human resources practice. Both the selection of authors and the instructions to them support this objective.

The Authors

The assembled authors are experienced, sophisticated human resources practitioners. Their headquarters span most of the United States: from Massachusetts (Harry Levinson), down the Northeast corridor to New

York (Warner Burke, Elise Walton, and David Nadler) and nearby New Jersey (Douglas Bray), west across Pennsylvania (Robert Rogers and William Byham), northwest to Minnesota (Ronald Zemke), west to Oregon (Kimball Fisher), and south to Arizona (James Walker and Thomas Bechet) and California (Edward Lawler). Regardless of their home base, the authors practice nationally and often internationally. The majority are external consultants, in firms large and small or in academically based centers. The lone representative of internal practitioners is Doug Bray, who relates his experiences at AT&T, although Kim Fisher also includes lessons from his past experiences as a team leader for Procter & Gamble.

The Authors' Instructions

The authors were asked to draw a picture of both the process and content of organizational diagnosis and to color it with case examples. Although some topics better lent themselves to this approach than others, the book is rich with real-life experiences that make organizational diagnosis palpable.

Some illustrations highlight companies and CEOs at the leading edge of organizational change. We will learn, for example, how John Welch linked General Electric's values to executive behaviors and how British Airways approached the difficult transition from a government-owned to a private enterprise.

Other examples reveal obstacles, unpleasant surprises, or serious misjudgments. We will find a large Fortune 500 company with a gimmicky quality day, a weapons manufacturer unable to implement teams, telephone company service representatives erroneously thought to have deficient skills, and a bank with dull leftover middle managers. A few case studies are more fully fleshed, though disguised to protect the dignity of organizations courageously confronting change. We will visit Vitech, wrestling with an overcontrolling founder to emerge from its entrepreneurial state; Xellence, using staffing to reinvigorate the organization while still trying to avoid layoffs; and, of course, Translines.

The Scope of Organizational Diagnosis

Time spent on problem identification is not uniform among those in different areas of human resources practice. In the SIOP membership study (Howard, 1991a), the more time a practitioner spent in organization development, the more time he or she spent on problem identification. Contrarily, the more time spent in training, the less time on problem identification. Trainers focused on implementation, while practitioners in individual evaluation spent relatively more time validating the effects of their work. This disproportionate use of time may explain why organizational diagnosis is more often associated with organization development than with other aspects of human resources practice.

This is not to say that those involved with training or individual evaluation spend *no* time in problem identification or diagnosis. There are well-established and frequently used methods in these domains. Job analysis, training needs analysis, performance analysis, and competency mapping all reflect diagnostic procedures, but they are not typically equated with organizational diagnosis, perhaps because they address more micro problems. Analysis can and does take place at the organizational, group, and individual levels (see Harrison, 1987), complete with models that spotlight their respective focal points (see Hausser, 1980).

There are many methods of organizational diagnosis, but they can generally be categorized into four types: interviews, questionnaires, observations, and records. All of the chapters in the main body of this book refer to at least one of these techniques, and many authors use all four. Each method has its own variations and subtypes. The four techniques are associated with different advantages and disadvantages, summarized briefly in the following paragraphs (for a more complete exposition, see Lawler et al., 1980). Often the negatives of one approach are the positives of another. Multiple methods are recommended not only to balance strengths and weaknesses but to capitalize on the unique nature of the data each method produces and to cross-check the validity of information.

Interviews

Interviews differ in degree of structure and formality and in whether they are conducted with individuals or focus groups. The interview is a common data-gathering method to diagnose functioning at the organizational, group, and individual levels.

The major advantage of interviews is the rich data they produce. They also offer an opportunity to establish rapport with participants, which, hopefully, evokes frank and honest replies. Interviews are subject to biases, however, both from the self-reports of participants and from the interpretations of interviewers. They can also be expensive because of the amount of time they consume.

Questionnaires

Questionnaires are typically structured, although questions can be open-ended as well. Surveys are quite popular for gathering perceptual and attitudinal data that can be aggregated at the group and organizational level. Questionnaires at the individual level encompass many psychological tests. If standardized, questionnaires offer high reliability and an opportunity to construct norms, but they may also be custom-tailored to gather data more specific to an organization. The authors in this volume tend to construct questionnaires for their distinct purposes but to use them repeatedly across organizations, allowing them to develop normative expectations. Questionnaires may be administered to samples from a variety of populations for comparative views. Rogers and Byham (Chapter 8), for example, use both internal and external scans to determine an organization's critical success factors, as well as 360° feedback instruments to evaluate individual behavior.

Questionnaires are particularly useful for gathering specific data from a large number of people. They are easily administered and scored and, once developed, are inexpensive. They do not offer the opportunities for rapport or explanation that the interview does, of course, and they suffer from self-report response biases.

Observations

Observations offer real, not symbolic, behavior and can thus eliminate self-report biases. They can reveal patterns of individual behavior as well as interpersonal and group behavior, as in meetings. Observations involve real-time behavior, not retrospective remembrances subject to reinterpretation and distortion. Like interviews and questionnaires, observations vary in degree of structure, from the open approach of the anthropologist to the structured simulations of the assessment center. The more open the structure, the more the method depends on the skill of the observer, and training can be a problem. Structure also reduces potential observer biases, although a price is paid in data richness.

Observations entail logistical problems, although modern technology is proving helpful for some of them. For example, personal computer software aided assessors in the developmental center at Translines by expediting report writing and the rating of key behaviors and assessment dimensions. Observational methods tend to be expensive and can intrude on the behavior they are designed to diagnose. Naturalistic observations can be quite time-consuming; simulations use time much more efficiently, but they limit the kinds of behaviors that can be observed.

Records

Records include various kinds of documents, accounts, journals, and other evidence subject to secondary analysis. The organization's files often contain data collected for a variety of purposes, some legal and regulatory and others for in-house tracking and use. Industrial/Organizational (I/O) psychologists have often been creative in their search for "hard" data to validate tests, delving into such areas as absenteeism, production, and turn-over. There is often other evidence, not collected for a specific purpose, that may reveal organizational characteristics (Mirvis, 1980a; Webb, Campbell, Schwartz, & Sechrest, 1966). Records do not have to be produced by the company; for example, Harry Levinson (Chapter 2) consults newspaper articles.

Records have the advantage of being generally free from bias, inexpensive, and unobtrusive. But they are not always easy to retrieve, may be of poor quality, and are subject to errors of coding or interpretation. Some may violate ethical principles of informed consent, so the diagnostician must proceed with care.

It is in the interpretation of data that the practitioner's skill is particularly critical. Diagnosis has been described as both an art and a science (Mirvis, 1980b). To understand culture, for example, the diagnostician must interpret symbolic behavior and rituals. Some even use stories and metaphors (Foules, 1988). Precisely because the practitioner must give them meaning, data must be collected meticulously and redundantly.

The Integration of Organizational Diagnosis

It is unfortunate that the term "diagnosis" is so identified with the practice of medicine, for it too easily leads to the inference that the organization is in some way "sick." But the popular wellness movement may be just as fitting a metaphor. Organizations seek help from behavioral science practitioners not necessarily because the social system is broken but because it could function better. Mills, Pace, and Peterson (1988) refer not to an organizational problem but to a "point of concern." Sometimes this is an activity provoking anxiety, but other times it is a "nagging desire or urge to do something better, to achieve something more than is currently being done" (p. 14). Those promoting continuous improvement as a means of remaining competitive transform the old saw "If it ain't broke, don't fix it" into "If it ain't broke, fix it anyway."

It is highly unlikely that any reader of this volume is unaware of the competitive pressures on today's organizations from the global economy. A combination of high technology and demographic and social changes have forced organizations to reconsider their business and human resources strategies in profound ways (Howard, 1991b). Renewed attention to servicing customers, quality, innovation, constituency management, and speed and efficiency of operations has stimulated organizations to restructure, reengineer, redesign, and retrain. Traditional organizations are undergoing more fundamental changes than at any time in the past (Beckhard & Pritchard, 1992).

These transformations support use of a holistic framework for viewing organizational problems and challenges. As organizations shed their traditional bureaucratic forms for the sake of greater flexibility, they cannot afford to leave any system untouched. Never before has it been so important to take an integrated approach to organizational diagnosis.

The open systems model, discussed more fully in Part I, makes clear that an organization comprises interrelated parts. Changes in one system violate another. Diagnosis of one part of an interrelated system in isolation gives a limited and distorted picture (Kotter, 1978; Lawler et al., 1980). Moreover, the types of problems identified correlate with the type of procedure used. "If your only tool is a hammer, everything looks like a nail" (Mills et al., 1988, p. 8).

But just as an organization's culture can thwart efforts to change, so too can a profession's traditions. A variety of specialists consult with work organizations, and they have traditionally focused on certain subsystems with little recognition of the importance of others (Kast & Rosenzweig, 1970). Within I/O psychology, there is a gap between the individual differences tradition of the "I" side and the group or organizational tradition of the "O" side. SIOP members from these traditions have tended to settle into different camps, according to survey results (Howard, 1991a). Those practicing subspecialties related to individual evaluation spent less time in subspecialties related to organization development and vice versa. One of the organization development models cited by Burke in Chapter 3 completely ignores the individual level of analysis. This is not atypical; a recent review of procedure-oriented OD theories showed that 14 out of 16 did not include individual behavior as a diagnostic variable (Porras & Robertson, 1992). Integrated organizational diagnosis appears highly desirable, but it will not necessarily come easily.

OVERVIEW OF THE VOLUME

The chapters ahead demonstrate the practice, scope, and integration of organizational diagnosis. The volume is divided into three major parts, with a concluding chapter at the end. The major subdivisions correspond roughly to the three types of problems or gaps identified by Mills, Pace, and Peterson (1988). The first covers what they call organization gaps, or how the organization is conceived and designed. Next come performance gaps, or deficiencies in the ways employees carry out and execute their duties. The third section centers on management gaps, or deficiencies in the way people are managed and motivated.

Part I features broad organizational perspectives. Harry Levinson, in Chapter 2, portrays the frequently unacknowledged role of the practitioner as his or her own diagnostic instrument. He stresses the importance of theory, which forms an undercurrent for the interpretation of data. Warner Burke, in Chapter 3, provides several examples of diagnostic models to guide organization development. He illustrates how both a simple and complex model can help the practitioner digest organizational data and pilot an appropriate intervention. In Chapter 4, Elise Walton and David Nadler also use a model to lay the groundwork for organization design. They steer us through the major elements of design and preview new organizational forms to meet the challenges of the future.

Part II shifts to the individual level of analysis. Continuing with structure, James Walker and Thomas Bechet in Chapter 5 demonstrate how to blueprint an organization chart and fill it with people. They link human resource planning with business strategy, showing how diagnosis in anticipation of radical change differs from one geared to more gradual development. Human resource planning frequently exposes training and development needs, which Ronald Zemke addresses in Chapter 6. Here, too, what used to be a straightforward process has taken a turn toward complexity. Like human resource planning, training has been elevated to a strategic initiative. In Chapter 7, Douglas Bray views individuals as reflections of their work environment. Using his personnel-centered diagnosis, an organization can capitalize on intensive evaluations of small groups of individuals to surface organization-level problems.

Each of the authors in Part III pursues yet a new content area of organizational diagnosis related to management and motivation. All, in addition, give special attention to the increasingly popular high-involvement workplace, where workers assume responsibilities and authority heretofore considered the province of management. Robert Rogers and William Byham introduce the concept in Chapter 8 and use it to illustrate how various systems must be aligned with an organization's culture. Their diagnosis of culture, from critical success factors to vision and values, applies to organizations whether or not they embrace employee empowerment. Edward Lawler scrutinizes one particular organization system—that of rewards—in Chapter 9. He explores various diagnostic issues, from the intent of reward systems to their structure and process. In Chapter 10, Kimball Fisher gets to the heart of empowerment with an analysis of work teams. He shows how to diagnose the appropriateness of teams for an organization as well as how to investigate team dysfunctions.

In the final chapter the authors cooperate in an exploration of integrated organizational diagnosis. They offer the benefit of their observations and experience to address such issues as client expectations, the specialization of expertise, and barriers to more integrated organizational diagnosis.

By emphasizing the practice, scope, and integration of organizational diagnosis, this book will, we hope, broaden the sights of internal and external human resources practitioners, whether in organization development, human resource planning, organization design, culture and climate, training, selection, career development, teams, reward systems, or other areas. All subspecialties of organizational practice are inescapably related, and all practice needs diagnosis.

The book should also be instructive for students in organizational *and* industrial psychology, organizational behavior, human resources management, and related fields. We hope it will also attract the attention of managers who are pursuing or flirting with organizational change, especially those who count on professional help to do so.

REFERENCES

Beckhard, R., & Pritchard, W. (1992). *Changing the essence: The art of creating and leading fundamental change in organizations*. San Francisco: Jossey-Bass.

Bray, D. W. (1991). The range of human resources practice. In D. W. Bray & Associates, *Working with organizations and their people* (pp. 1–12). New York: Guilford Press.

Foules, D. F. (1988). Methods of documentation, organizational systems analysis: Interpretive approaches. In G. E. Mills, R. W. Pace, & B. D. Peterson (Eds.), *Analysis in human resource training and organization development* (pp. 193–207). Reading, MA: Addison-Wesley.

Harrison, M. D. (1987). *Diagnosing organizations: Methods, models, and processes*. Newbury Park, CA: Sage.

Hausser, Doris L. (1980). Comparison of different models for organizational analysis. In E. E. Lawler III, D. A. Nadler, & C. Cammann (Eds.), *Organizational assessment: Perspectives on the measurement of organizational behavior and the quality of work life* (pp. 132–161). New York: Wiley.

Howard, A. (1991a). Industrial/organizational psychologists as practitioners. In D. W. Bray & Associates, *Working with organizations and their people* (pp. 13–44). New York: Guilford Press.

Howard, A. (1991b). New directions for human resources practice. In D. W. Bray & Associates, *Working with organizations and their people* (pp. 219–252). New York: Guilford Press.

Kast, F. E., & Rosenzweig, J. E. (1970). *Organization and management: A systems approach*. New York: McGraw-Hill.

Kotter, J. P. (1978). *Organizational dynamics: Diagnosis and intervention*. Reading, MA: Addison-Wesley.

Lawler, E. E. III, Nadler, D. A., & Cammann, C. (1980). *Organizational assessment: Perspectives on the measurement of organizational behavior and the quality of work life*. New York: Wiley.

Mills, G. E., Pace, R. W., & Peterson, B. D. (1988). *Analysis in human resource training and organization development*. Reading, MA: Addison-Wesley.

Mirvis, P. H. (1980a). Assessing physical evidence, documents, and records in organizations. In E. E. Lawler III, D. A. Nadler, & C. Cammann (Eds.), *Organizational assessment: Perspectives on the measurement of organizational behavior and the quality of work life* (pp. 418–443). New York: Wiley.

Mirvis, P. H. (1980b). The art of assessing the quality of life at work: A personal essay with notes. In E. E. Lawler III, D. A. Nadler, & C. Cammann (Eds.), *Organizational assessment: Perspectives on the measurement of organizational behavior and the quality of work life* (pp. 471–489). New York: Wiley.

Porras, J. I. (1987). *Stream analysis: A powerful way to diagnose and manage organizational change.* Reading, MA: Addison-Wesley.

Porras, J. I., & Robertson, P. J. (1992). Organizational development: Theory, practice, and research. In M. D. Dunnette & L. M. Hough (Eds.), *Handbook of industrial and organizational psychology* (2nd ed., Vol. 3, pp. 719–822). Palo Alto, CA: Consulting Psychologists Press.

Webb, E. J., Campbell, D. T., Schwartz, R. D., & Sechrest, L. (1966). *Unobtrusive measures: Nonreactive research in the social sciences.* Chicago: Rand McNally.

Weisbord, M. R. (1978). *Organizational diagnosis: A workbook of theory and practice.* Reading, MA: Addison-Wesley.

PART I

ORGANIZATIONAL PERSPECTIVES

Introduction

The three chapters that constitute this section undertake diagnosis with macro perspectives, guided by the conceptualization of organizations as open systems. This organic metaphor has been especially popular in recent years (Clancy, 1989; Morgan, 1986). First proposed for physics and biology (Von Bertalanffy, 1950), the power of this concept for the behavioral and social sciences was early recognized by Fred Emery of the Tavistock Institute (Weisbord, 1991). The primary thesis of the conceptualization of organizations as open systems is that the organization is in a dynamic relationship with its environment: It receives various inputs, transforms these inputs in some way, and exports outputs (Kast & Rosenzweig, 1970). Moreover, all the systems within organizations are interrelated and responsive to each other.

Diagnosis of an organization from an open systems perspective must take into account a large sweep of internal and external variables and how they influence each other. It is no surprise, then, that the three chapters in this section make much of models and theory.

THE PRACTITIONER AS DIAGNOSTIC INSTRUMENT

As Harry Levinson makes clear at the outset of Chapter 2, the data for diagnosis are frequently subjective—feelings, opinions, and perceptions subject to inference and interpretation. The wise practitioner, then, not only attempts to gather confirming data but proffers a diagnosis with proper humility, borne of the understanding that another practitioner may have come to a different conclusion from the same data. It is the diagnostician's interpretation that requires a coherent theory, one that the practitioner clearly recognizes is guiding the way.

We lead off with Levinson's chapter because he so vividly portrays the *process* of diagnosis. He takes us from the initial signing of the client contract, through preliminary and in-depth analyses, to interpretation and prognosis, to the feedback report, and to preparation for intervention. Along the way we follow Levinson the detective, absorbing every clue to the organization's past, present, and future. We observe the furniture, inspect the bulletin boards, read 10K financial reports, interview people inside and outside the company's boundaries, administer surveys, and attend to hundreds of other signs, symbols, and details. We come to appreciate not only the variety and ingenuity of his methods but the thoroughness with which he approaches the task.

Of particular interest is his scrutiny of the organization's leadership. "All organizations are the lengthened shadows of their leaders," he reports. Interviews, observations of executives at work, media stories, and external contacts—all are grist for this skilled psychologist's mill. His analysis inevitably invokes leaders' paranoid hostility, he reports, but with planfulness and equanimity he brings this reaction under control.

DIAGNOSTIC MODELS
FOR ORGANIZATION DEVELOPMENT

While Levinson emphasizes the importance of theory, Warner Burke, in Chapter 3, illustrates some of the models that guide organization development practitioners. His chapter is not intended to be an exhaustive review: "Pick 100 organizational consultants, and we would have 100 diagnostic models," he reports. But he cogently illustrates how a model can help to gather and categorize data, enrich understanding, and suggest the proper intervention.

Burke provides a thoughtful overview and critique of several organizational models, including the popular 7S framework by McKinsey, with special attention to the open systems models of Weisbord, Nadler–Tushman, Tichy, and Hornstein–Tichy. A highlight of the chapter is an exposition of the Burke–Litwin model, which predicts behavior and performance consequences. This model embodies the complexity and interrelatedness of organizational phenomena and the consequent difficulty of a comprehensive organization diagnosis. The arrows flow from everywhere to everywhere, charting the energy that sweeps from one organizational factor to every other. Two spatial dimensions are deemed insufficient; Burke would prefer arrows circling in a hologram—a dizzying representation, even if true to life.

Taking a cue from the leadership literature, the Burke–Litwin model neatly distinguishes between transformational and transactional dynamics, singling out the heavyweights that propel organizational change. Culture and climate part company in this analysis, which has implications for their diagnosis and change. Burke ends the chapter by offering criteria to select a diagnostic model for organization development. But his primary message is clear: Use a model.

DIAGNOSIS FOR ORGANIZATION DESIGN

One of the models mentioned in Burke's chapter, the Nadler–Tushman congruence model, forms the springboard in Chapter 4 for Elise Walton and David Nadler's launch into organization design. Actually, they approach diagnosis from two levels. Their first look with the congruence model covers all systems, because design choices must consider the broader framework. This initial diagnosis of inputs, outputs, and the transformation process "often indicates that organization design is not the solution," they note. Moreover, identifying key relationships helps them anticipate likely responses to change in the organization design itself.

The second level of diagnosis addresses design, or decisions about the formal organization. Most critical are the grouping decisions, which are determined by strategy, task requirements, or current problem areas. Grouping necessarily creates boundaries; thus the organization must next consider linking mechanisms to ensure information flow and achievement of superordinate goals.

While providing a systematic view of diagnosis and organization design, Walton and Nadler write with the specter of change peering over their shoulders. "The organization of the future will bear little resemblance to what we have traditionally thought of as organizations," they predict. Design burgeons into organizational architecture, encompassing all the transformational elements of the congruence model, not just the formal structure and processes. Walton and Nadler offer a sampler of the new organizational forms they expect to become increasingly common in the next decade, from networks and fuzzy boundaries to work teams at the organizational bottom and top.

A NOTE ON CONSISTENCY AND CHANGE

While absorbing the three chapters of Part I, keep in mind a dilemma of organizational perspectives on diagnosis. Open systems make adaptation possible; they draw energy and stimulation from the outside, which is advantageous, even necessary, for survival (to the extent that systems are closed, self-contained, and unable to import energy, they are subject to entropy or running down). At the same time, open systems bend toward equilibrium; internal or external forces that disrupt the system are countered by forces to restore it to its previous state (Katz & Kahn, 1966). As Levinson notes in Chapter 2, the organization is continually striving for both internal and external equilibrium. How, then, does the organization adapt and change? Burke raises this issue in Chapter 3 in his critique of models that emphasize congruence and alignment. Similarly, Harrison (1987) argues that incongruities often characterize organizations in which some systems are changing more rapidly than others; the resulting tensions may foster innovation and adaptation to external change. In Translines (Chapter 1), for example, the Carrier vice president's introduction of empowered teams was incongruent with the preexisting authoritarian culture but offered genuine hope for change. Yet lack of congruence threatened to sabotage efforts to develop the area managers.

Several authors in this book specifically search for congruence or alignment, including Walton and Nadler in Chapter 4. A textbook resolution to this dilemma of open systems is a dynamic equilibrium or steady state, not motionless, that preserves the character of the system through growth and expansion (Katz & Kahn, 1966). Practically, the diagnostician faces the task of ensuring reasonable internal consistency while not freezing the organization into an unchangeable state. The Burke–Litwin model deliberately avoids the goal of high congruence in an effort to ward off the latter possibility. Harrison (1987) suggests evaluating lack of fits against explicit effectiveness criteria to determine if they are truly detrimental.

Walton and Nadler admit that the organization's tendency toward equilibrium may undermine planned change as other elements of the organization try to bring the deviant back into alignment. Similarly, Kotter (1978) argues that nonalignments, if not corrected, drain energy out of the system and that organizations try to correct them by taking the path of least resistance. But because fit doesn't necessarily lead to long-run effectiveness, he looks for congruence in the moderate run (6 months to 6 years) but structural openness to adaptation in the long run.

Clearly, organizations do suffer from countervailing forces toward stagnation. In Levinson's terms (Chapter 2), the cohesion that unites organizational members can also foster organizational narcissism, regression into narrower functions, and a decline of adaptive capacity, as witnessed in more than one large American corporation in recent years. The diagnostician, then, must be ever alert to adaptability as a goal, especially in today's cutthroat and chronically changing environment.

For a first look at an open system, join Harry Levinson in Chapter 2 on a diagnostic organizational tour. Just watch out for the blob of grease headed your way.

REFERENCES

Clancy, J. J. (1989). *The invisible powers: The language of business*. Lexington, MA: Lexington Books.

Harrison, M. D. (1987). *Diagnosing organizations: Methods, models, and processes*. Newbury Park, CA: Sage.

Kast, F. E., & Rosenzweig, J. E. (1970). *Organization and management: A systems approach*. New York: McGraw-Hill.

Katz, D. , & Kahn, R. L. (1966). *The social psychology of organizations*. New York: Wiley.

Kotter, J. P. (1978). *Organizational dynamics: Diagnosis and intervention*. Reading, MA: Addison-Wesley.

Morgan, G. (1986). *Images of organization*. Beverly Hills, CA: Sage.

Von Bertalanffy, L. (1950). The theory of open systems in physics and biology. *Science, 3*, 23–29.

Weisbord, M. R. (1991). *Productive workplaces: Organizing and managing for dignity, meaning, and community*. San Francisco: Jossey-Bass.

CHAPTER 2

The Practitioner as Diagnostic Instrument

HARRY LEVINSON

Organizational diagnosis is a systematic method for gathering, organizing, and interpreting information about organizations for the purpose of helping them anticipate or ameliorate their adaptive problems. It is carried out by individuals, whether as single practitioners or in a team. The individual practitioner is his or her most important instrument or device for gathering data, making inferences, interpreting those data and inferences, and evolving modes of acting on his or her conclusions.

FRAMEWORKS FOR DIAGNOSIS

The independent practitioner or human resources specialist within an organization who is undertaking diagnosis may use a wide variety of methods to gather information. Inasmuch as many of the data are subjective (feelings, opinions, perceptions), the diagnostician must require confirming sources of information to accept data as valid. When there is agreement about the data from various perspectives and different sources, the practitioner is likely to have greater confidence in them. Once sufficient data are gathered, the next task is to give them meaning.

The Use of Theory

Giving meaning to diagnostic data involves two steps that must be clearly differentiated. The first is making inferences from the data. The second is interpreting the data and the inferences. The latter task requires that the practitioner have a guiding theory because of the necessarily subjective nature of interpretation and the fact that the same data may have different meaning according to the scientific or professional discipline within which the practitioner operates.

For example, assume that you, an organization consultant, are passing an automobile assembly line with the plant manager. While he is explaining aspects of the work to you, a blob of grease suddenly comes flying through the air toward you. You manage to step out of the way and avoid being smeared by it. You don't understand why this has happened, but the fact that it has makes you uneasy. Your host is embarrassed. He may offer an excuse, such as a sudden increase in pressure in the compressed air gun held by the operator, an increase that forced out a blob of grease. Without checking, he is making an inference about the cause of the event. One could make other inferences. Perhaps the gun is heavy and therefore difficult for an operator to handle. Or its mechanism may be worn and thus difficult to control. Perhaps the operator ejected the grease deliberately out of anger with the management; conceivably, he wanted to symbolize tension and disagreement in the plant. Any of these inferences could be valid.

When the plant manager checks these varied inferences, he discovers that the gun is not too heavy, it is not unduly worn, and there was no sudden surge of air pressure. You, the observer, then develop the hypothesis that there is hostility toward the manager, if not management in general. Assuming that the blob of grease did in fact turn out to be an act of hostility toward the management, you will pursue that issue further before you can answer the question of why the hostility exists.

If you are a Marxist economist, you will likely assert that the hostile act is a product of the class struggle between the owners and the workers. If you are a sociologist, your discipline might lead you to the conclusion that social class differences are endemic in such large plants and that management and employees are treated differently by the corporation, to the envious anger of the latter. If you are a social psychologist, you might attribute the act to tensions that arise between groups, particularly when one group is given a disproportionate share of scarce resources. If you are an industrial/organizational psychologist, you might conclude that the employee is bored and angry because higher management denigrates his competence and keeps him in a passive, overcontrolled role. If you are a clinical psychologist, you might theorize about the worker's attitude toward those in power because of his chronic hostility to his father. In short, the meaning you attribute to the act, and the interventions you might make to cope with the problem that you think lies behind the act, would be determined by your theoretical frame of reference.

It is imperative, therefore, that practitioners be aware of the theory that guides them and that they differentiate fact from inference from interpretation. They must recognize that others might understand an incident—or a whole set of data—differently. Such recognition might enable practitioners to maintain a certain humility about what they believe to be the focal problem and what they propose to do about it.

In trying to understand matters psychological, the practitioner will proceed backward from behavior to thoughts to feelings. In the preceding example, the worker shot the grease in your direction. That was the behavior. We don't know why it occurred. To approach an answer to that question, we must ask, "What was he thinking?" Had we asked him that question, he might have replied, "I think the manager of this plant is an SOB." However, if we are to understand why he thinks that, we must know what his feelings are and what gave rise to them. In some cases, individuals can explain the sources of their feelings. In other cases, the explanations offered mask some other motivation of which the individuals themselves are unaware, like unconscious rivalry with the person to whom they report. Ideally, our theory helps us understand the feelings and thoughts that lead to behaviors whose rationale at first appears obscure.

An important implication of the subjective nature of consultation is that all diagnosis is hypothesis. Like any scientific finding, an organizational diagnosis is a best guess. That's why the practitioner's conclusions must be refined and tested continuously and are subject to change on the basis of additional information.

A View of Organizations

Organizational diagnosis assumes that an organization is a living organism because it comprises people. If it has a long history, that history is a product of successive cadres of people. One may therefore think of an organization in terms of biological analogies: An organization necessarily has energy, a structure, a history, and a developmental or evolutionary pattern (Greiner, 1972). Embedded in a society and composed of a collective of people, an organization also has a character, or consistent modes of acting on the basis of a set of values, and its own culture (Schein, 1985; Trice & Beyer, 1984), which includes a unique language, symbols, practices, rites, and myths.

The feelings, thoughts, and behavior in an organization give it its life and are the bases of the human interactions within it. Despite efforts to make organizational decisions rational and to attenuate individual differences by structure, policies, procedures, and technical proficiency, in the last analysis organization direction, function, and activity are based on human judgment. Feelings, therefore, are its fundamental currency.

An organization, like any biological organism, is an open system. That means, among other things, that it receives information from outside itself, as well as from within itself, and processes and acts on that information. It is composed of interrelated components that affect each other and, in turn, affect the whole. It will respond to its external world on the basis of its internal processes, abilities, and capacities, and those same internal processes lead it to act on the world outside itself in certain ways. It is therefore continuously engaged in maintaining an internal equilibrium among its components and an equilibrium in relationship to its external environment.

An organization necessarily requires the integrated effort of people. The devotion of people to a common effort fosters their attachment to the organization and vice versa. Cohesion is the psychological glue of integration. That sense, however, fosters organizational narcissism (Schwartz, 1991). It also leads to regression into narrower functions (Miller, 1991) and to decline of the adaptive capacity that is a product of diversity. Such major American corporations as IBM, AT&T, and General Motors, that is, corporations that narcissistically continued to do what they had always done while the world changed around them, are cases in point.

Yet an organization and the people in it are constantly undergoing change. Change inevitably occurs partly as a product of evolution and growth, partly because of technical or cultural change, and partly as a result of the vicissitudes of the marketplace.

People become attached to the organizations in which they work, to their roles, to their technical proficiency, to the people they work with, and to the symbols that represent all of these. They derive affectional input or support for their self-images from these attachments, which become a significant part of the meaning of their lives. When the attachments are disrupted, people experience psychological loss. Almost all change is loss, and, as reflected in the many social devices we have for dealing with it, all loss must be mourned or the ensuing depression is unrelieved. The emotional burden of unrelieved depression inhibits the successful adaptation of individuals and organizations to their losses. All organizations, therefore, should incorporate methods for coping with the losses brought about by continuous change. Few, however, recognize this issue and do so.

All business organizations are, by definition, accountability hierarchies with levels of power, responsibility, and authority. The definition of these levels constitutes the organization's formal structure, as contrasted with its shape (by product line, by function, by geographical area, by customer, by tasks). Organizations recapitulate the family structure in the cultures in which they operate. Authority patterns and styles of managerial behavior in any organization must be consistent with those of the family structure in that culture or they will create difficulties.

An organization must have a purpose—an overarching aspiration that is never achieved—and a view of the world framed for that purpose that constitutes its vision. It must evolve a focus within that vision that constitutes its mission. For example, a pharmaceutical corporation may well want to provide means for conquering illness. Obviously, its vision includes the recognition that it can't possibly deal with all of the many kinds of illnesses throughout the world. Therefore, it will concentrate its efforts on two or three, perhaps cancer, heart disease, and tuberculosis. Having delimited its thrust or mission, it then establishes goals (long-term steps toward mission, vision, and purpose) and objectives (short-term steps toward those goals). These, taken together, constitute the integrated logic of its mission. Without such an integrated logic, such practices as management by objectives become limited exercises.

All organizations necessarily are attack mechanisms; they are created to attack some kind of problem. The vitality of an organization is reflected in the effective intensity with which it attacks the problems for which it was created. To sustain our biological metaphor, adaptation is aggressive attack on the environment for survival. Fundamentally, all organizations, unless deliberately created for short-term goals, must be engaged in perpetuating themselves.

UNDERTAKING THE DIAGNOSIS

If the practitioner comes from outside the organization as a consultant, the first step is to negotiate the contract. This usually involves defining what one proposes to do, the amount of time one proposes to spend doing it, how one proposes to go about doing it, what other people will be involved in the consultation, how confidentiality is to be assured, how one is to be introduced into the organization, how and to whom the subsequent report is to be fed back, and the projected end point of the consultation. Of course, a critical element is the statement of costs, which should include the cost of questionnaires and other instruments that one might use, if any, and the time necessary for report preparation.

In many cases it is wise to undertake a brief preliminary study by reviewing with the person who is the contracting agent the definition of the problem that precipitates the consultation. This should be followed by interviews with senior executives or administrators, a review of several of the organization's recent annual reports, and a description of the organizational symptoms that reflect its pain. The practitioner might make a proposal for the initial exploratory effort, to be followed then by a more comprehensive proposal for the diagnostic study per se.

In the course of reviewing the statement of the initial problem, the practitioner may well discover that the presenting complaint is not necessarily the basic cause of the organization's pain. Conflict between components of an organization, for example, may reflect conflict between two of its senior officials. A strike may be the product of poor management of change rather than the result of differences about wages, hours, and working conditions. The practitioner will develop initial hypotheses to guide the selection of consultation methods and the formulation of the consultation design.

If the practitioner is a human resources specialist within the organization or has a similar role, probably it will be important to clear what he or she is doing with higher management and to clarify with others in the organization why such a consultation is being undertaken and with what intent, what method, and what feedback. Otherwise, there will be great suspicion when one delves into data that ordinarily are not part of one's professional role. Furthermore, one is likely to be conducting a diagnosis to bring about organizational change, which will require, in turn, the assent and participation of key figures in the organization. In fact, the practitioner may find it helpful to involve some of those key figures in the diagnostic effort as interviewers or compilers of data because they, by sharing in the diagnostic effort, will then have a more direct appreciation of the issues and give more active leadership to the change process.

If the practitioner is a consultant from outside the organization, it will be important to consider the question of why he or she was chosen for this particular consultation, rather than some other person or consulting group. Even if the question cannot be answered initially, the practitioner should develop an answer along the way. That question should give rise to others: Why does this consultation arise at this time rather than some other time? What makes it imperative now? What does the highest-ranking executive with whom one is dealing expect from this diagnostic effort? Sometimes the expectation is not readily apparent and may become clear only after repeated contact with that person. There is always the risk that the expectations may exceed what is possible. Therefore, the practitioner will have to temper and focus the expectations in keeping with the realities of time, resources, costs, and organizational complexities.

At this time, too, it will be important to assess what boundaries, limitations, and prohibitions the client executive imposes so far as which areas and functions can be observed and which persons or groups can be interviewed, observed, questioned, or even contacted. For example, in one company the chief executive was reluctant to have the consultant contact the union business agent. He said that he had worked so hard to establish an effective relationship with that person that he didn't want to have it disrupted by the consultant. Later it turned out that he was uneasy about a member of the consulting staff whom he regarded as brash and immature and capable of upsetting the relationship. When he had greater confidence in the consultant, he posed no further resistance to that interview.

Internal consultants or external practitioners who undertake a diagnosis to precede addressing an organizational problem should have their own ideas of what questions the diagnosis is expected to answer. Practitioners should also assess whether they can undertake such a diagnosis objectively, whether they should do it alone or mobilize other resources in the organization or other consultants to help, and what the political ramifications might be of undertaking such an effort.

Scanning the Organizational Horizon

As their own most important diagnostic instrument, practitioners should begin the diagnostic process immediately by forming initial impressions of the organization which are tentative hypotheses. What do you see? What do you sense? What are your feelings about your initial contact? The practitioner should have a notebook at all times and write such impressions down, however vague, illusory, or tentative they may seem. For example, a consultant's initial impression of a new major research laboratory was that it looked like a prison, leading to a preliminary hypothesis that it was autocratically managed; the hypothesis was further validated when the director said proudly that he had chosen every aspect of the design of the building, down to the color of the chair seats in the cafeteria. The practitioner should note what people's attitudes are toward him or her, ranging from the person who authorized the diagnosis to potential recipients of the results. What occurred in those contacts that made you feel good, bad, or indifferent?

Usually the practitioner is taken on an initial tour of the premises. In that tour, one gets a sense of the psychological and physical atmosphere of the organization. How does the tour guide address the employees that you meet? Does he or she introduce you to them? Are they sullen or smiling? Do they treat each other courteously, informally, with a sense of humor, or does the atmosphere seem to be cold, distant, and austere? Is the setting noisy, making communications difficult? Do people have to operate at an almost frenzied pace to keep up with the equipment? Is the lighting adequate and the temperature appropriately controlled? Are the safety practices honored, the food resources and eating facilities adequate and clean, the grounds neatly kept? The feelings you experience about these matters are likely to be experienced similarly by employees, even if they have become inured to the factors that generate those feelings.

During the tour, it is useful to examine bulletin boards not only for their content but also for the manner in which people are addressed. In one company such notices are posted in the ladies' and men's rooms, to be sure that everyone sees them. In another the language simulates military commands. The reception lobby of one company has several large display cases with trophies of the company's employee athletic teams, reflecting a paternalistic orientation. In another company there are no seating arrangements for visitors to await their appointments; people move back and forth through the reception room, both behind and in front of the receptionist's desk. Open doors on both sides of the desk and the easy movement of people indicate informality. That same informality reflects a lack of formal controls and suggests that the organization is operated in a sloppy manner.

In the course of the initial tour and in subsequent contacts, employees will react to the practitioner. Some will be guarded and hostile, others will be open and friendly; some will seek to become the practitioner's ally, others will avoid contact. Inasmuch as these reactions occur without prior contact with the practitioner, obviously they must arise out of people's feelings about themselves, the organization, and the present context. People will then attribute motives and attitudes to the practitioner that will represent their unconscious attitudes toward people in positions of power. We speak of such attitudes as "transference." That is, there is a transfer of attitudes from earlier experiences to the present situation. People's reactions to the practitioner reflect their own personalities, conflicts, and crises that have occurred in the organization, and perhaps an earlier history with consultants. Variations in these attitudes will occur throughout the diagnostic effort, and the practitioner must make note of them and try to understand their significance. In the process, people also will be testing the diagnostician's neutrality. Sometimes this will occur in the form of questions, for example, about whom the practitioner is going to interview, who will get the report, and what the practitioner has learned from other interviewees.

The practitioner will bring to the diagnostic relationship attitudes resulting from his or her own personal experiences with authority and with people who are suspicious or hostile or rivalrous and competitive. The practitioner also will have feelings about the way the client organization does its business, manages its people and processes, and shares or disdains the practitioner's values. Sometimes feelings aroused in the practitioner are subtle, and the practitioner will become aware of them only retrospectively or when he or she blunders. These attitudes we speak of as "countertransference." The practitioner should note them in as much detail as possible. The practitioner should be particularly alert to the degree to which the organization's conflicts and problems touch on his or her own history and feelings. Also, the practitioner should note the degree to which organization conflicts, problems, divisions, and resistances stimulate a sense of helplessness in him or her and should identify those responses that intrude into the diagnostic process.

The practitioner will begin to accumulate factual information. Most immediately available factual information can be found in annual reports and other formal publications of the organization. For a more comprehensive view of the financial condition of a publicly held corporation, one should review the company's 10K report, a public report that such a company submits to the Securities and Exchange Commission. From these reports the practitioner will be able to discern how the company manages its money, how much it depends on stocks or bonds or loans for financing, and how those financial arrangements facilitate or inhibit its flexibility for cash management and investment. For publicly held corporations, credit information is available in the directories of Dun & Bradstreet, Inc. Often there is detailed discussion of a company's performance in business publications like *Forbes, Business Week*, and *Fortune*. The 10K report also will list executives' salaries, outstanding obligations, litigation, government actions against the organization, and similar matters.

Whether from these reports or others, one will need to learn the numbers of employees in the various organizational locations, together with demographic information. In large companies, headquarters are often located in metropolitan areas distant from manufacturing plants and operations. These, together with the diversity of the work force, will point to questions about communication, cultural differences, and particular problems the organization may face in dealing with ethnic groups. For example, a corporate headquarters group in Philadelphia employing a largely Hispanic group in South Carolina would have to understand the complexities facing these employees in that particular rural environment, where Spanish is not the local language, where Hispanics are experienced as rivals by local African-Americans, and where the traditions of the community make them feel alien.

The practitioner will also want to get organizational charts early on. These will reflect not only who reports to whom but also the range of roles and functions that ultimately will have to be sampled. Interestingly, when one asks a given interviewee to draw an organization chart, that person's view of the organization may differ significantly from the formal chart. This will be especially true if one asks who the interviewee's boss is. The response will not necessarily be the person to whom the interviewee ostensibly reports but the person who is a conceptual level above the interviewee (Jaques, 1991).

The practitioner will then want to compose a description of the various work settings and tasks. This will provide a sense of who does what, what the nature of the work flow is, what kinds of differences exist in style of work, time frames, criteria for performance, and other dimensions of the work. For example, a research unit will likely have people of a higher conceptual level who operate without the same time demands and efficiency requirements as workers on an assembly line (Lawrence & Lorsch, 1967). Those who are developing products do not have the same time urgency as marketers whose task is to get the product to market as quickly as possible. These subcultural differences may make for problems among different work groups. Much of the contemporary effort to involve manufacturing people in discussions with customers and to bring marketing staff into early consultation with those in product development are efforts to cope with such differences.

Exploring Organization Direction

All organizations necessarily anticipate the future and are directed toward coping with it. They invest in buildings and equipment, in marketing and advertising, in developing their employees. Many engage in long-term projects like building nuclear power plants or developing oil fields. Most acquire capital either by equity (selling stocks and bonds) or debt (borrowing). It is important, therefore, to understand how an organization perceives its future and focuses its anticipatory efforts. A significant component of that understanding is developing a sense of the organization's trajectory. What is its history? What is its evolutionary pattern? What have been the stages in its development, and how has it managed its transitions (Greiner, 1972)? How would you describe its trajectory, its momentum, its focus? In short, where has it come from and where is it going? With what speed and toward what target?

The most critical aspect of an organization's evolution is the changes in its leadership. How has it managed succession? Entrepreneurs do a notoriously poor job of choosing successors. Political conflicts in an organization may well result in power struggles and the compromise choice of a passive leader who will not favor either faction. In family businesses often the rule of primogeniture is followed, which means that the eldest son takes over, even though another child may be more competent. Some organizations do a very careful job of developing succession with formal executive development programs. Some use psychological testing or assessment centers. Others, however, leave succession to chance. Some organizations recognize that no leader can do everything well, and succession becomes an effort to compensate for the weaknesses of previous leaders and perhaps to confront new market conditions. For example, when John F. Welch succeeded Reginald Jones as chief executive of General Electric Co., Welch quickly sold off many of GE's businesses and concentrated its efforts on those that were most profitable. The GE of the Welch era is vastly different from what GE was before.

One can get a sense of how seriously an organization is concerned with its perpetuation by the attention it gives to formal management and executive development programs, to assignments for training and development, to the money it invests in such programs, and to the degree of systematic effort it makes to assure its own adaptive perpetuation. Major organizations, like IBM, GE, Motorola, and Procter & Gamble, spend millions of dollars in training and development. They give careful attention to succession planning. Some do so well at this that they are the suppliers of talent to other organizations. Consumer products businesses frequently turn to Procter & Gamble for managerial candidates. Manufacturing organizations often do the same with GE. In fact, one way to judge how well an organization does in this respect is to learn how frequently other companies seek to attract its managers and executives. Usually, this issue will arise spontaneously as interviewees discuss the organization's history and where superiors or peers have gone. Sometimes it becomes evident in the statistics of managerial turnover. For example, although for many years Digital Equipment was a highly successful organization, few other corporations tried to win away its executives, as contrasted with the experience of IBM. The reason simply was that Digital was dominated by its founder, Kenneth Olsen, and its structure was deliberately created to diffuse authority. As a result, no one could judge how well any Digital manager would do when he or she became responsible for the total managerial role.

Another important index of how and to what degree an organization anticipates its future is its financial investment in that future. Some wise organizations have systematic plans for capital investment and reinvestment in facilities. Others can't or don't. The latter are therefore likely to lose out in competition that requires increasing efficiency and productivity and lowering costs.

Organizations usually have a core skill that, properly understood, can become their dominant competitive edge. For example, for many years AT&T thought of its core skill as developing telecommunications products. It did not readily recognize that billing millions of customers as it had done for many years was a core skill. Recognizing that fact and taking advantage of it, AT&T quickly became a serious competitor of other credit card companies that didn't have its established mailing lists and collection procedures.

Not only must an organization have a focus, but it also must have an equally widely shared understanding of how it intends to reach its goals. Although there is much talk about vision, mission, goals, and so on in most organizations, in too many those issues are not adequately articulated. Top management may have a sense of where the organization is going, but often, even only a few levels below, not many people understand fully what the thrust is. In some cases processes have not been organized carefully around that thrust. As a result, one of the contemporary buzz words in the organization literature is "reengineering," meaning aligning the structure and processes of an organization in keeping with what it hopes to be able to accomplish.

All organizations are bombarded with continuous communications from the outside. There is a plethora of information of all kinds. Some inputs, such as newspapers, are broad, while others, such as highly technical reports, are narrow. What kind of information does this organization get, and how does it use that information? Any visitor to a corporation can readily observe on the reception room coffee table and sometimes in the offices of managers and executives a wide array of business magazines—mostly unread. Typically, managers don't read much. (Even organization development consultants seem not to read very much.) To what extent does the organization make use of the information that comes its way? How does it do that? What information is the basis for common discussion and shared decision making? Who brings what specialized information from which sources into the common pool? What critical information seems to be ignored? For example, General Motors had to lose 35% of its market share before it took Japanese competition seriously. In sum, how does this organization keep up with the external world? And how rapidly does it respond to threats from various kinds of competitors and from economic conditions and political circumstances? For example, in the face of recession, many companies downsized drastically. Others couldn't seem to face their reality directly and undertook limited downsizing that necessitated their repeating that process again and again, to the demoralization of their people.

THE DIAGNOSTIC PROCESS

Having undertaken the initial exploration and developed a sense of the organization's key figures, directions, financial status, and physical and employee distribution, and of the multiple facets of its work, the practitioner must create a method for organizing the information that he or she will gather. The most convenient way is to create a set of file cards or similar files on a computer, one for each critical topic. Then, as the practitioner gathers data, information can be placed under the appropriate heading immediately, thus avoiding the complex and cumbersome task of later sorting the myriad facts that the diagnostic effort will yield. Overlapping topic categories make it possible for the practitioner to perceive phenomena from several different vantage points and simultaneously to have the confirmation necessary for credible inferences.

There are myriad ways of organizing information. I prefer to do so from the beginning forward, so to speak. The origins of an organization give rise to all else that follows because so much of what ensues grows out of those origins. Few organizations are wiped out, to become only legal shells from which another is later constructed. The evolutionary path of an organization reflects is adaptive methods and patterns. Its communications patterns are an analog to the human nervous system.

The following topics are those under which I gather and organize information (see Levinson, 1972, for a complete outline). The first three topics emphasize gathering facts while the fourth puts heavy emphasis on inferences.

1. Genetic data (identification and description of the organization, its history, and the reasons for the consultation).
2. Structure data (the formal organization, plant and equipment, finances, personnel demographics and policies, general policies and practices, and time cycles).
3. Process data (communications and information transmission).
4. Interpretative data (how the organization perceives itself and its environment; its basic knowledge and how it makes use of that knowledge; the emotional atmosphere of the organization and its capacity to act; attitudes and relationships toward multiple stakeholders, toward the consultant, toward things and ideas, toward power, and toward itself).

The facts and inferences are eventually integrated into an analysis and set of conclusions, followed by a summary and recommendations.

Developing a Sample

Once a method for organizing data has been established, the next step is to develop a sample for individual and group interviews, questionnaires, and observations. Developing a sample is fundamental to diagnosis. The practitioner wants to know that his or her information truly represents the organization. The client system wants to be assured of the validity of the information. Though various members of the organization may differ with the practitioner's interpretations, none will fault his or her fundamental work if they can trust that the data truly are representative and verifiable. (That is, another diagnosis would yield the same data.)

As a rule of thumb, I usually interview all of the members of top management (however that is defined), a representative sample (usually about 10%) of middle management (those below what has been defined as top management and above first-level supervisors), and a sample of line employees (usually about 5%). Depending on the size of the organization, these percentages may vary. In any event, one wants to be certain of sampling the range of organizational activities with sufficient comprehensiveness that when the sample is subsequently described, people in the organization will accept it as truly representative. Sometimes a comprehensive sample is neither necessary nor possible for certain kinds of focal problems. In such instances, it will be important to point out the limits of the sampling.

Interviews

It is particularly helpful for the practitioner to construct an interviewing schedule with the names of people whom he or she has chosen for the sample. The practitioner can then make specific appointments, clearing them with the person to whom the interviewee reports and making it clear to the interviewee that the interview content is confidential and participation is voluntary. In practice, I find it useful to allow 2 hours for each executive and managerial interview and one hour for those at the line level.

Sometimes interviewees will be dubious about confidentiality and the prospect that anything constructive will come of the consultation. The practitioner can explain that leaks undermine the diagnostic effort and therefore the work of the practitioner and can encourage the interviewee to hold doubts in abeyance until the final results are in.

To provide the basis for a comprehensive grasp of the organization, I ask a series of open-ended interview questions (Levinson, 1972). These questions touch on such issues as the history of the organization, feelings about the organization and coworkers, the organization's image, help and training for employees, performance evaluation, benefits, rules, time pressures, communications, sources of information about the work, what the organization stands for and pays attention to in the outside world, and the organization's future. Interviewees seem most intrigued by (and later discuss among themselves) my request that they construct a personified visual image of the organization and describe that "person" to me. Related questions ask how peppy or energetic the organization is and how strong it is.

Questionnaires

In large organizations it is helpful to have a complementary questionnaire. The practitioner may use a commercially available attitude or morale instrument or the Organization and Job Attitude Inventory (Levinson, 1972) that is intended to complement the open-ended interview questions. Commercial instruments that provide for computer scoring may be more efficient, even though the resulting information may be less psychologically sophisticated.

It is unwise to use questionnaires without personal interviews. The reasons are simple. A questionnaire provides answers to questions one asks but not to those one doesn't ask. Furthermore, the subtleties of response are necessarily missed by the simple responses allowed on questionnaires, which are more expedient for scoring than for understanding complexity.

Diagnosing Leadership

All organizations are the lengthened shadows of their leaders. Sometimes that shadow lasts for generations. Inevitably, it is heavily cast by incumbent leaders. Therefore, it is important for the practitioner to assess and describe the behavior of leading figures in the organization and to examine the influence of their behavior on the organization's performance. This assessment is inferred from the responses to questions in the interview about the organizational image and communication of information. It also derives from spontaneous comments of interviewees and from individual interviews with leaders. Sometimes there are business media stories about the leadership. In other instances such information comes from members of the board or contacts outside the organization.

There may be significant differences among the organization's leaders that offer the disadvantage of conflict or the advantage of complementary effort. In one entrepreneurial organization the chief executive was widely noted for his flood of creative ideas. One of his two lieutenants concentrated his efforts on winnowing those ideas and translating the best into products. The second, whose emphasis was on the immediate and practical, attended to the day-to-day business of the organization. None of the three could carry on the roles of the others; all were necessary to achieve the organization's goals.

Overcontrolling leaders will rigidify an organization. Charismatic leaders will tend to overshadow it. Manipulative leaders will be likely to exploit it for their own gain (Kets de Vries, 1989; Kets de Vries & Miller, 1984, 1988). Of course, significant differences in behavioral style, perceptions, and values among organization leaders and managers will make it difficult for the organization to evolve and sustain a coherent competitive thrust.

Observations

From time to time it is useful to observe people at work to see exactly what they do and how it fits into the larger context of the organization. Sometimes, if the work is not too complex or difficult, employees will allow the practitioner to do some of it and experience its requirements firsthand. The greater the immersion one has in the work process itself, the more likely one is to understand some of the issues and problems related to it.

This method also helps to evaluate leadership. By sitting in the office of a chief executive one can observe both the flow of contacts and the content of the issues that arise. Such observations will soon provide a sense of what that particular person thinks is important and how he or she goes about dealing with those issues. There may be a significant difference between what an individual says is important and what he or she actually does in the course of a day's work (Kotter, 1982; Mintzberg, 1973).

Written and Other Information

The practitioner may want to gather all kinds of information: human resources policies and practices; historical data, both formal and from public media sources; references to the organization in trade or professional journals; reports or discussions in industrial or medical histories or similar volumes to understand the place of the organization in its industry, field, or community. Exit interviews are an informative source of information about experiences in the organization. Interviews with competitors, with clients or customers, or with political or other officials with whom the organization has contact add additional perspectives.

Organizations use many different kinds of consultants, and reports by these consultants often yield important data. Sometimes such reports indicate that the same issues have arisen repeatedly and have not been resolved—or, in some cases, even addressed. In some organizations, consultants' reports sit on shelves. In others they will have resulted in important and sometimes drastic changes, echoes of which may now be reverberating for the practitioner. Change, for example, is poorly managed in most organizations, and its effects may remain as residual problems for years. In any event, the practitioner will want to review such reports, particularly after arriving at his or her own conception of the organization's problems and strengths.

The practitioner should review organization communications in some detail. These include external publications for customers and the public at large, such as the annual report, brochures, advertising, news releases, and similar devices. One might ask of an annual report, for example: What does the management want the reader to think and believe about the organization? What kind of an image is it trying to present? With what success? How realistically? How large is the gap between how the organization wants to be perceived and how, in fact, it is perceived? Organizational communication also includes internal publications such as bulletins and memoranda. What issues are emphasized in these and other internal communications? What are the repetitive themes? How effective and persuasive are these communications? How much do they contribute to giving employees the information they need and want, as contrasted with superficial pronouncements?

In particular, what is the substance of the communications to customers or clients, to political figures, to regulatory bodies? How does the organization engage its competitors? How does it relate to the communications media and to the respective communities of which it is a part? And what is its attitude toward itself? For example, "Sensor was a giant hit because of Gillette's willingness to spend heavily on its own brand name—and its ability to deliver a product good enough to live up to it" ("The Best a Plan Can Get," 1992).

THE LOGIC OF DIAGNOSIS

Having gathered all the diagnostic information and organized it under the critical topics, the practitioner must now construct inferences from what he or she has learned. That means assessing the strengths and weaknesses of the organization, its resources (financial, intellectual, market position, reputation, and similar facets), its mode of interacting with its environment, its awareness and understanding of the problems it is encountering, and the level of conceptual ability at which it understands those problems. Since the organization's leadership is crucial to its capacity to resolve its problems, the practitioner must assess how far ahead the leadership can conceive of and anticipate issues, how aggressive it is in taking a competitive position, and how well it has developed followership within the organization. The Gillette example cited earlier is a case in point ("The Best a Plan Can Get," 1992):

> Gillette undertook a high-risk option to launch Sensor throughout both America and Europe.... It added to its risk by planning to back Sensor's simultaneous American and Pan-European launch with an advertising and promotional blitz featuring identical television commercials (apart from language) in every market.... Such campaigns often fail; ads that work in one place can flop in others. (pp. 59–60)

Clearly, the Gillette top management conceived of a worldwide strategy to turn the razor blade from a commodity to a product by adding luster to its brand name.

Inferences and Interpretation

The practitioner must be careful in following the path from fact to inference to interpretation. By this time the practitioner will have recorded all of the facts and made the appropriate inferences. The practitioner should be able to cite the facts from which the inferences were made, specify the alternative inferences that were possible, and explain the reason for choosing one over another. This is neither the time nor place to introduce new information. Furthermore, the practitioner must be able to defend his or her conclusions. One can do so only if there is a clear path from the data to the interpretations.

The diagnostic formulation is a comprehensive summary of the practitioner's logic and the conclusions that the practitioner draws from it. The conclusion will also include recommendations about what change efforts are necessary and how they might be accomplished in this organization.

A critically important aspect of the diagnosis is the prognosis. This should be a statement of what kinds of changes are likely to be undertaken by the practitioner and the organization, or by the organization alone, in what period of time and with what resources, limits, and prospective outcome. Unfortunately, this is usually not done. As a result, practitioners frequently are overwhelmed with a sense of the impossible nature of their work. They expect too much of themselves and the organization and therefore frequently are disappointed with the limits of what they and the organization can do. A careful evaluation of a prognosis and a formulation of its boundaries helps to contain the work within realistic limits and to alleviate the sense of overwhelming inadequacy that often follows a diagnosis. Neither the organization nor the practitioner is going to be as good as either would like in its problem-solving efforts. This realistic recognition should not, however, destroy the good that either or both can do.

Feedback Report

The next logical step is the practitioner's feedback report. This should include three basic considerations: (1) a brief history of the organization and its context as a setting for the problem that was posed to the practitioner, (2) what the practitioner did to obtain the information that forms the basis for his or her recommendations, and (3) how the practitioner understands the information and what recommendations he or she makes about what might be done to cope with the perceived problem.

The report then is presented to the chief executive officer or whoever is in an equivalent role. Several cautions must be observed in reporting to that person. First, the practitioner must insist that the chief executive reserve the last 2 hours of a working day and the first 2 hours of the next morning for the report feedback and subsequent discussion. If the practitioner does not insist on such a condition, the consultation is likely to be lost. The reason is simple. No matter how much a given executive wants accurate information, he or she is and has been doing the best he or she can. Consequently, a consultant's report, no matter how gently couched, is perceived to be an indictment.

Therefore, I do not give a client a report; rather I read it aloud, asking the client how it might sound to others. I encourage taking notes during my reading, and then after the reading, I clarify any points about which the client has questions. I ask the client to take the report home, read it during the evening, and come back prepared to discuss it the next morning. Inevitably, the sense of indictment will swell into paranoid hostility when the client reads the report. Meeting together the next morning will temper that paranoid reaction, and the subsequent review of the report will bring the reaction back to realistic proportions. I ask the client to review both what has been said in the report and how it has been said. I offer the opportunity for the client to suggest appropriate language changes, if necessary, that will not alter the substance of the report. In one case, I had to review the report word by word, line by line, in three 2-hour sessions with the chief executive.

Having clarified the report with the chief executive, the report is then presented to each successive level of the organization. It may be necessary to modify the report for successively lower levels so that it is specific and concrete enough for employees to understand clearly what is reported. Discussion then follows. In some cases, there will be no discussion; the recommendations stand as presented. In other instances, the report may serve as the basis for discussion within the organization about possible options for action. In still others, particularly when there has been no commitment to report throughout the organization, only the person who asked for the consultation will decide on any action to be taken. It is important for the practitioner to understand that the chief executive is the person responsible for the organization and the one who must necessarily determine how to manage the impact of the report on the organization and the subsequent action processes. The practitioner must be extremely careful not to undermine the role of the chief executive.

For example, in a community service organization, the heads of the various departments saw themselves as a collective that made the decisions on behalf of the organization. A major problem in that organization was the failure of the chief executive to demarcate his role and exercise his power appropriately. The department directors protested when I announced that I was to report to the CEO and subsequently to them. They felt, in effect, that they were a collective CEO and that they should all hear the report at the same time. I pointed out that they were not a collective CEO, that the chief executive was indeed the chief executive, and my obligation was to him in that role. I would not collude with them against their leader, however willing he had been to collude with them against his own authority and the interests of the organization that depended on his leadership.

From time to time people will want to quarrel with the practitioner about the validity of the data, the diagnostic method, or the conclusions. It is here that the practitioner's comprehensive sources of information, careful inferences, and logical conclusions will enable him or her to feel comfortable about the solidity of the effort.

Frequently, those who had earlier voiced doubts about the degree to which the practitioner would report what was learned now come forward to applaud the integrity of the work and its results. There can be a highly useful corollary effort. In the case cited earlier, where the chief executive required three review sessions, his conviction about the conclusions was such that he followed each presentation he made to successive parts of his organization with a statement of what he was going to do about the recommendations. His actions subsequently validated his promises.

Having the practitioner then help the organization implement the recommendations usually calls for renegotiating the contract to define what is to be done, within what period of time, with what costs, and what checks on the outcome. If the organization's leadership is left to its own devices to follow up the practitioner's recommendations, the practitioner will have to take leave of the people with whom he or she has worked. It is important to say good-bye to as many of those one has interviewed as is reasonable—to those who have demonstrated their work activities, those who have provided special information, and those who have been generally helpful, such as secretaries, administrative assistants, and others who have assisted with accommodations and logistics. All should have a sense of having been personally respected and appreciated for their contributions to the effort. The practitioner, too, will want to close the relationship on a positive note with a gratifying sense of having left something useful behind.

AN ILLUSTRATIVE CASE: THE VITECH CORPORATION

Vitech makes measurement and control systems, precision optical products, and glass and medical devices. It comprises four divisions: Graphic Measurement, Precision Measurement, Imprinting Devices, and Government Systems. The first three of these manufacture and sell high-tech instruments, while Government Systems does technical design work for the military services. At the time of the consultation there were 769 employees, of whom 50 were in corporate headquarters and 400 in Government Systems, the largest division. The company was started by its president, Vernon Lambertson, 25 years ago in a garage.

Vitech had recently been experiencing difficulties. In 1987 the commercial products divisions accounted for 45% of sales. The latest figures showed that 90% of profits came from the Government Systems division.

The president had ordered both pay and working hours reduced in the commercial divisions, in some cases to a 4-day week. There had been continued indecision about closing the Graphic Measurement division because of low profits, poor management, and inadequate marketing. Layoffs had been announced in the Precision Measurement and Imprinting Devices divisions, but the Government Systems division worked a 50-hour week. Employees in the commercial divisions were disgruntled and worried about their future.

The board of directors had been concerned about these and other matters and felt that Lambertson was spread too thin. He took on a controller and a vice president of human resources, Greg Edwards, as a response to this criticism. The latter felt that outside consultation was needed and turned to The Levinson Institute.

The Course of Consultation

The Levinson Institute had one previous contact with Vitech. Lambertson had agreed to consultation a year previously, but had changed his mind. Now Edwards's urging had pushed him into grudging acceptance. It was felt, however, that Lambertson might abort the consultation at some point and might not support critical activities in the consultation.

The Vitech building was one story of red brick, unpretentious, and approximately 100 feet long. A small sign with a logo stood in front of the building but gave no indication of what the company did. The reception area was small and poorly lighted, and nothing in it described or pictured Vitech. Management offices were small and modestly furnished. Linoleum took the place of carpeting. The cafeteria consisted of a long row of vending machines, a microwave oven, and simple chrome and plastic tables and chairs.

These arrangements proved to reflect Lambertson's philosophy and Spartan way of life. He saw no need for fancy trappings or advertising. In winter he drove a jeep with a snowplow in case a driveway needed clearing or an employee's car had to be helped out of a drift.

The consulting team reviewed annual reports, 10K reports, previous consultation reports, policy manuals, contracts, government comments, corporate publications, and similar materials. Also available were the results of an annual attitude survey conducted by another consultant. A four-person team interviewed all of the top management, the six members of the board of directors, 16 department heads, and a random sample of 5% of the employees in corporate headquarters and each division. The team devoted 332 hours (the equivalent of 8 weeks) to interviews, analysis, report preparation, and feedback.

Four divisions in one building made for a task-oriented, functional, but cluttered physical layout. Thus, initial questions for the team included the following: How does one define one's place and meaning at Vitech? One's boundaries, autonomy, and support relationships? One's divisional and organizational identity (is there one)? What are the factors that make Vitech a "family," and how do they affect the functioning of the organization, the president, management, and the employees?

Attitudes and Opinions

The need for management development was mentioned by several of the executives who reported to the president. One cited the lack of managers who were aggressive and decisive and could plan. Another pointed to a lack of really skilled and experienced people. The president himself was considered by some to be part of the problem. He was seen as unable to delegate and let go, a trait that hindered Vitech's growth.

At a lower level, engineering managers who were relatively new to Vitech stated that in comparison to their previous companies Vitech had a low level of technological expertise and that their own expertise and creativity were not welcomed. Promotion was seen by this group and others as haphazard and dependent upon seniority and getting along with the president.

Employees had mixed views about Vitech. They were proud of its professionalism. However, relations with customers were tainted by difficulties in responding quickly enough to customers' needs. Although they thought that the Government Systems division and the Graphic Measurement division responded quickly, they viewed Precision Measurement less favorably and the responses of Imprinting Devices as poor. When employees were asked to describe Vitech as though it were a person, responses included the following: an adolescent unsure of where he or she was going; a freight train out of control; an honest, sincere person, competent but not brilliant, who stumbled around hoping things would fall into their proper places.

The culture of the organization was defined as easygoing and informal. There were comparatively few official policies and procedures and a lack of uniformity in the application of policies from division to division. The informality was also reflected in the lack of punctuality about coming to work and a casual attitude about setting objectives and evaluating performance.

Although opinion surveys and market surveys were a regular feature of the operation, Vitech didn't seem eager to accept much advice, particularly from the employee surveys. There was a question about how deeply Lambertson wanted to listen. That attitude was reflected further down the organization by the lack of regular meetings for most work groups. Division managers seemed to have little interest in understanding employees' perceptions. Most supervisors tried to ignore problems until they blew up.

The President

Vernon Lambertson was in his 50s, tall, and stockily built. He was quiet-spoken and seemingly shy. He worked in shirtsleeves. His shoes were scuffed, and he had a number of pens in his pocket. He looked like a hands-on engineer and appeared uncomfortable with social banter.

Lambertson was aware of the poor interpersonal skills of many of his managers. He said they were so good with tangible gear that they thought they were good with people, but he found some of them to be awful managers who produced work situations that were hard to correct. Many middle managers were older employees who had been promoted into their positions and lacked the skills to perform effectively in the present business environment. Lambertson was troubled over this fact and sensitive to his responsibility to these employees who were not able to function as productively and as creatively as newly trained managers might. His loyalty to them, his protectiveness, and his inability to solve the problem resulted in his leaving the situation as it was.

Lambertson himself was not very open to change, but he was not intransigent. For example, 3 years previously he had not thought it important, or even appropriate, to share information with employees. However, working with consultants who conducted the regular employee attitude survey led him to change his mind, and communications had improved. On the other hand, Lambertson's tight control meant that nothing got done unless he wanted it done, and managers had to approach him individually and try to get his approval. This tended to stifle creativity and produce frustration.

Lambertson was the first to admit that he was neither a good manager nor a good salesman, but employees had a great deal of respect and affection for him as a person and as an engineering genius. Employees saw him as sincere, honest, and concerned, but also as somewhat incompetent, an opinion they felt guilt in expressing.

Lambertson appeared to hold two ego-ideals. On the one hand, he embodied the traditional image of the compulsive, detail-oriented engineer who was dedicated to results, comfortable with the abstractions of numbers and the specificity of tasks, but uncomfortable with interpersonal relationships and the surfacing of emotions. He was satisfied by task accomplishment and being valued by others who appreciated his solutions to their technical problems. But circumstances from within and without had thrust him into the role of president of a growing and troubled high-tech company. He therefore, on the other hand, aspired to be a good president. He saw that his role logically demanded monitoring of the outside world, developing managers and teams of managers, and exercising broad conceptual management skills. However, at 59 years of age and after 10 years of coaching by consultants, he did not think he had changed much, nor was he apt to change, although he had tried and was still trying.

Summary, Inference, and Interpretation

This was an organizational family that had a clear sense of identity, was troubled by and concerned over a member who was very ill (the Graphic Measurement division), and was looking to the future with feelings of apprehension and hope. Whether it would survive the near future in its present form; how it would meet the internal and external challenges it now faced; and how the family heads would ensure its cohesion, health, and growth were questions that weighed heavily on all the members. The company, like its founder, in many ways was hidden from the outside world. Both were unable to explicitly assess and state what they were, what they did, and how well they did it. They were resistant to self-knowledge while making attempts to learn about themselves and hoping to change.

Vitech was described as an organization in the adolescent phase of its life. It had now outgrown its old clothes; the informal management procedures and methods of operation were no longer working. The time for introspection had arrived. Responding to the question of imagining the organization as a person and describing what that person was doing, one employee described Vitech as a teenage boy engaged in his first fistfight: finding himself slugged and stunned, he knew he must fight back, but he was not exactly sure how.

Vitech had not been able to move successfully from its entrepreneurial state to one that was fully professional (Greiner, 1972). It was inhibited by the inability of its chief executive to let go. The chief executive's overcontrol of his own aggression and his need to punish himself were reflected in his severe superego, his overcontrol of others, and the minimal comforts of the work environment. He was able to tolerate neither the expression of his aggression nor the expression of more affectionate feelings, except through a paternalistic sense of noblesse oblige. Furthermore, he was heavily dependent on his professional skill not only for his self-esteem but also as a means of avoiding being dependent on others. This lifelong personality pattern was not susceptible to significant change, but inasmuch as the chief executive was responsive to the opinions of the consultants and was face-to-face with economic circumstances that threatened to compel him to contract his company, the consultants believed it might well be possible, with sensitive support, to assist him in taking gradual steps to distance himself from operations. Although Lambertson's paternalism and technical proficiency created conditions for identification that could hold the company together, the changes would have to take place, for Vitech had to differentiate itself more clearly and become more competitive. The prognosis was optimistically guarded.

Recommendations

Numerous recommendations were made for improving Vitech's functioning in many areas. The central recommendation was that Vernon Lambertson be provided with a more permanent form of managerial assistance than had been available to him in the past. That assistance would take the form of an executive vice president or chief operating officer. He or she would provide managerial expertise, complement Lambertson's technical strength, and spare him the extraneous problems he had to deal with under the present structure.

Although Lambertson seemed to understand his own limitations as a manager, it did not follow that he could easily accept the addition of an intervening executive, as his overcontrolling character and past reactions to such suggestions indicated. It was believed that a psychological consultant would be helpful in supporting Lambertson in his relationship to the new executive and in enabling him to anticipate his inevitable retirement. Careful, sensitive support would be needed to preserve Lambertson's self-esteem while helping him recognize his limitations and their cost to the organization.

The central issue for Vitech was the development of a more sophisticated approach to management. Vernon Lambertson could not do it alone. The provision of additional managerial expertise to support the CEO was the foundation upon which the other recommendations rested; implementation of all the other recommendations without addressing the core problem in this manner would mean little for the future of Vitech.

CONCLUSION

Management, like all disciplines, is subject to fads as executives seek quick and easy solutions to complex problems (Levinson, 1992). But there are no quick and easy solutions. Various managerial techniques are applied to organizations without addressing the following basic questions: What is the specific problem in the organization? What are its multiple causes in the context of the economy, its own industry, and its unique organizational history? How well is the organization able to cope with its problem?

An ethical consultant must answer such questions, report what he or she has learned in a manner that can be understood, and recommend steps for change. These recommendations can be the basis for discussion within the organization and for evolving a plan of change that is in keeping with the organization's capacities and competence. All this requires a formal, comprehensive diagnostic process, such as outlined in this chapter, and solid psychological skill.

REFERENCES

The best a plan can get. (1992, August 15). *The Economist*, pp. 59–60.

Greiner, L. (1972, July–August). Evolution and revolution as organizations grow. *Harvard Business Review*, pp. 37–46.

Jaques, E., & Clement, S. D. (1991). *Executive leadership*. Arlington, VA: Cason Hall.

Kets de Vries, M. F. R. (1989). *Prisoners of leadership*. New York: Wiley.

Kets de Vries, M. F. R., & Miller, D. (1984). *The neurotic organization*. San Francisco: Jossey-Bass.

Kets de Vries, M. F. R., & Miller, D. (1988). *Unstable at the top*. New York: New American Library.

Kotter, J. P. (1982). *The general managers*. New York: Free Press.

Lawrence, P. R., & Lorsch, J. W. (1967). *Organization and environment*. Boston: Harvard University, Graduate School of Business Administration, Division of Research.

Levinson, H. (1972). *Organizational diagnosis*. Cambridge, MA: Harvard University Press.

Levinson, H. (1992). Fads, fantasies, and psychological management. *Consulting Psychology Journal, 44*(1), 1–12.

Miller, D. (1991). *The Icarus paradox*. New York: Harper Business.

Mintzberg, H. (1973). *The nature of managerial work*. New York: Harper & Row.

Schein, E. H. (1985). *Organizational culture and leadership*. San Francisco: Jossey-Bass.

Schwartz, H. S. (1991). *Narcissistic process in corporate decay: The theory of the organizational ideal*. New York: New York University Press.

Trice, H. M., & Beyer, J. M. (1984). Studying organizational cultures through rites and ceremonials. *Academy of Management Review, 9*(4), 653–669.

CHAPTER 3

Diagnostic Models
for Organization Development

W. WARNER BURKE

In the process of making a presentation to a group of executives recently, I asked them to take a stab at naming the most popular organizational model in North America today. One person named the family, another the army, and a third nominated the Catholic church. They were using the first dictionary definition of model, namely a standard or example to imitate, rather than the second definition (the one I was seeking); that is, a representation of something. Obviously, I did not ask the question very well. The answer to my question is the McKinsey 7S model, but more about that later.

An organizational model is therefore a representation, usually metaphorically, of an organization. As we observe people in an organization going about their duties and interactions with others, it can be quite useful to have an organizational model to help us understand more clearly and quickly what we are observing. An organizational model can also trap us, however. Becoming overly dependent on a model for understanding can cause us to see things that may not be there. But I am getting ahead of myself.

I will first briefly examine the ways that organizational models can help us and hinder us. I will then, in the bulk of this chapter, describe and evaluate several organizational models, concentrating on those that primarily serve diagnostic purposes, especially for organization development (OD). Finally, in an attempt to integrate much of what we know about diagnostic models for OD purposes, I will define and explain the Burke–Litwin model of organizational performance and change.

Thus, the purpose of this chapter is to provide a deeper understanding of diagnostic models for OD. I will cover some pros and cons of the more prominent models, but certainly not all organizational models. Pick 100 organizational consultants, and we would have 100 different diagnostic models. In an advanced OD training program with which I have been associated for many years, we conduct an exercise on the second day that asks each participant to depict on an easel pad his or her diagnostic model of organizations. After having seen at least as many as 500 of these models, I have yet to see two that are the same.

To choose only a handful of models to examine in this chapter is to be highly selective indeed, and I have limited myself to what has been published—and to only some of those. Ninety-nine percent of organizational diagnostic models are not in print, only in practitioners' heads or perhaps in notes they carry in their attaché cases. A further purpose of this chapter, then, is to learn how to use organizational models more efficiently for diagnostic purposes, not to argue that one is better than another—although I will in each case provide at least a brief critique of each model that is covered.

THE DIAGNOSTIC PHASE
IN ORGANIZATION DEVELOPMENT PRACTICE

Once a practitioner/consultant has established a contract with a client to perform OD work, the next phase is to conduct an organization diagnosis. The diagnosis consists of data gathering followed by analysis; that is, a diagnosis seeks to answer the question, "What do all of these data that we have gathered mean?"

Data gathering usually takes more than one form. Interviewing organization members is the most common. Using a questionnaire is also popular. In addition, many of us consultants like to include in our data gathering the reading of certain organizational papers, especially strategic plans, vision/mission statements, and policy documents. And, of course, there is always what the practitioner observes.

After the data have been collected, the OD practitioner must then summarize all the information. This summarizing process ideally should be done in two steps. The first is to create a simple summary of how many people said what and/or of average responses and percentages from a questionnaire, and perhaps to show how this summary ties in with—or does not relate to, as the case may be—certain organizational plans, policies, and so forth. The second step is to categorize the data into some organizational framework, or model.

The OD practitioner may ask broad open-ended questions at the data-gathering stage and later see how the information fits within a particular model. One might choose a certain model from among a number of frameworks, depending on the kind of organization one is consulting with and how the data appear to be arrayed or clustered. The other alternative is to choose a model a priori and ask the data-gathering questions accordingly.

Either way there are trade-offs. Asking broad, open-ended questions has the advantage of not "leading the witness," yet it may produce such wide-ranging information that one may have a difficult time making sense of it all, regardless of what model is chosen later to help with the analysis. On the other hand, asking questions at the outset according to some model has the advantage of rapidly organizing the data gathered, but the potential problem is that the model used may be too limited in scope.

It is important, in any case, to use a model. A model can help to make sense out of what may seem after an initial data-gathering step to be nothing more than a massive buzzing state of confusion. By way of summary, let us now examine more specifically the reasons for using a model in OD practice.

Uses of Organizational Models

Organization models are useful in several ways:

- *Models help to categorize data about the organization.* It is far easier to deal with six or eight categories than to consider 100 bits of information all at once.
- *Models help to enhance our understanding.* If we have a model with, say, seven categories and we find that most of the organization's problems cluster in two of the seven, then we have a better idea of where to begin to improve matters than if we had 100 bits of information.
- *Models help to interpret data.* Suppose in our model we have the two categories of strategy and structure (most models do indeed include these two categories). Let us further assume that from our data we have found a problem with the organization's structure (i.e., the hierarchy, reporting relationships, decision-making accountability, etc.). We know from the literature (e.g., Chandler, 1962) that to achieve organizational effectiveness, strategy and structure must be linked. In other words, to fix the structure problem without consideration first of the organization's strategy would lead to ineffectiveness.
- *Models help to provide a common shorthand language.* For example, the terms culture, shared values, networks, helpful mechanisms, and transactional factors all come from one model or the other. Greater efficiency in communication among organization members can be realized from the use of a model.

Finally, a note of caution: It is possible to become trapped by one's chosen model. If one particular viewpoint drives the diagnostic process,

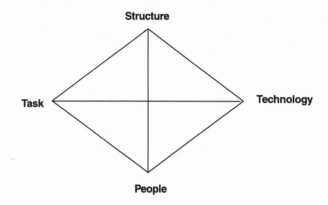

FIGURE 3.1. Leavitt's organizational systems model.

we can easily miss important issues in the organization. We cannot afford to allow our model to become ideology, to proceed, as Morgan (1986) has warned, so that our "way of seeing is a way of not seeing" (p. 73).

Earlier Organizational Models

Some time ago Harold Leavitt (1965) conceptualized organizations as "multivariate systems" and provided an organizational model with four interacting variables. His model is shown in Figure 3.1.

With the diamond shape, Leavitt meant to convey that the four variables were highly interdependent, that change in any one would result in compensatory (or "retaliating," as he put it) change in the other three. *Task* means the organization's reason for being, that is, manufacturing products and/or providing service. *People* are those who carry out the tasks. *Technology* refers to tools—computers, drill presses, and so forth. And *structure* means systems of communication, authority, and work flow. With only four variables, the Leavitt model is obviously fairly simple. Except for the notion of interdependence—the idea that organizational variables are dynamic and interact, thus conveying some degree of cause and effect—this representation of an organization is primarily descriptive.

Leavitt's earlier thinking actually influenced the creation of the highly popular McKinsey 7S Framework developed by Pascale and Athos (1981) and Peters and Waterman (1982). These organizational thinkers and consultants "stretched" their ideas into seven words beginning with an "S" to facilitate one's remembering and to explain their variables more easily. To quote Peters and Waterman (1982): "Hokey as the alliteration first seemed, four years' experience throughout the world has borne out our hunch that the framework would help immeasurably in forcing explicit thoughts about not only the hardware—strategy and structure—but also about the software of organization—style, systems, staff (people), skills, and shared values" (pp. 9,11). Similar to Leavitt's depiction, the McKinsey 7S model was presented as seven circles, all interconnecting.

The model's popularity is no doubt due to certain strengths: the framework's inclusion of seven key organizational variables (strategy, structure, systems, style, staff, skills, and shared values) and the creators' recognition of the importance of the interrelationships among all the dimensions. However, there are problems with the 7S Framework, as we have pointed out (Burke & Litwin, 1992):

> [The model] does not contain any external environment or performance variables. The model is a description of these seven important elements and shows that they interact to create organizational patterns, but there is no explication of how these seven dimensions are affected by the external environment. Nor do we know how each dimension affects the other or what specific performance indices may be involved. (p. 524)

To be fair, the 7S creators were clear that they wanted to keep matters simple so that organizational managers could quickly remember these important variables and easily understand their meaning. The emphasis on the "software" variables, as Peters and Waterman (1982) put it, was a significant influence on managerial thinking at the time—and probably remains so today.

Back to the problem alluded to earlier. Neither Leavitt's model nor the 7S Framework account for an organization's external environment and outcomes, or performance. Many of us organizational psychologists have an open system bias; that is, organizations are like living organisms in that there is input (the external environment), throughput (the variables Leavitt and others include), and output (organizational performance). Moreover, to complete the open system framework, there is a feedback loop that connects output with input. For me, the Bible (or at least the Old Testament) on organizational thinking is *The Social Psychology of Organizations*, by Katz and Kahn (1978). These authors were very explicit in their explanation of organizations as open systems.

The models I have chosen to describe in some detail in this chapter are organismic frameworks. While the open system notion is, to me, critical to understanding organizations, this mode of thinking, this organizational metaphor, is nevertheless a biased one. There are organizational metaphors other than the organism, as Morgan (1986) has explained—for example, machine, brain, culture, political system, and psychic prison—and, as Morgan points out, there are advantages and disadvantages to each of these metaphorical ways of conceptualizing organizations.

With this bias in mind, let us proceed with descriptions of organizational models that are important for purposes of diagnosis and are more specifically germane to organization development.

ORGANIZATION DEVELOPMENT MODELS

OD models serve at least two purposes: One purpose is to categorize data according to dimensions that the OD practitioner believes are important. A second purpose of an OD model is to explain—that is, not only to help the client understand how organizational issues and problems may be classified and localized but to provide at least some clue as to what action to take, where to intervene to change things for the better. A good diagnosis determines the proper intervention. The models to be considered will be described in these two ways, that is, in their data-categorizing and explanatory aspects.

Weisbord's Six-Box Model[1]

Weisbord's (1976) framework is highly visual. He depicts the model as a radar screen, with blips that inform us about key organizational variables and issues, good and bad. But just as air traffic controllers use the screen as a whole and avoid concentrating exclusively on individual blips, so too must the OD practitioner to avoid focusing on any particular box (see Figure 3.2).

As Figure 3.2 shows, Weisbord's six organizational categories are encircled by the external environment with arrows—input and output—pointing in both directions. Weisbord believes that for each box, the organization should be diagnosed in terms of both its formal and informal systems. A key aspect of any organizational diagnosis is recognition of the gap between the formal dimensions of an organization, such as the organization chart (the structure box), and its informal policies, such as how authority is actually exercised. The larger this gap, the more likely it is that the organization is functioning ineffectively.

Weisbord provides key diagnostic questions for each of the six boxes. For the Purposes box, the two most important factors are goal clarity (the extent to which organization members are clear about the organization's mission and purpose) and goal agreements (whether people support the

---

[1]This section and the one on the emergent pragmatic model are based in part on pages 169–173 and 179–182 from Burke (1982).

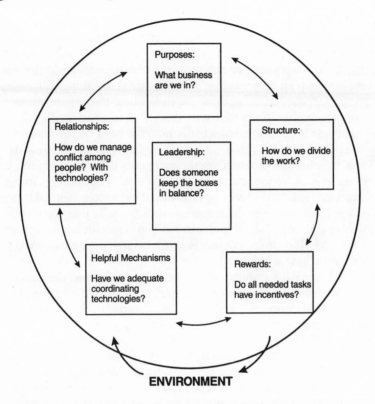

FIGURE 3.2. Weisbord's six-box model. From Weisbord (1976). Copyright 1976 by Sage Publications. Reprinted by permission.

organization's purpose). For Structure, the primary question is whether there is an adequate fit between the purpose and the internal structure that is supposed to serve that purpose. With respect to Relationships, Weisbord contends that three types are most important: between individuals, between units or departments that perform different tasks, and between people and the nature and requirements of their jobs. He also states that OD consultants should "diagnose first for required interdependence, then for *quality of relations*, and finally for modes of conflict management" (Weisbord, 1976, p. 440). In determining possible blips for the Rewards box, the consultant should diagnose the similarities and differences between what the organization formally rewards (the compensation package, incentive systems, and the like) and what organization members *feel* they are rewarded or punished for doing.

Weisbord places the Leadership box in the middle because he believes that a primary job of the leader is to watch for blips among the other boxes and to maintain balance between them. To help the OD consultant in diagnosing the leadership box, Weisbord refers to an important book published some years ago by Selznick (1957) that cites the four most important leadership tasks. According to Selznick, the consultant should determine the extent to which an organization's leaders are (1) defining purposes, (2) embodying purposes in programs, (3) defending the organization's integrity, and (4) maintaining order with respect to internal conflict.

For the last box, Helpful Mechanisms, Weisbord (1976) refers analogously to "the cement that binds an organization with separate needs" (p. 443). Thus, helpful mechanisms are the processes that every organization must attend to in order to survive: planning, control, budgeting, and other information systems that meet organizational objectives. The OD consultant's task is to determine which mechanisms (or which aspects of them) help members accomplish organizational purposes and which seem to hinder more than they help. When a helpful mechanism becomes red tape, it probably is no longer helpful.

Table 3.1 gives a summary of the six-box model and the diagnostic questions to be asked. These questions could be asked in a survey, but individual or group interviews are preferable because of the opportunity to probe further with each question. Diagnostic questions may be asked on two levels:

1. How big a gap is there between formal and informal systems? (This speaks to the fit between individual and organization.)
2. How much discrepancy is there between "what is" and "what ought to be"? (This highlights the fit between organization and environment.)

Weisbord (1978) has produced a workbook based on his model that provides an array of questions to use in the diagnostic phase of OD work.

An actual example should help to explain how the Weisbord model is applied. Some years ago I consulted with a regional general manager within a large financial services corporation. Ron (not his actual name) was new in the job and requested help in getting to understand his organization as quickly as possible and in identifying the strengths and weaknesses of his region. I interviewed the top eight people, including Ron himself. An additional purpose of the interviews was to determine the objectives for a planned off-site meeting for Ron and his seven direct reports. At the meeting feedback from the interviews would be provided, and then work would proceed on the agreed-upon objectives. Table 3.2 is a summary of the interview results, and Table 3.3 is a categorization of the interview data from Table 3.2 within the six-box model.

Note that some of the interview summary phrases are categorized within more than one box. I should also point out that some classifications

TABLE 3.1.   Weisbord's Matrix for Survey Design or Data Analysis

	Formal system (work to be done)	Informal system (process of working)
Purposes	Goal clarity	Goal agreement
Structure	Functional, program, or matrix?	How is work actually done or not done?
Relationships	Who should deal with whom on what? Which technologies should be used?	How well do they do it? Modes of conflict management?
Rewards (incentives)	Explicit system What is it?	Implicit, psychic rewards What do people *feel* about payoffs?
Leadership	What do top people manage? What systems are in use?	How? Normative "style" of administration
Helpful Mechanisms	Budet system Management information (measures?) Planning Control	What are they actually used for? How do they funtion in practice? How are systems subverted?

Note. From Weisbord (1976, p. 445). Copyright 1976 by Sage Publications. Reprinted by permission

are easier than others. It was difficult, for example, to classify S-8, Creativity. I chose Helpful Mechanisms–Informal because it seemed that some informal mechanisms within Ron's organization must help foster creativity, but my classification was arbitrary. In practice, the client will have more to say about the appropriate boxes in such instances. It is also not absolutely necessary to classify everything.

Once the data are classified and the client has agreed or has rearranged some of the categories, we are in a position to formulate a diagnostic picture of the organization. What Table 3.3 shows us, among other things, is that our primary problem areas—the blips on the radar screen—are in the Purposes box, both Formal and Informal, the Structure–Formal box, the Relationships–Informal box, the Helpful Mechanisms–Formal box, the Relationships–Informal box, and the Rewards box, both Formal and Informal. A clear strength is in the Leadership–Informal box, and there are strengths in some of the same boxes that have problems.

The priorities of the meeting were to work on goals (Purposes), strategy, and priorities (Purposes), and on building a senior management team (Relationships). Follow-up activities included some changes in the struc-

TABLE 3.2. Partial Summary of Eight Interviews Conducted with a Regional Senior Management Group

Strengths of the Region

1. Senior management group is highly experienced in the business (7)
2. Commitment of work force; community spirit (5)
3. Considerable opportunity; natural market area (3)
4. Good people throughout (3)
5. Last 4 years we have experienced success in many areas (3)
6. Have become more of a marketing organization (3)
7. We are technologically superior and a market leader as compared with our competitors (3)
8. Creativity (2)
9. Managers think entrepreneurially (2)

Weaknesses

1. Our marketing and services system (6)
2. Try to do too many things at once; do not establish priorities (3)
3. Region priorities are always secondary to individual manager's (3)
4. Lack of management depth (3)
5. Little planning (3)
6. Structure (2)
7. High costs (2)
8. Overly change-oriented (2)
9. Poor reward system (2)
10. Low morale (2)
11. Internal competition (2)
12. High degree of mistrust (2)

Objectives of Off-Site Meeting

1. Agree on the regional structure (7)
2. Set financial objectives for next 2 years (6)
3. List of things we need to do and stop doing (4)
4. Must hear from Ron about his team notions, ideas, expectations (4)
5. Some ventilation of feelings needed (3)
6. Must come together more as a top management team (3)
7. Establish standards for performance (3)
8. Increase mutual respect (2)

Note. The number in parentheses after each item indicates the number of respondents who specifically mentioned that point.

ture and reward system and installation of some improved "helpful mechanisms," such as a more formal planning function. The strength of the leadership was instrumental in bringing about significant and rapid change.

My diagnostic summary of the case example within the framework of the six-box model is obviously cursory. I have simply shown how the

TABLE 3.3. A Classification of Interview Data from Table 3.2 According to Weisbord's Six-Box Model

	Formal system			Informal system		
1. Purpose	S-3	W-2 W-8	M-2	S-9	W-2 W-3	M-3
2. Structure		W-1 W-6	M-1	S-6 S-8		
3. Relationship				S-2 S-4	W-11 W-12	M-5 M-8
4. Rewards		W-9		S-2 S-5	W-10	
5. Leadership		W-4	M-4	S-1 S-7 S-9		M-6
6. Helpful Mechanisms		W-1 W-5 W-7		S-8		

Note. The symbols S-1, S-2, W-2, M-1, M-2, and so forth refer to the summary phases in Table 3.2: S-1 is the first strength listed, S-2 the second strength, W-1 the first weakness, M-1 the first objective for the off-site meeting, and so forth.

model may be used and how its use may help point to the parts of the client system that need the most immediate attention.

In summary, Weisbord's model is particularly useful (1) when the consultant does not have as much time as would be desirable for diagnosis, (2) when a relatively uncomplicated organizational map is needed for quick service, or (3) when the client is unaccustomed to thinking in systems terms. In the latter case, the model helps the client to visualize his or her organization as a systemic whole without the use of strange terminology. I have also found Weisbord's model particularly useful in supervising and guiding students in their initial OD consultations. (For another case example using the Weisbord model, see Burke, 1991, pp. 107–115.)

Some of the strengths of the model are also its weaknesses. To categorize everything into only six boxes is quick and easy to understand, yet we know that organizations are far more complicated. And it is clear from the model that if we have strong, negative blips in the Leadership box, we have some serious problems due to the key coordinating function of leadership. We also can see that Purposes links most directly with both Structure and Relationships, but what about the other boxes? And other than the causal implication of Leadership, other potential cause–effect linkages are not mentioned. In short, then, the model is quite useful for quick, simple diagnostic purposes, but when deeper analysis is required, the six boxes and their uncomplicated linkages are not enough.

The Nadler–Tushman Congruence Model

When there is more time for diagnosis and where the client is accustomed to thinking in systemic and fairly sophisticated terms about organizations, a model that covers more ground and explains more is desirable. In such instances, the Nadler–Tushman (1977) model can be useful (see Figure 4.2 in Chapter 4).

Nadler and Tushman make the same assumptions as Weisbord, namely, that an organization is an open system and therefore influenced by its environment (inputs) and that it also shapes its environment to some extent by outputs. An organization thus is the transformation entity between inputs and outputs. For a description of the model and how it is applied, see the chapter by Walton and Nadler in this volume.

The dimensions of the Nadler–Tushman model are quite comprehensive and have face validity. Moreover, their notion of congruence suggests certain cause–effect linkages. For example, little or no congruence between, say, strategy and structure in their model produces poor organizational performance. Also, a mismatch between what's going on in the organization's environment and strategy (e.g., no plan for dealing with a recent change in government regulation) would imply a causal relationship to performance. Many other congruences or lacks thereof could be mentioned; the number of possibilities is large. Nadler and Tushman, however, do not provide ideas or, say, a formula for determining which variables in their model are central. For example, they include under the single heading Organizational Arrangements quite a number of components, any one of which could easily be central. And, finally, they do not suggest any means for knowing when congruence has occurred or what levels of congruence or incongruence produce desirable or undesirable effects.

To be fair, more recently Nadler and Tushman (1989) have had some second thoughts about their congruence position:

> While our model implies that congruence of organizational components
> is a desirable state it is, in fact, a double-edged sword. In the short term,
> congruence seems to be related to effectiveness and performance. A system with high congruence, however, can be resistant to change. It develops ways of insulating itself from outside influences and may be unable
> to respond to new situations. (p. 195)

Tichy's TPC Framework[2]

With his organizational framework, Tichy (1983) focuses explicitly on the management of change. He states that there are nine organizational

[2]This section is taken in part from a portion of Chapter 6 in Burke (1994).

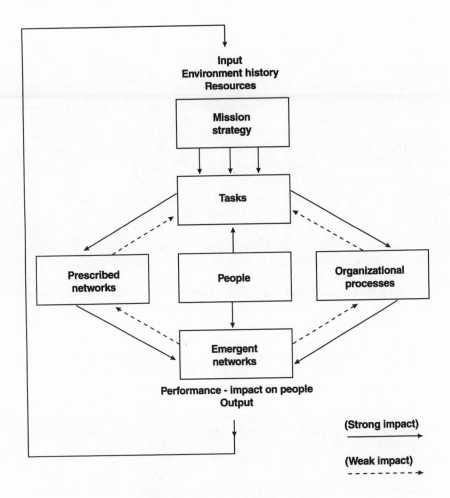

FIGURE 3.3. Tichy's framework.

change levers: (1) external interface, or the organization's external environment (input); (2) mission; (3) strategy (Tichy combines mission and strategy in the model but he considers them distinct levers); (4) managing organizational mission/strategy processes (that is, realistically engaging the relevant interest groups); (5) task (change often requires new tasks); (6) prescribed networks (more or less the formal organizational structure); (7) organizational processes (communicating, problem solving, and decision making); (8) people; and (9) emergent networks (more or less the informal organization). Figure 3.3 shows how Tichy arranges these nine levers. Managing is not depicted in the figure but as a lever it permeates the entire model. He assumes "that organizational effectiveness (or output) is a function of the characteristics of each of the components of the model, as well as a function of how the components interrelate and align into a functioning system" (p. 72).

Even more important in Tichy's thinking about organization change is his TPC framework. The model in Figure 3.3 is not especially unique. What is unique is Tichy's overlay of the three systems—*technical, political,* and *cultural*—across the nine-lever model. He contends that there have been three dominant yet fairly distinct traditions guiding the practice of organization change. The technical view is rational, based on empiricism and the scientific method. The political view is based on the belief that organizations have dominant groups, and bargaining is the primary mode of change. The cultural view is the belief that shared symbols, values, and "cognitive schemes," as Tichy labels them, are what tie people together and form the organization's culture. Change occurs via altering norms and the cognitive schemes of organization members. Taking only one or two of these views for managing organizational change is dysfunctional. All three must be adjusted and realigned for successful change. The metaphor that Tichy uses to capture this thinking is a rope with three interrelated strands. The strands, or three views, can be understood separately but must be managed together for effective change.

For diagnostic purposes, Tichy uses a matrix like the one shown in Figure 3.4. This format summarizes what he calls "the analysis of alignments." Tichy (1983) describes the use of the matrix this way:

> Based on the diagnostic data collected, a judgment is made for each cell of the matrix regarding the amount of change needed to create alignment. Working across the matrix, the alignment is within a system: technical, political, or cultural. Working down the matrix, the alignment is between systems. The 0 (no change), 1 (moderate change) or 2 (great deal of change) ratings represent the amount of change needed to align that component. (p. 164)

In summary, Tichy's model includes many, if not most, of the critical variables important to understanding organizations. His model is unique with respect to the strategic rope metaphor and is particularly relevant to OD work since the emphasis is on change. Moreover, Tichy is clear about what he considers to be the primary organizational levers that must be pushed or pulled to make change happen effectively. Instead of congruence, alignment is the operational term. And Tichy provides a way of analyzing the key alignments that are necessary according to his framework. Data are first collected and then categorized within his matrix (Figure 3.4).

There is a people component in Tichy's model, but for the most part his framework ignores issues at the individual level. He admits this omis-

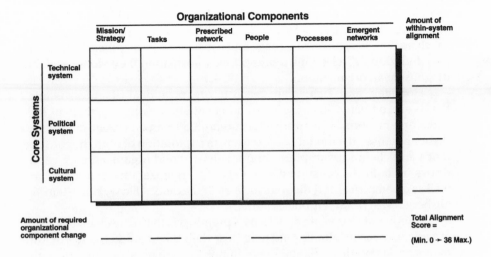

FIGURE 3.4. Tichy's TPC matrix.

sion at the end of his book by stating that he skimmed over the psychological aspects of change. The political and cultural strands are, of course, people concerns but at a larger, more macro, level than, say, job–person match (or alignment) and local work unit activities such as teamwork. Finally, the criticism of too much congruence potentially working against change could also apply to Tichy's insistence on alignments.

Hornstein and Tichy's Emergent Pragmatic Model

The emergent pragmatic model of organizational diagnosis (Hornstein & Tichy, 1973; Tichy, Hornstein, & Nisberg, 1977) is based on the premise that most managers and consultants carry around in their heads implicit theories or models about organizational behavior and about how human systems actually operate. These notions are usually intuitive, ill-formed, and difficult to articulate. Because they are largely intuitive and idiosyncratic, different observers and members of organizations have different theories, which gives rise to conflicts between consultants or between consultants and clients about what is really wrong with the organization and how to fix it.

To deal with these intuitive notions, Hornstein and Tichy have developed a procedure for helping managers and consultants conceptualize and eventually articulate their implicit models, thereby making them explicit. The procedure, known as an emergent pragmatic theory or model, consists of using a workbook and either selecting items from among 22 sample labels or creating one's own labels from 28 blank labels that are provided. The sample labels include such items as informal groupings, fiscal characteristics, turnover, goals, and satisfaction of members with their jobs. Individuals' selections represent the information they would seek in diagnosing an organization.

Hornstein and Tichy's approach to organizational diagnosis is one that is shared between consultant and client and among members of the client organization. The approach is identified as an emergent pragmatic theory because "the model *emerges* from an exploration of both the consultant's and client's assumptions about behavior and organizations . . . and draws on both the consultant's and client's organizational *experiences* as well as on empirical and theoretical work in the field" (Tichy, Hornstein, & Nisberg, 1977, p. 367; emphasis added).

Another of Hornstein and Tichy's premises is that, consciously or not, organizational consultants tend to impose their theories and models of human systems on their clients. These impositions may or may not fit with the client members' perceptions and beliefs, and may or may not correspond to the client organization's underlying values. To assure better congruence, Hornstein and Tichy advocate a highly collaborative approach between consultants and clients, one that results in an emergent model that represents different perspectives and experiences.

In the emergent pragmatic approach the consultant guides the client group through five phases:

1. *Exploring and developing a diagnostic model.* The first step of this phase is for members of the client group to work individually in the workbooks. They select labels for the organizational items they believe represent the most important dimensions of organization for the purpose of diagnosis.

The second step of this initial phase is for all members of the client group to agree on a common list. This agreement process consists largely of eliminating overlapping labels and arriving at a final list that represents all individuals' selections.

The third step is to develop categories of organizational components from the common list of labels. This step is a group activity. Categories of labels representing organizational components might include such elements as formal structure, hard data (e.g., a profit-and-loss statement), environmental interface, and organization member characteristics. A secondary but important consequence of this step is that the group begins to develop a common language, a shared organizational vocabulary. The terms and categories are therefore concrete, pragmatic, and more meaningful for the client members.

The final step of this initial phase is to make the model dynamic. For this activity, the group members first imagine that change may occur in one component of their model and then trace the effects of this change on all other components. They do this for each component of their model. The resulting matrix shows which components the group members believe are the most and the least significant in terms of impact on other components. The model is then used as the basis for developing change strategies.

2. *Developing change strategies.* Since different components of the model will probably have different impacts, client members are in a position to determine potential levers for change. "For instance, if a model included a category called formal structure which contained such items as authority structure, reward system, and formal communication structure, the category might be considered a good leverage point if changes in this category produced desirable changes in a number of other categories" (Tichy, Hornstein, & Nisberg, 1977, p. 372). Thus, the change strategy is a statement of what is to be changed, the method of change, and the sequence of events constituting the change steps.

3. *Developing change techniques.* This phase consists of exploring potential techniques, determining which are most appropriate, and then matching the selected techniques with each organizational component that has been designated for change.

4. *Assessing the necessary conditions for assuring success.* The final selection of change techniques is based on criteria developed in this phase. These criteria usually stem from such conditions as the system's readiness for change, the available resources, budget considerations, and the system's history regarding change, especially whether OD has been attempted before.

5. *Evaluating the change strategies.* For this final phase, criteria are generated for evaluating the success or failure of the overall change strategy, and measurement procedures are developed.

Comparing the Models

The three models described earlier—Weisbord's six-box model, the Nadler–Tushman congruence model, and Tichy's TPC framework—are fairly generic and do not necessarily fall prey to the problems of Hornstein and Tichy's two premises. When the consultant and the client do not find the Weisbord, Nadler–Tushman, Tichy TPC, or other formal models to their liking, however, the emergent pragmatic approach offers a clear alternative. It is a do-it-yourself model, and if both consultant and client are willing to spend the time required to do it right, a mutually satisfying and appropriate model for the client organization is likely to result. One must bear in mind a rather critical point: Formal models that are based on sound theory, research, and practice provide the benefit of tested knowledge; with the emergent pragmatic process the outcome in the final analysis is only as good as the expertise and skill of the consultant and client groups.

Descriptively, the three explicit OD diagnostic models—Weisbord, Nadler–Tushman, and Tichy—have more similarities than differences. All three include the external environment, direction (variously labeled purpose, mission, strategy), structure (formal organizational arrangements, prescribed networks), people (relationships, individual), and performance (outputs and Weisbord's arrow going out toward the external environment). At least two of the models include resources, history, task, informal organization (emergent networks), and organizational processes (Weisbord's "helpful mechanisms"). Tichy's model is unique in including political and technical factors, and Weisbord's is the only one that explicitly mentions rewards and leadership. Tichy includes culture and the others do not, although Nadler and Tushman argue that their informal organization component includes culture and Weisbord might couch relationships as culture, at least in part.

With regard to explanation, Weisbord argues that leadership is critical, Nadler and Tushman advocate congruence (but not too much of it), and Tichy espouses alignment. The Weisbord and the Nadler–Tushman models present more of a contingency viewpoint whereas Tichy takes a strong normative stance. Tichy's strategic rope, consisting of technical, political, and cultural strands, must indeed be a braided rope; that is, the strands must be aligned, the three systems, as he labels them, must be aligned with his key levers (organizational components), and the levers themselves must be aligned with one another.

THE BURKE–LITWIN MODEL[3]

The final model presented in this chapter is more normative than contingent but does not stress congruence or alignment. In presenting the Burke–Litwin model (1992), I am attempting to provide yet another perspective while at the same time demonstrating that this more recent framework captures some of the best qualities of previous models. Like Tichy's TPC framework we take certain positions about organization change; thus, the model *predicts* behavior and performance consequences and therefore deals with cause (organizational conditions) and effect (resultant performance). Important background regarding the development of the model (the concepts of organizational climate and culture) will be presented first, followed by a description of the model. Finally, suggestions for ways to use the model, as well as case examples, will be provided.

Background

Climate

The original thinking underlying the model came from George Litwin and others during the 1960s. In 1967 the Harvard Business School sponsored a

---

[3]This section is taken in part from Burke and Litwin (1989).

conference on organizational climate. Results of this conference were subsequently published in two books (Litwin & Stringer, 1968; Tagiuri & Litwin, 1968). The concept of organizational climate that emerged from this series of studies and papers was that of a psychological state strongly affected by organizational conditions such as systems, structure, and managerial behavior. In their theory paper Tagiuri and Litwin (1968) emphasized that there could be no universal set of dimensions or properties for organizational climate. They argued that one could describe climate along different dimensions, depending on what kind of organization was being studied and what aspects of human behavior were involved. They described climate as a molar, synthetic, or changeable construct. Further, the kind of climate construct they described was relatively malleable; it could be modified by managerial behavior and by systems and was strongly influenced by more enduring group norms and values.

This early research and theory development regarding organizational climate clearly linked psychological and organizational variables in a cause–effect model that was empirically testable. Using the model, Litwin and Stringer (1968) were able to predict and control the motivational and performance consequences of various organizational climates established in their research experiment.

Culture

The concept of organizational culture is drawn from anthropology and is used to describe the relatively enduring set of values and norms that underlie a social system. These underlying values and norms may not be entirely conscious. Rather, they describe a "meaning system" that allows members of a social system to attribute meaning and value to the various external and internal events they experience. Such underlying values and meaning systems change only as continued culture is applied to generations of individuals in that social system.

It is necessary to recognize the distinction between climate and culture. The Burke–Litwin model attempts to describe both climate and culture in terms of their interactions with other organizational variables and builds on earlier research and theory with regard to predicting motivation and performance effects.

In addition, the variables that influence and are influenced by climate need to be distinguished from those influenced by culture. There are two distinct sets of organizational dynamics. One set is associated primarily with the transactional level of human behavior, or the everyday interactions and exchanges that create the climate. The second set of dynamics is concerned with processes of human transformation, that is, sudden "leaps" in behavior. These transformational processes are required for genuine change in the culture of an organization. Efforts to distinguish transactional and transformational dynamics in organizations have been influenced by the writings of James McGregor Burns (1978) and by consulting efforts to change organizations.

Before we leave this climate and culture discussion, it should be pointed out that if we examine the literature, we do not find as much of a distinction made between climate and culture as the Burke–Litwin model suggests. Reichers and Schneider (1990), having examined this body of literature, believe "there is substantial overlap between the two concepts. This is especially true when climate and culture are viewed as reciprocal processes, the one causing the other in an endless cycle over time. . . . Climate . . . is both the manifestation of culture . . . and the data on which culture comes to be inferred and understood" (p. 42).

Climate and culture are indeed reciprocal processes. Yet useful distinctions, perhaps with the aid of analogies, can be made. Comparing the organization to the individual, one might say that personality bears the same relationship to behavior as culture does to climate. Culture is background, climate is foreground. Yet both are parts of a larger whole—the organization. While difficult to differentiate clearly between the two conceptually and empirically, some distinction is nevertheless useful.

To understand how to change large, complex organizations, especially the culture of an organization, it is important and practical to draw a distinction between culture and climate. As I have theorized before (Burke, 1993), one does not attempt to change organizational culture directly. The consultant and client begin with managerial behavior change, which in turn affects climate and, if applied consistently and persistently, eventually and ever so gradually has an impact on the culture; meaning that norms and values are influenced. Thus, the distinction is most important for purposes of applying the Burke–Litwin model toward organization change, especially culture change. Moreover, some recent evidence, albeit somewhat "soft" with respect to research method, suggests that culture, not necessarily climate, relates significantly to long-term financial performance of a corporation. And an adaptive culture, amenable to change, is related to high financial performance (Kotter & Heskett, 1992). In any case, conceptually and from what we know from research, we need to maintain the perspective that while there are similarities between climate and culture, understanding the difference is important to understanding organization change.

The Model

As noted in the preceding section, the Burke–Litwin model (Figure 3.5) owes its original development to the work of Litwin and his associates

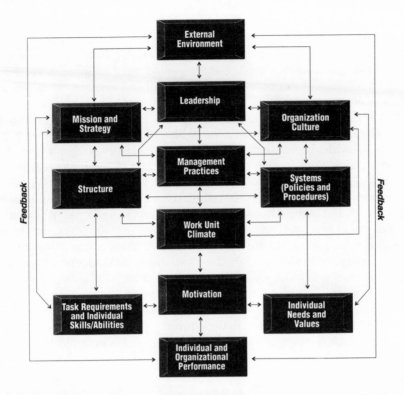

FIGURE 3.5. The Burke–Litwin model of organizational performance and change. From the Burke–Litwin Model of Organizational Performance and Change. Copyright 1987, 1992 by W. Warner Burke Associates, Inc. Reprinted by permission.

(Litwin & Stringer, 1968; Tagiuri & Litwin, 1968); it has been refined through a series of studies directed by Burke (Bernstein & Burke, 1989; Fox, 1990; Michela, Boni, Schechter, Manderlink, Bernstein, O'Malley, & Burke, 1988). Recent collaboration has led to the current form of this model, which attempts to (1) specify the interrelationships of organizational variables and (2) distinguish transformational and transactional dynamics in organizational behavior and change.

The Burke–Litwin model is complex, as is the rich intricacy of organizational phenomena. However, this model, exhibited two-dimensionally, is still an oversimplification; a hologram would be a better representation. In accordance with accepted thinking about organizations from general systems theory (Katz & Kahn, 1978), the external environment box represents the input and the individual and organizational performance box represents the output. Feedback loops go in both directions. The remaining boxes of the model represent the throughput aspect of general systems theory. Arrows in both directions convey the open systems principle that change in one factor will eventually have an impact on the others. If the model could be diagrammed so that the arrows are circular (as they would be in a hologram), reality could be represented more accurately. Yet this is a *causal* model. For example, although culture and systems affect one another, culture has a stronger influence on systems than vice versa.

The model could be displayed differently. External environment could be on the left and performance on the right, with all throughput boxes in between, as with the Nadler–Tushman model. However, displaying it as shown makes a statement about organizational change: Organizational change stems more from environmental impact than from any other factor. Moreover, with respect to organizational change, the variables of strategy, leadership, and culture have more weight than the variables of structure, management practices, and systems; that is, having leaders communicate the new strategy is not sufficient for effective change. Changing culture must be planned as well as aligned with strategy and leader behavior. How the model is displayed does not dictate where change could start; however, it does indicate the weighting of change dynamics. The reader can think of the model in terms of gravity, with the push toward performance being in the weighted order displayed in the figure.

In summary, the model, as shown in Figure 3.5, portrays the following:

- The primary variables that need to be considered in any attempt to predict and explain the total behavioral output of an organization.
- The most important interactions among these variables.
- How the variables affect change.

The variables in the model can be described as follows:

- *External environment*: Any outside condition or situation that influences the performance of the organization, including such things as marketplaces, world financial conditions, and political/governmental circumstances.
- *Mission and strategy:* What employees believe is the central purpose of the organization and the means by which the organization intends to achieve that purpose over an extended time.
- *Leadership*: Executive behavior that provides direction and encourages others to take needed action (for purposes of data gathering, this variable includes perceptions of executive practices and values).
- *Culture*: The collection of overt and covert rules, values, and principles that guide organizational behavior and that have been strong-

ly influenced by history, custom, and practice ("The way we do things around here").

- *Structure*: The arrangement of functions and people into specific areas and levels of responsibility, decision-making authority, and relationships, an arrangement that assures effective implementation of the organization's mission and strategy.
- *Management practices*: What managers do in the normal course of events with the human and material resources at their disposal to carry out the organization's strategy.
- *Systems*: Standardized policies and mechanisms that are designed to facilitate work and that primarily manifest themselves in the organization's reward systems and in control systems, such as the organization's management information system, goal and budget development, and human resource allocation.
- *Climate*: The collective current impressions, expectations, and feelings of the members of local work units, all of which in turn affect members' relations with supervisors, with one another, and with other units.
- *Task requirements and individual skills/abilities*: The behavior required for task effectiveness, including specific skills and knowledge required for people to accomplish the work assigned and for which they feel directly responsible (this variable concerns what is often referred to as job–person match).
- *Individual needs and values*: The specific psychological factors that provide desire and worth for individual actions or thoughts.
- *Motivation*: Aroused behavioral tendencies to move toward goals, take needed action, and persist until satisfaction is attained, that is, the resultant net energy generated by the combined desires for achievement, power, affection, discovery, and other important human values.
- *Individual and organizational performance*: The outcomes or results, with indicators of effort and achievement including productivity, customer or staff satisfaction, profit, and service quality.

Transformational and Transactional Dynamics

The concept of transformational change in organizations, usually identified with leadership, is suggested in the writings of Bass (1985), Burke (1986), Burns (1978), McClelland (1975), and Tichy and Devanna (1986). Figure 3.6 displays the transformational variables, those in the upper half of the Burke–Litwin model. "Transformational" refers to areas in which alteration is usually caused by interaction with environmental forces (both within and without) and therefore require entirely new behavior sets on the part of organization members.

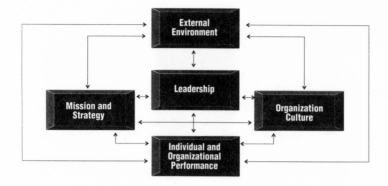

FIGURE 3.6. The transformational factors.

Figure 3.7 shows the transactional variables, those in the lower half of the Burke–Litwin model. These variables are very similar to those originally isolated by Litwin and Stringer (1968) and those later identified by Michela et al. (1988). They are *transactional* in that alteration occurs primarily via relatively short-term reciprocity ("You do this for me and I'll do that for you") among people and groups.

In the causal model, climate results from transactions whereas culture change requires transformation. Day-to-day climate is a result of transactions related to issues such as the following:

- *Sense of direction* (the effect of mission clarity, or lack thereof, on one's daily responsibilities).
- *Role and responsibility* (the effect of structure, reinforced by managerial practice).
- *Standards and commitment* (the effect of managerial practice, reinforced by culture).
- *Fairness of rewards* (the effect of systems, reinforced by managerial practice).
- *Focus on customer versus internal pressures or standards of excellence* (the effect of culture, reinforced by other variables).

In contrast, the concept of organizational culture has to do with those underlying values and meaning systems that are difficult to manage, alter, and even to articulate (Schein, 1992). Moreover, instant change in culture seems to be a contradiction in terms. By definition, those things that can be changed quickly are not the underlying reward systems but the behaviors that are attached to the meaning systems. It is relatively easy to alter superficial human behavior; it is undoubtedly quite difficult to alter some-

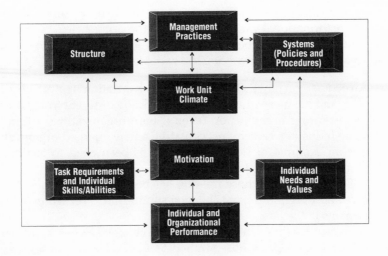

FIGURE 3.7. The transactional factors.

thing unconscious that is hidden in symbols and mythology and that functions as the fabric helping an organization to remain together, intact, and viable. To change something so deeply imbedded in organizational life does indeed require transformational experiences and events.

Using the Model: Data Gathering and Analysis

Distinguishing transformational and transactional processes in organizations has implications for planning organizational change. Unless one is conducting an overall organizational diagnosis, preliminary interviews will result in enough information to construct a fairly targeted survey. Survey targets would be determined from the interviews and, most likely, would be focused on either transformational or transactional issues. Transformational issues call for a survey that probes mission and strategy, leadership, culture, and performance. Transactional issues need a focus on structure, systems, management practices, climate, and performance. Other transactional probes might involve motivation, including task requirements (job–person match) and individual needs and values. For example, the Job Diagnostic Survey (Hackman & Oldham, 1980) might be appropriate in this case.

A consultant helping to manage change would conduct preliminary interviews with, say, 15 to 30 representative individuals in the organization. If a summary of these interviews reveals that significant organizational change is needed, additional data would be collected related to the top or *transformational* part of Figure 3.5. Note that in major organizational change, transformational variables represent the primary levers, those areas in which change must be focused. The following examples represent transformational change (involving the variables in Figure 3.6):

- An acquisition in which the acquired organization's culture, leadership, and business strategy are dramatically different from those of the acquiring organization (even if both organizations are in the same industry), thereby necessitating a new, merged organization (for an example of how the model has been used to facilitate a merger, see Burke & Jackson, 1991).
- A Federal agency whose mission has been modified, whose structure and leadership have changed significantly, yet whose culture remains in the past.
- A high-tech firm whose leadership has changed recently and is perceived negatively, whose strategy is unclear, and whose internal politics have moved from minimal (before the leadership change) to predominant (after); the hue and cry here is "We have no direction from our leaders and no culture to guide our behavior in the meantime."

For an organization in which the presenting problem requires more of a fine-tuning or improving process, the variables presented in the lower part of the Burke–Litwin model (i.e., the transactional factors depicted in Figure 3.7) serve as the area of concentration. Examples of fine-tuning include changes in the organization's structure; modification of the reward system; management development (perhaps in the form of a program that concentrates on behavioral practices); and the administration of a climate survey to measure job stratification, job clarity, degree of teamwork, and so on.

British Airways (BA), which became a private corporation in 1987, is a good example of an organization for which almost all of the Burke–Litwin model was used, providing a framework for executives and managers to understand the massive change they were attempting to manage. (For an overview of the BA change effort, see Goodstein & Burke, 1991.) Changing from a government agency to a market-driven, customer-focused business enterprise is a significant change. All variables in the model have been, and are still being, affected. Data based on most of the variables have been gathered and summarized in a feedback report for many BA executives and managers. This feedback, organized according to the model, helped executives and managers understand which of the variables within their domains needed attention.

Another example involves a large, government-sponsored organization based in Europe. A survey was conducted in 1993 with a stratified random sample of almost 5,000 people from the total population of ap-

TABLE 3.4. Sample Questions for a Survey Based on the Burke–Litwin Model

Variable	Sample question
External environment	Regarding the pace of change (from static to very rapid), what would you say the organization as a whole is experiencing?
Mission and strategy	How widely accepted are the organization's goals among employees?
Leadership	To what extent do senior managers make an effort to keep in personal touch with employees at your level in the organization?
Culture	To what extent are the standard ways of operating in the organization difficult to change?
Structure	To what extent is the organization's structure clear to everyone?
Management practices	To what extent does your manager communicate in an open and direct manner?
Systems	To what extent are the following communication mechanisms in the organization effective? (e.g., grapevine, company newspaper, staff meetings, bulletin boards, etc.)
Climate	Where you work in the organization, to what extent is there trust and mutual respect among employees?
Skills–job match	How challenged do you feel in your present job?
Motivation	To what extent do you feel encouraged to reach higher levels and standards of performance in your work?
Needs and values	I have a job that matters. (Indicate extent to which this statement is true for you, from "disagree strongly" to "agree strongly.")
Performance	To what extent is the organization currently achieving the highest level of employee performance of which it is capable?

proximately 23,500 employees. The survey was constructed on the basis of the Burke–Litwin model, with at least four questions asked per variable, and a maximum of 28 questions on management practices. A total of 150 items, using a five-point scale, constituted the survey, with three additional open-ended write-in questions at the end. Table 3.4 provides a sample question from the survey for each variable of the model. The response rate was almost 60% and, amazingly, 93% of the respondents chose to answer our three questions at the end (e.g., "If you could change one thing to improve your effectiveness on the job, what would it be?").

A factor analysis of the respondents' answers to the 150 items showed that people's responses were easily categorized according to the 12 variables of the Burke–Litwin model. Figure 3.8 is a partial summary of the survey results. The arrows indicate strength of relationship according to a number of regression analyses. Notice that there is a clear top-down relationship. These analyses were far stronger than in the opposite, bottom-up direction. This outcome could, at least in part, be a function of the kinds of questions that we asked. In any case, what was clear from an action standpoint was the need for the following:

- Stronger teamwork, inspiration, and visibility at the senior management level.
- More involvement of employees in the goals of the organization.
- A culture that is more adaptive to change and less bureaucratic.
- More consistency in managerial decision making.
- A more clearly defined structure that facilitates horizontal relationships.
- Mechanisms to help people feel more valued in their work.

These are only a few of the most critical recommendations, which, if implemented, could change the organization's effectiveness significantly. As suggested by the top-down nature of the survey results, changes would need to begin at the transformational level, changes that in turn would affect the transactional categories.

One additional point is important to note about these results. This government-sponsored organization is in the early stages of significant change, which was brought about by pressure from the nation's elected government representatives. Conditions such as goals not being fully accepted (these goals are highly associated with changes the organization needs to make), senior management not being together, strong bureaucracy, unclear structure, and organization members being poorly informed are common problems during early stages of change.

As can be seen from this example, it is useful to consider the model in a vertical manner. For example, Bernstein and Burke (1989) examined the causal chain of culture, management practices, and climate in a large manufacturing organization. In this case, feedback to executives showed how and to what degree cultural variables influenced management practices and, in turn, work-unit climate (the dependent variable).

In a survey based on the Burke–Litwin model and conducted a few years ago with the National Aeronautics and Space Administration, the most negatively rated variable within the model was in the systems, or policy and procedures, domain. The issues concerned rewards, performance evaluation, and career development. Following the survey feed-

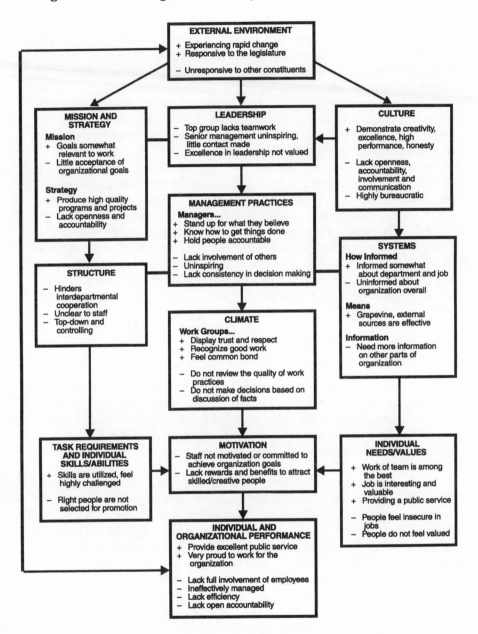

FIGURE 3.8. Summary of survey results including the positives and negatives for a large government-sponsored organization categorized according to the Burke–Litwin model.

back, action was taken to address the problems in these three areas. These changes were transactional, not transformational. In other words, the changes made were attempts to improve existing systems, not efforts to overhaul them as a consequence of larger, more fundamental, changes in culture, leadership, and/or strategy.

To summarize, considering the Burke–Litwin model in horizontal terms emphasizes the fact that organizational change is either transformational or transactional. Considering the model from a vertical perspective entails hypothesizing causal effects and assuming that the weight of change is top-down; that is, the heaviest or most influential organizational dimensions for change are, first and foremost, external environment and then mission/strategy, leadership, and culture.

As with other models, the Burke–Litwin model has its limitations. For example, the model does not account for the organization's technical strengths, those core competencies that make it competitive in the marketplace and/or effective in accomplishing its mission. Since technology largely pervades the entire organization, displaying the Burke–Litwin model three-dimensionally with technology as the third dimension might improve its validity.

CONCLUSION

Provided we do not allow ourselves to be trapped by a particular model—and, as a consequence blind to certain critical information about an organization—using a model for diagnosis is highly beneficial. A sufficiently comprehensive model can help us to (1) organize data into useful categories and (2) see more easily and quickly domains in the organization that need attention.

What model to choose should depend on at least three criteria: First, the model you choose to work with should be one that you as a practitioner thoroughly understand and feel comfortable with as you work with organization members. Second, the model you choose should fit the client organization as closely as possible; that is, it should be comprehensive enough to cover as many aspects of the organization as appropriate yet simple and clear enough for organization members to grasp fairly quickly. Third, the model you choose should be one that is sufficiently comprehensive to enable you to gather data about the organization according to the model's parameters without missing key bits of information.

Finally, remember not to make the mistake I recently made with a group of executives: Be clear with your client at the outset that your use of the term "model" means a representation (the second dictionary definition), not a standard or example (the first dictionary definition).

REFERENCES

Bass, B. M. (1985). *Leadership and performance beyond expectations.* New York: Free Press.

Bernstein, W. M., & Burke, W. W. (1989). Modeling organizational meaning systems. In R. W. Woodman & W. A. Pasmore (Eds.), *Research in organizational change and development* (Vol. 3, pp. 117–159). Greenwich, CT: JAI Press.

Burke, W. W. (1982). *Organization development: Principles and practices.* Boston: Little, Brown.

Burke, W. W. (1986). Leadership as empowering others. In S. Srivastva & Associates (Eds.), *Executive power: How executives influence people and organizations* (pp. 51–77). San Francisco: Jossey-Bass.

Burke, W. W. (1991). Practicing organization development. In D. W. Bray & Associates, *Working with organizations and their people: A guide to human resources practice* (pp. 95–130). New York: Guilford Press.

Burke, W. W. (1993). The changing world of organization change. *Consulting Psychologists Journal: Practice and Research, 45,* 9–17.

Burke, W. W. (1994). *Organization development: A process of learning and changing.* Reading, MA: Addison-Wesley.

Burke, W. W., & Jackson, P. (1991). Making the SmithKline Beecham merger work. *Human Resource Management, 30,* 69–87.

Burke, W. W., & Litwin, G. H. (1989). A causal model of organizational performance. In J. W. Pfeiffer (Ed.), *1989 Annual: Developing human resources* (pp. 277–288). San Diego: University Associates.

Burke, W. W., & Litwin, G. H. (1992). A causal model of organizational performance and change. *Journal of Management, 18*(3), 523–545.

Burns, J. M. (1978). *Leadership.* New York: Harper & Row.

Chandler, A. (1962). *Strategy and structure.* Cambridge, MA: MIT Press.

Fox, M. M. (1990). *The role of individual perceptions of organizational culture in predicting perceptions of work unit climate and organizational performance.* Unpublished doctoral dissertation, Columbia University, New York City.

Goodstein, L. D., & Burke, W. W. (1991). Creating successful organizational change. *Organizational Dynamics, 19*(4), 5–17.

Hackman, J. R., & Oldham, G. R. (1980). *Work redesign.* Reading, MA: Addison-Wesley.

Hornstein, H. A., & Tichy, N. M. (1973). *Organization diagnosis and improvement strategies.* New York: Behavioral Science Associates.

Katz, D., & Kahn, R. L. (1978). *The social psychology of organizations* (2nd ed.). New York: Wiley.

Kotter, J. P., & Heskett, J. L. (1992). *Corporate culture and performance.* New York: Free Press.

Leavitt, H. J. (1965). Applied organizational change in industry. In J. G. March (Ed.), *Handbook of organizations* (pp. 1144–1170). New York: Rand McNally.

Litwin, G. H., & Stringer, R. A. (1968). *Motivation and organizational climate.* Boston: Harvard Business School Press.

McClelland, D. C. (1975). *Power: The inner experience.* New York: Irvington.

Michela, J. L., Boni, S. M., Schechter, C. B., Manderlink, G., Bernstein, W. M., O' Malley, M., & Burke, W. W. (1988). *A hierarchically nested model for estimation of influences on organizational climate: Rationale, methods, and demonstration.* Working paper, Teachers College, Columbia University, New York City.

Morgan, G. (1986). *Images of organizations.* Newbury Park, CA: Sage.

Nadler, D. A., & Tushman, M. L. (1977). A diagnostic model for organization behavior. In J. R. Hackman, E. E. Lawler III, & L. W. Porter (Eds.), *Perspectives on behavior in organizations* (pp. 85–100). New York: McGraw-Hill.

Nadler, D. A., & Tushman, M. L. (1989). Organizational frame bending: Principles for managing reorientation. *Academy of Management Executive, 3,* 194–204.

Pascale, R. T., & Athos, A. G. (1981). *The art of Japanese management.* New York: Simon & Schuster.

Peters, T. J., & Waterman, R. H. Jr. (1982). *In search of excellence: Lessons from America's best-run companies.* New York: Harper & Row.

Reichers, A. E., & Schneider, B. (1990). Climate and culture: An evolution of constructs. In B. Schneider (Ed.), *Organizational climate and culture* (pp. 5–39). San Francisco: Jossey-Bass.

Schein, E. H. (1992). *Organizational culture and leadership* (2nd ed.). San Francisco: Jossey-Bass.

Selznick, P. (1957). *Leadership in administration.* New York: Harper & Row.

Tagiuri, R., & Litwin, G. H. (Eds.). (1968). *Organizational climate: Explorations of a concept.* Cambridge, MA: Harvard University Press.

Tichy, N. M. (1983). *Managing strategic change: Technical, political, and cultural dynamics.* New York: Wiley.

Tichy, N. M., & Devanna, M. A. (1986). *The transformational leader.* New York: Wiley.

Tichy, N. M., Hornstein, H. A., & Nisberg, J. N. (1977). Organization diagnosis and intervention strategies: Developing emergent pragmatic theories of change. In W. W. Burke (Ed.), *Current issues and strategies in organization development* (pp. 361–383). New York: Human Sciences Press.

Weisbord, M. R. (1976). Organizational diagnosis: Six places to look for trouble with or without a theory. *Group and Organization Studies, 1,* 430–447.

Weisbord, M. R. (1978). *Organizational diagnosis: A workbook of theory and practice.* Reading, MA: Addison-Wesley.

CHAPTER 4

Diagnosis for Organization Design

ELISE WALTON
DAVID A. NADLER

In the late 1990s, organizations will undergo radical transformations of their shape and functioning. The organization of the future will bear little resemblance to what we have traditionally thought of as organizations. Few of the successful, thriving companies will be the traditional hierarchical models built up after the industrial revolution (Chandler, 1962).

These changes derive from three basic causes. First, environmental changes are forcing executives to consider radical transformations. Competition has forced companies to search for ways to decrease the cost in both time and money of internal coordination. Customer demand for quality has led companies to recognize the need to energize employees by providing them with better tools and an increased sense of the meaning of their work. The need for competitive innovation has required many firms to search for ways to increase both the sense of accountability and the degree of empowerment for teams at all levels. The global economy has pushed corporations to search for their true competitive advantage and to broaden their reach and scale without creating the "mass" that traditionally has been required.

In industry after industry, senior managers are dealing with conditions that make success more elusive. The days of easy and effortless global dominance by U.S. firms clearly have passed, replaced by conditions that require executives to use every possible tool at their disposal to create and maintain organizational effectiveness. Changes in the labor force and the very social infrastructure on which the corporations rest also make changes necessary. Political changes—from increased civil actions, increased board-of-director activity, and federal regulatory changes—also present new demands. These conditions create the *need* to improve organization designs.

Second, social and technological changes now enable the design of very different types of organizations. The reduction in the cost of technology, as well as its increasing functionality, now allows organizations to manage in ways previously unimaginable. These conditions create the *ability* to develop new organization designs.

Finally, there is an increased *willingness* to try new organizational designs. While academics have long talked about different approaches for organizations, managers only began implementing them in the late 1980s. In many different settings, industries, and markets, companies are searching for new designs that will serve them more effectively in a new and changing environment.

Organization design is one of the key levers executives have to create an adaptive, competitive organization. In our work, design begins with diagnosis, since any design must be relevant to the organization's strategy and context. Therefore, we begin this chapter with our fundamental diagnostic model. After this grounding we review our approach to organization design and the key decisions designers have to make. Finally, we consider *organizational architecture*, an emerging way of thinking about organization design.

ORGANIZATIONAL DIAGNOSIS

Organization design is just one aspect of organizations. It has great impact, but it would be a mistake to consider design choices and decisions without a broader framework. Thus, in thinking about an organizational design, it is important to start with an overall diagnosis of the organizational system.

In approaching the diagnosis, we believe it is important to use a framework to structure the information. Our framework, the *congruence model* (Nadler & Tushman, 1980), emphasizes the transformation process and reflects the critical system property of interdependence. It views organizations as made up of components or parts that interact with each other. These components exist in states of relative balance, consistency, or "fit" with each other. The different parts of an organization can fit well together and function effectively, or they can fit poorly and lead to problems, dysfunctions, or performance below potential. Our view is that organizational effectiveness is based on how well the organization's components fit together, that is, the congruence among the components.

It is important to remember that we are concerned about creating a model for the *behavioral* system of the organization, the system of elements that ultimately produces behavior patterns and, in turn, organizational performance. Put simply, we need to deal with questions of the inputs the system has to work with, the outputs it must produce, the major components of the transformation process, and the ways in which these components interact.

Ideally, all organization design efforts should begin with a diagnosis. The diagnosis often indicates that organization design is not the solution. We repeatedly find executives planning a structural solution for a problem rooted elsewhere in the organization. For example, one client, frustrated by his organization's inability to increase worldwide sales, felt that a new structure was warranted. The diagnosis revealed that while the structure was causing some problems, the lack of a clear strategy and disagreements over the customer base were the primary drivers of organizational dysfunction.

However, design efforts are often part of a broader set of organizational actions. For example, in the process of redefining its strategy, a high-technology company came to realize that it could not execute its new strategy with its existing organization. Therefore, the organization redesign was a reaction to a broader organizational assessment. In this case, diagnosis was not a separate activity but part of ongoing activities. Only rarely should design be undertaken without an in-depth diagnosis.

A final reason for starting with an overall diagnosis is the systems properties of organizations. Systems properties play a prominent role in implementing new organizational designs (Nadler & Tushman, 1988). For example, the *internal interdependence* of the components and the tendency toward *equilibrium* frequently undermine planned changes. That is, when one aspect of the organization (its design) changes, other components of the organization may react by trying to bring the deviant back into alignment with the prior arrangements. Therefore, the diagnosis is extremely helpful when planning the implementation of the design, because it can identify key relationships and anticipate the likely responses to change.

In the following paragraphs we describe the content areas a diagnosis should typically consider. We use a variety of methods to assess these content areas: interviews, surveys, observations, archival data, and so on. However, we typically consolidate the information into a system map in order to identify the primary organizational issues and misfits.

Inputs

Inputs are factors that at any one point in time make up the givens facing the organization. They are the material that the organization has to work with. There are several different types of inputs, each of which presents a different set of givens to the organization (see Table 4.1 for an overview of inputs).

The first input is the *environment*, or all factors outside the organization being examined. Every organization exists in a larger environment that includes individuals, groups, other organizations, and even larger social forces. All of these have a potentially powerful impact on how the organization performs. More specifically, the environment includes markets (clients or customers), suppliers, governmental and regulatory bodies, labor unions, competitors, financial institutions, special interest groups, and so on.

Three critical features of the environment affect organizational diagnosis. First, the environment places *demands* on the organization; it requires, for example, certain products or services at certain levels of quality or quantity. Second, the environment may *constrain* organizational action. These constraints range from limitations imposed by scarce capital to prohibitions set by government regulations. Third, the environment *provides opportunities* that the organization can explore. Thus, when we analyze an organization, we need to consider the factors in the organization's environment and determine how those factors, singly or collectively, create demands, constraints, or opportunities.

The second input is the organization's *resources*. Any organization has a range of different assets to which it has access. These include employees, technology, capital, information, and so on. Resources can also include less tangible assets, such as the perception of the organization in the marketplace or a positive organizational climate. A set of resources can be shaped, deployed, or configured in different ways by an organization. For diagnostic purposes two features of an organization's resources are of interest: (1) the relative quality or value of those resources in light of the environment, and (2) how flexible or fungible the resources are.

The third input is the organization's *history*. There is growing evidence that the way organizations function today is greatly influenced by past events. It is particularly important to understand the major phases of an organization's development over a period of time, as well as the current impact of past events, for example, key strategic decisions, the acts or behavior of key leaders, crises and the organization's responses to them, and the evolution of core values and norms of the organization.

The final input, *strategy*, is somewhat different from the others. It reflects both determinate environmental givens (environment, resources, history) and managerial choices (Hitt & Tyler, 1991). We use strategy in its broadest context to describe the whole set of decisions that are made about how the organization will configure its resources against the demands, constraints, and opportunities of the environment within the context of its history. Strategy makes the fundamental decision of "What business are

TABLE 4.1. Key Organizational Inputs

Input	Definition	Critical features for diagnosis
Environment	All factors outside the organization (institutions, groups, individuals, events, etc.) that have a potential impact on that organization	1. What demands does the environment make on the organization? 2. How does the environment put constraints on organizational action?
Resources	Various assets to which the organization has access (resources, technology, capital, information, etc.) as well as less tangible resources (recognition in the market, etc.)	1. What is the relative quality of the different resources to which the organization has access? 2. To what extent are resources fixed rather than flexible in their configuration(s)?
History	The patterns of past behavior, activity, and effectiveness of the organization that may affect current organizational functioning	1. What have been the major stages or phases of the organization's development? 2. What is the current impact of such historical factors as strategic decisions, acts of key leaders, crises, and core values and norms?
Strategy	The stream of decisions about how organizational resources will be configured to meet the demands, constraints, and opportunities within the context of the organization's history	1. How has the organization defined its core mission, including the markets it serves and the products or services it provides to these markets? 2. On what basis does it compete? 3. What supporting strategies has the organization employed to achieve the core mission? 4. What specific objectives have been set for organizational output?

we in?" and determines how the organization's resources should be matched against the environment. For purposes of analysis, we usually assess the organization's mission, vision, tactics, and measurements. This includes the markets, the offerings, the customers, and other elements crucial to strategy.

Strategy may be the most important single input for the organization. On one hand, strategic decisions implicitly determine the nature of the work the organization should be doing or the tasks it should perform. On the other hand, strategic decisions, and particularly decisions about objectives, determine the system's outputs. The pattern of strategic decisions about how to apply organizational resources and capabilities to changing environmental demands is the critical variable in explaining sustainable competitive advantage (Williams, 1992).

In summary, there are three basic inputs—environment, resources, and history—and a fourth derivative input, strategy, which determines how the organization responds to or deals with the basic inputs. Strategy is critical because it determines the work to be performed by the organization and defines desired organizational outputs.

Valuable insight lies in understanding the organization's inputs as well as the organization's strategy, or strategic response. Data from customer interviews, market experts, environmental scans, and competitive analyses are useful for diagnosing environmental inputs. Human resource audits and other employee assessments can help evaluate the human resources the organization has at its disposal. Clearly, financial analysis is an important aspect in understanding the organization's inputs. A firm's financial strength or weakness tells a great deal about the pressure for change the organization is experiencing. Finally, a diagnosis of history may be done via case studies or culture audits. Often, accurate chronologies are less important than the stories and messages that are conveyed in the hallway folklore.

In many cases, the problem of assessing inputs is in the conflicting evaluations of the inputs. For example, one group considers the organization's human assets healthy, another group considers them weak. We find the problem of conflicting evaluations particularly prevalent in the area of strategy. As one client put it, "As soon as we present a study proving the value of a strategic initiative, we find someone else studied it last year and proved it was no good." Because strategy is particularly important in directing organizational activity, conflicting views of strategy create a great deal of organizational ineffectiveness. These problems are often uncovered in a diagnosis. The diagnosis makes explicit the implicit differences in strategy and the differences between the espoused strategy and the strategy-in-use. As such, it provides an important key to understanding how the organization currently functions.

Outputs

Outputs are what the organization produces, how it performs, and how effective it is. We think about outputs at different levels. In addition to the system's basic output, its products, we consider other outputs that contribute to sustained organizational performance, such as the functioning of groups or units within the organization and the functioning of individual organization members.

At the organizational level, three factors help evaluate organizational performance: (1) goal attainment, or how well the organization meets its objectives; (2) resource utilization, or how well the organization makes use of available resources; and (3) adaptability, or whether the organization continues to position itself favorably with respect to its environment and environmental changes.

Obviously, the functioning of groups (departments, divisions, or other subunits in the organization) and individuals contribute to these organization-level outputs. We also look for specific group- and individual-level outputs as indicators of longer-term organizational viability. Specifically, do activities enhance and maintain the functioning and commitment of groups and teams? Does the organization maintain individual commitment, work life satisfaction and self-esteem? Has the organization built a strong culture consistent with its strategy and task? While these may not contribute directly or substantially to annual marketplace or financial performance, they prognosticate organizational vitality over the long run.

The Organization as a Transformation Process

So far, we've defined the nature of the inputs and outputs of the organizational system. This brings us to the transformation process. Given an environment, a set of resources, and history, the question is how to implement a strategy to produce effective performance at the organization, group, and individual level. In the congruence model, the major components are the system that transforms the inputs into outputs.

We use a four-point model, including the following specific organizational subsystems: (1) the work, (2) the people, (3) the formal organization, and (4) the informal organization (see Figure 4.1 for an overview of the model). Like other models of organizations (Galbraith, 1977; Peters & Waterman, 1982), this model provides a framework for sorting and categorizing activities in organizations. Like any categorizing scheme, this model is designed to provide insight and review key subsystems rather than provide perfect classification or sorting precision.

Work is the first component of the model. This component is the basic activity the organization is engaged in, with emphasis on the specific work activities and their inherent characteristics rather than the specific config-

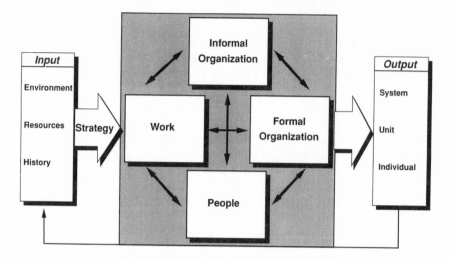

FIGURE 4.1. The congruence model.

uration of the work process at any moment in time. An analysis of an organization's work should characterize the different tasks required, the specific work flows, and the required task outputs. In addition, the organizational diagnosis may look at job design, competency requirements, task uncertainties, boundaries, and constraints. Because it is assumed that a primary (although not the only) reason for the organization's existence is to perform the task consistent with strategy, the task is the starting point for the organizational diagnosis. As we will see, the assessment of the adequacy of other components depends to a large degree on an understanding of the nature of the tasks to be performed.

People, those who perform the organizational tasks, form the second component of this model. The most critical issue here is to identify the organization members' characteristics. We consider the nature of individual knowledge and skills; the different needs, preferences, and expectations among members; and demographic characteristics of the human assets of the firm.

The third component is the *formal organization*. This includes the range of structures, processes, methods, procedures, and so forth that are explicitly and formally developed to get individuals to perform tasks consistent with organizational strategy. The broad term *formal organization* encompasses four factors: (1) the way jobs are grouped together into units, the internal structure of those units, and the coordination and control mechanisms used to link those units together; (2) the way jobs are designed within the context of organizational designs; (3) the work environment, which includes a number of factors that characterize the immediate environment in which work is done, such as the physical working environment, the available work resources, and so on; and (4) the organization's formal systems for attracting, placing, developing, and evaluating human resources. Together, these factors constitute the set of formal organizational arrangements; that is, they are explicitly designed and specified, usually in writing.

The final component is the *informal organization*, the arrangements that develop or emerge over a period of time. These arrangements are usually implicit and unwritten, but they influence a good deal of behavior. They include the different structures, processes, and elements that emerge while the organization is operating. For example, different types of informal working arrangements (including rules, procedures, methods, and so on), as well as various communication and influence patterns develop. The behavior of leaders (as opposed to the formal creation of leader positions) is an important feature of the informal organization, as are the patterns of relationships that develop both within and between groups. The components of the informal organization sometimes complement formal organizational arrangements by providing structures to aid work where none exist. In other situations they may arise in reaction to the formal structure to protect individuals from it. They may therefore either aid or hinder the organization's performance. The informal organization has a particularly critical effect on behavior and is potentially the most difficult to change.

In recent years, corporations have developed an increasing awareness of the importance of the informal organization in creating organizational effectiveness. In 1982, Peters and Waterman made the point that culture (shared values, vision) is a key success factor in excellent companies, and recent research (Kotter & Heskett, 1992) makes the point even more powerfully: The "right" culture—one that fits with the environmental, strategic, and task demands—correlates with financial performance. However, more important than the research has been corporations' experience during the 1980s. Massive restructurings, layoffs, and investments in productivity-enhancing technologies did not seem to lead to the expected improvements, and executives came to recognize that effective change required not only an alteration in the formal organization, but modifications in the informal organization (i.e., culture), informal work practices, and work communities as well.

In summary, organizations can be thought of as a set of components: the work, the people, the formal organization, and the informal organization. In any system, however, the critical question is not what the components are, but what the nature of their interaction is. The congruence model raises the question, What are the dynamics of the relationships among the components? To deal with this issue, we must return to the concept of congruence or fit.

The Concept of Congruence

The congruence between two components is defined as the degree to which the needs, demands, goals, objectives, and/or structures of one component are consistent with the needs, demands, goals, objectives, and/or structures of another component. Congruence, therefore, is a measure of consistency, or how well pairs of components fit together. Consider, for example, two components—the task and the individual. At the simplest level the task presents some demands (i.e., for skill or knowledge) on individuals who would perform it. At the same time, the set of individuals available to do the task have certain characteristics (their levels of skill and knowledge). Obviously, if the individual's knowledge and skill match the knowledge and skill demanded by the task, performance will be effective. Obviously, too, the individual/task congruence relationship encompasses other factors besides knowledge and skill. Similarly, each congruence relationship in the model has its own specific characteristics. Research and theory can guide the assessment of fit in each relationship. For an overview of the critical elements of each congruence relationship, see Table 4.2.

DIAGNOSIS FOR DESIGN

Organization design consists of the decisions about the formal organization, including formal structures, processes, systems, roles, and relationships. Specifically, design involves job content and boundaries, reward systems, measurement systems, information systems, control systems, methods and procedures, management processes, shape of work units, groups, and hierarchy.

The purpose of design is to enable the successful execution of strategy through the following mechanisms: First, design can enable strategy via the appropriate specialization, coordination, and scope (e.g., to gain cost benefits of scale or differentiation); second, design can make possible the effective coordination of diverse efforts; and, finally, design should motivate and enable desired behaviors. Overall, the organization must meet the multiple demands of the work for coordination, specialization, and cycle time.

Organizing creates value by aggregating sets of individuals or groups who all do the same thing—by moving beyond "cottage industries." Economies and advantages come from bringing together individuals, jobs,

TABLE 4.2. Definitions of Fit Among Components

Fit	Issues
Individual/ organization	How are individual needs met by the organizational arrangements?
	Do individuals hold clear perceptions of organizational structure?
	Is there a convergence of individual and organizational goals?
People/ work	How are individual needs met by the tasks?
	Do individuals have skills and abilities to meet task demands?
People/ informal organization	How are individual needs met by the informal organization?
	How does the informal organization make use of individual resources consistent with informal goals?
Work/ organization	Are organizational arrangements adequate to meet the demands of the task?
	Do organizational arrangements motivate behavior that is consistent with task demands?
Work/ informal organization	Does the informal organization structure facilitate task performance?
	Does it help meet the demands of the task?
Organization/ informal organization	Are the goals, rewards, and structures of the informal organization consistent with those of the formal organization?

and roles related to doing the same thing or using the same resources. Benefits accrue from specialization, leveraging of resources, shared support, and common practices. As learning is formalized in processes and procedures, individuals can build on previous learning without having to invent solutions from scratch.

Organizing also creates value by structuring and processing information. By this we mean moving information between individuals and groups who need it to do their work or who need it for coordinating their activities, as well as for monitoring, control, sensing, understanding customer requirements, producing the work, and so forth. By structuring information and activity, organization design shapes the behavior of the people in the firm. It does this, in part, by focusing the attention of people in key areas (customer, activities, products). It motivates people by signaling what is important, and it also can provide important empowering and enabling structures.

The fundamental problem is how to build a design that will fit the other components of the organization. Of primary importance is a design that will enable the organization to perform its tasks effectively. This implies the need to find a way of organizing that reflects the requirements posed by the work and the strategy of the organization. At the same time, the formal organization needs to fit the people and the informal organization. Often, perfect fit cannot be achieved, and the designer must balance the demands of the strategy and work against the needs of the individuals and the informal organization.

In a certain sense, organization design goes on all the time. As part of their day-to-day work, managers make decisions involving the distribution of work, the assignment of people, and the core values of the organization. There are times, however, when significant, systematic redesign efforts are called for, such as in the following situations:

• *Strategic shift*. Strategic shifts may occur as a result of environmental changes, resource changes, or a new management vision. They usually prescribe a change in mission or task and often in the formal organization design.

• *Work redefinition*. In some situations the work is redefined not because of strategy but because of new technologies, changed expectations, or a change in the cost or quality of resources. Restructuring, benchmarking, and work reengineering efforts typically change the way work is done but need not reflect a change in strategy.

• *Cultural/political change*. An organization may be redesigned as a way of influencing the informal organization. For example, cross-functional teams, a structural solution, addresses an informal problem of functional boundaries and conflicts. Co-locating sales or service people with customers may create a more customer-responsive culture. Management succession can also impact the informal organization.

• *Growth/shrinkage*. Companies facing dramatic growth or dramatic declines inevitably have to redesign themselves to keep up with the changes required in coordination and differentiation.

• *Changes in people*. Over time, the skills, knowledge, motivation and demographic profile of the work force may change and require rethinking existing organization designs. For example, the increasing demand for individual influence and rights in the workplace fueled the development of more innovative, participative work designs. In high-technology firms, the skills and knowledge of the work force frequently become outmoded over time and require continuing structural redeployment.

• *Organization-caused problems*. When the organization is performing poorly, redesign may be appropriate. Redesign may be a countermeasure to a specific coordination or specialization problem. Some of the frequent

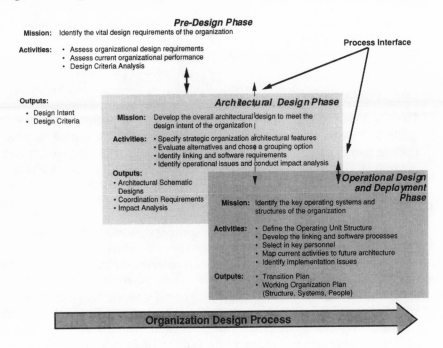

Pre-Design Phase

Mission: Identify the vital design requirements of the organization

Activities:
- Assess organizational design requirements
- Assess current organizational performance
- Design Criteria Analysis

Process Interface

Outputs:
- Design Intent
- Design Criteria

Architectural Design Phase

Mission: Develop the overall architectural design to meet the design intent of the organization

Activities:
- Specify strategic organization architectural features
- Evaluate alternatives and chose a grouping option
- Identify linking and software requirements
- Identify operational issues and conduct impact analysis

Outputs:
- Architectural Schematic Designs
- Coordination Requirements
- Impact Analysis

Operational Design and Deployment Phase

Mission: Identify the key operating systems and structures of the organization

Activities:
- Define the Operating Unit Structure
- Develop the linking and software processes
- Select in key personnel
- Map current activities to future architecture
- Identify implementation issues

Outputs:
- Transition Plan
- Working Organization Plan (Structure, Systems, People)

Organization Design Process

FIGURE 4.2 Organization design process.

indicators of design dysfunctions are coordination difficulties, intergroup conflict, unclear roles and responsibilities, reduced responsiveness, and the proliferation of extra-organizational units.

The Design Process

There is a logical sequence for organizational design decisions, beginning with an assessment of organizational needs, continuing through the key decisions, and concluding with implementation (see Figure 4.2). This process has been used in many different settings, and we find that following it rigorously has led to good results in redesign efforts. Most important, it helps managers design organizations that respond to their competitive requirements and helps them avoid choices based on familiarity or current fads.

In this process it is important to maintain some continuity between the phases so that the learning is transferred and the handoffs are smooth. The process usually requires executive involvement, either by the CEO or by an executive board. However, it is often valuable to pull together diverse perspectives in the design teams. We typically use high-potential junior managers as well as more seasoned executives on a design team. In addition, representatives from the different units within the current organization are included. When undertaking organization design there are some key decisions that designers face. These are grouping decisions and linking decisions, to which we now turn.

Grouping Decisions

The single most important decision designers face is grouping. This is particularly true at the top levels of an organization. Grouping involves putting some functions or tasks together and necessarily suggests separating others. Grouping addresses specialization in that the people working together will discuss, plan, and perform a common task. It also creates reward systems and career paths. In addition, it affects the way people see information, process information, and learn.

Assuming that an individual has primary membership in only one group, there are just three ways to group people or tasks:

1. *Grouping by activity.* The most common example of this sort of design is the functional organization. People who perform the same function are grouped together. The function that provides the sameness may be knowledge, skills, occupation, or time. For example, individuals who are working on projects with short time frames might constitute one group, while those working with longer time frames might constitute another.

2. *Grouping by output.* When grouping by output, people are put together based on the offering, service, or product they provide. The product organization is a classic illustration of grouping by output. Each product organization includes people who engage in different activities and have different knowledge or skills but who work toward the delivery of a common product or service.

3. *Grouping by user or client.* People who perform different activities and provide different products or services may be grouped together because they all service the same user or client. Geographic organizations usually fall into this category.

Grouping decisions have a dramatic impact on the organization because these divisions establish the boundaries where information will be easily exchanged (within groups) and where it will not be easily exchanged (between groups). Within the groups, there will be increased information processing, shared resources, common goals, and common supervision. Across boundaries, groups will have decreased information exchange, poorer coordination, duplicated resources, and potentially unaligned objectives.

Grouping decisions derive from three sources. First, *strategic requirements* dictate the required organizational capabilities, priorities, and concerns and should be the primary driver of these key decisions. Second, *inherent task requirements* may drive grouping decisions. Where the work shares similar properties, it may make sense to group tasks together. For example, work that requires high information processing, complex analysis, and frequent redirection might not be grouped with work that requires continuous processing and incremental improvements. Third, in thinking about redesign, managers should consider *current problem areas*. For example, ongoing lack of coordination between product development and marketing might suggest that these groups should be grouped together.

In a recent reorganization, Xerox moved from a functional grouping to a business division grouping (Howard, 1992). Its primary business, selling and servicing copiers, was going through a transformation as end users looked to alternative print and copy methods. In addition, the advent of digital copying enabled new approaches to copying. This environmental change drove Xerox to look at how the product was used by customers: Was it for production (such as in a copy center), or was it for a local work group (the hallway copiers used by work groups)? Was it plugged into a network, or was it stand-alone? Xerox worked through the grouping decision first by deciding that grouping by line of business was the best choice. The company then identified distinct business groups by asking specific questions about the products that formed a business division. Did the grouping have an identifiable set of competitors? Was there a definable decision maker or customer? Did the products tend to have the same economic or business model (product life cycle, hardware/software value-added, margins, etc.)? Were the products substitutes for each other? This led to decisions about grouping products into nine different business divisions—ranging from Software, to Printing Systems, to Business Services, to Personal Document Products—and with a well-defined market space to pursue.

Linking Decisions

Linking decisions reflect the organizational requirement of spanning the boundaries created by the grouping decisions. Once the key grouping decisions have been made, the next step is to coordinate or link the different groups so that the organization can function as an integrated whole. The objective of linking mechanisms is to provide for adequate information flows and an organization competence of achieving common, superordinate goals.

There are numerous structural linking mechanisms, many of which are commonly used. A *liaison role* is a common linking mechanism in which the person's job is to work across the boundaries of groups to ensure communication and problem solving across boundaries. A systems analyst, for example, often works the boundary between the users and their needs, and the systems designers' needs. *Cross unit groups*, either permanent or temporary, can be formed of members from different units. They can provide an extensive forum for exchange of information, coordination, and conflict resolution. An *integrator role or department* can have the responsibility for coordinating the activities of multiple work units around the performance of a task. The integrator is not part of any one unit and has no formal reporting authority, but must oversee the process using expertise and personal influence. *Matrix structures* are frequently used to integrate whole groups. For example, members of the finance department may report directly to the chief financial officer but must also report to the business managers they serve.

Groups can also be linked through *management processes*, including linking by formal systems, such as planning or goal-setting systems, rules and procedures, processes, and information flows. These mechanisms serve to coordinate actions of different groups by monitoring activity and giving direction. They frequently are adjuncts or enhancements for hierarchy as a means of coordination.

These mechanisms have become quite popular in the past decade. Horizontal processes such as time to market (Stalk & Hout, 1990), supply chain, or order-fulfillment administration systems (Davidow & Malone, 1992) have focused management attention on designing operating processes that allow the organization to accomplish tasks that cross group boundaries.

Finally, the *informal organization* may be used to create linkages between groups. Educational events and forums that bring different groups together have become increasingly popular. In these forums members of different, even competing, groups are expected to work to understand and shape common strategies and goals. Recently, organizations are exploring and supporting the emergence of communities of practice. These are learning communities that emerge informally as different employees discover a shared need to understand and learn about a given technology, process, or competence (Brown, 1991). Other examples include individual relations/direct contact, culture-shaping events, and intergroup exchanges.

In the Xerox case, Paul Allaire, the CEO, recognized that the new organization design would be weak at nurturing core competencies, particularly the technology competencies and platforms on which printers and copiers are built. The redesign effort created the Technology Decision-Making Board, a forum that brought together those in research and in development, business presidents, and key corporate staff to make decisions about technology choices and investments. This linking mechanism brought together the separate groups who could and should share common infrastructure and platforms.

GOING FORWARD: ORGANIZATIONAL ARCHITECTURE

In recent years organizations have been facing conditions of chronic discontinuities in the environment. This means that assumptions about the environment and resources are short-lived, if they can even be made. It also means that strategy must be evergreen, or continually renewed based on continuous learning about the environment and resources. Therefore, a process based on clearly understood and constant organizational requirements may not always work.

Historically, when executives talked about organization, they focused on the elements of organizational design, that is, the formal structures and systems that they created to execute strategies. During the past few years, forward-thinking executives have become less interested in the specifics of organizational structure—what is in the boxes and which lines connect them—and more interested in a broader concept called *organizational architecture*. By architecture we mean a much more inclusive view of the elements of design of the social and work systems that make up a large complex organization. Architecture therefore includes the formal structure; the design of work practices; culture or operating style; and the processes for selection, socialization, and development of people. In terms of the congruence model, architecture means designing all the organizational components.

What has become clear is that it is the organizational architecture—not the design alone—that is a source of competitive advantage. The well-architected organization motivates, facilitates, and enables individuals and groups to interact more effectively with customers, the work, and each other. As companies gain equal access to capital, as technologies become generic, and as customers become more globally aware, organizations will gain a sustainable competitive advantage from the *system* they have created. The people, the way they work together, and the organizational design that supports them can provide a formula that, even when understood by the competition, cannot be copied. This is evidenced by the growing interest in organizational *capabilities* as a strategic advantage and by a declining interest in typical economic or structural advantages.

What this means for managers is a new way of thinking about their role in the organization. The manager is now the architect of the organization. The manager must have a design intent for the organization. That is, the executive, as architect, must have the overall picture of what the organization must do and the fundamental function and objective of organizing. The executive architect must also design fit into the system, that is, design not only the structures and processes but the culture, the norms, and the people requirements and design internal consistency between the components.

Perhaps the largest single influence on organizational architecture and design has been the evolution of information technology. Most modern theories of organizational design view the core task of organizational structure as information processing, that is, moving information among individuals and groups in the organization to coordinate their work activities.

The traditional information-processing device is hierarchy, built through the grouping of jobs and roles into work units that are linked through common reporting relationships and successive levels of management control. Organizations can also coordinate via standardization or formalization, that is, by means of sets of rules or contracts that allow people to process information in a structured, common way. Finally, organizations process and communicate information informally through "conversations around the coffee pot."

Information technology has begun to revolutionize organizational design choices by providing alternatives to hierarchy as the primary means of coordination. Information systems, common architectures, shared data bases, decision support tools, and expert systems facilitate the coordination, in part by building in greater formalization (of information and procedures) and greater informal communications (via e-mail, videoconferencing, and groupware). It also allows more loose coupling (vs. tight coupling) without the risks of lost coordination and control. The combination of the great potential of information technology with the great demands of the competitive environment has led to innovations in organizational design.

Because of these and other changes, we believe the organizational forms discussed in the following paragraphs will become fairly commonplace over the next decade. These eight architectural elements do not constitute an all-inclusive list. By definition, the responses of organizations to increased uncertainty are difficult to predict; however, we should expect to see these features. Those companies that are creative in designing new organizational architectures will be those that gain significant competitive advantage in this new era of change.

1. *Autonomous work teams.* Self-managed teams that are responsible for an entire piece of work or a complete segment of a work process will become more prevalent. Such teams provide their own supervision, cross-train and change roles, and may be empowered to take responsibility for their own process and results. Autonomous work teams have been used extensively in factory settings, but they will start to become more prevalent, first with respect to the production elements of the office and then in knowledge-intensive work.

2. *High-performance work systems.* As organizations and the people in them become familiar with technology-based advances (expert systems, knowledge-based power tools), the productivity implied by the new tech-

nologies will be realized. What this means is that the social interactions in and around the new technology will be aligned with or will take advantage of the capabilities new technology enables.

3. *Alliances and joint ventures.* An increasing number of companies will find they cannot go it alone. They will recognize the need to focus their talents, particular strengths, and resources on those areas in which they have a competitive advantage and to let others perform functions that can be done better elsewhere.

4. *"Spinouts."* As corporations search for the means to promote and leverage innovation, many will find that when they unleash human creativity, they end up with many more opportunities than there is time, attention, and capital to support. Rather than lose the innovators, they will stake entrepreneurs in the creation of new organizational entities in which they retain some equity. These spinouts may evolve into joint ventures, become fully independent companies, or continue to be associated with the parent, but they usually will not end up as fully integrated operations. Companies of the future will be surrounded by many of these satellite spinouts, with various degrees of coupling to the core.

5. *Networks.* Those companies that become particularly adept at shaping themselves to face uncertainty will evolve into a combination of wholly owned operations, alliances, joint ventures, spinouts, and acquired subsidiaries. They will not be holding companies but will be linked together in what will be called organizational networks through shared values, people, technology, financial resources, and operating styles. Dell Computer, for example, has experienced dramatic growth but has done so in part by networking with suppliers. Its virtual warehouse actually consists of an elaborate information-processing capability that can order, assemble, and ship to a customer's requirement without an employee even touching the product. Novell, a small firm competing in the computer industry, used a network of third parties (chains, value-added resellers) to duplicate the coverage IBM got with a massive sales force.

6. *Fuzzy boundaries.* The boundaries that define organizations will become less clear. The architectural elements of joint ventures, spinouts, and networks will contribute to this fuzziness. The main factor, however, will be technology. When a customer can hook into networks and interact with organizational tools and become a codesigner of products by participating in the design and development process, who is in and who is out become less clear. Xerox, in another example, codesigned document architecture and management with a pharmaceutical company.

7. *Self-designed organizations.* Accompanying the increasing rate of change is the need for organizations to develop the capacity to redesign themselves to meet different conditions. Thus, mechanisms will evolve that enable organizations to learn from their successes and failures and to

reshape themselves in response to changes. To help groups solve problems organizations will increasingly use technology and software ranging from straightforward applications like computer-aided brainstorming to distributed intelligence collection systems like those offered by Corporate Memory.

8.*Teamwork at the top*. Lastly, as all of these new forms evolve, a change will occur at the top of the organization. The diversity, uncertainty, and multiple relationships to be managed will place greater demands on the executive level of management. Although institutions will still require the single chief executive officer, fewer companies will find themselves with a single chief operating officer (COO). Instead, team structures will emerge at the top of organizations, and collective intellect and collaborative action will become more evident. These have emerged at AT&T and Xerox.

SUMMARY

In this chapter we have discussed how diagnosis leads to and supports organization design. In addition we have looked at some of the basic principles of design and introduced the new concept of organization architecture. We believe that in the future companies will redesign faster and more broadly than in the past. For us this means that consultants must have the fundamentals of design firmly in hand but must now complement them with the capability of redesigning the whole system (including culture, people, management practices, etc.). Furthermore, all this must occur more rapidly than in the past. This means that we must learn how to diagnose, design, and implement almost concurrently.

One aid to speed is recognizing some of the emergent forms and the capabilities and difficulties associated with them. We have outlined some of these new forms and structures, and consultants must continue to build an understanding of the different emerging forms. This requires a renewed understanding of structure, organization, systems (particularly information systems) and people and a fresh approach to diagnosis and design. Again, consultants can build on the knowledge and approaches they have used in the past, but they must broaden their scope and implement more rapidly. Although this may present a formidable challenge, it also presents an exciting opportunity.

REFERENCES

Brown, J. S. (1991, January–February). Reinventing the corporation. *Harvard Business Review*, pp. 102–111.

Chandler, A. (1962). *Strategy and structure: Chapters in the history of the American industrial enterprise*. Cambridge, MA: MIT Press.

Davidow, W. H., & Malone, M. S. (1992). *The virtual corporation*. New York: Edward Burlingame Books/HarperBusiness.

Galbraith, J. (1977). *Organization design*. Reading, MA: Addison-Wesley.

Hitt, M. A., & Tyler, B. B. (1991). Strategic decision models: Integrating different perspectives. *Strategic Management Journal, 12*, 327–351.

Howard, B. (1992, September–October). The CEO as organizational architect: An interview with Xerox's Paul Allaire. *Harvard Business Review*, pp. 107–121.

Kotter, J., & Heskett, J. (1992). *Corporate culture and performance*. New York: Free Press.

Nadler, D., & Tushman, M. (1980, Summer). A model for diagnosing organizational behavior: Applying a congruence perspective. *Organizational Dynamics*, pp. 35–51.

Nadler, D., & Tushman, M. (1988). *Strategic organization design*. Glenview, IL: Scott, Foresman.

Peters, T., & Waterman, R. H. Jr. (1982). *In search of excellence*. New York: Harper & Row.

Stalk, G., & Hout, T. (1990). *Competing against time*. New York: Free Press.

Williams, J. (1992). How sustainable is your competitive advantage? *California Management Review, 34*(3), 29–51.

PART II

PERSPECTIVES
ON HUMAN TALENT

Introduction

In this section we burrow to a deeper level of analysis—the individual. Although people materialize in the macro organizational models presented in Part I, OD practitioners seldom analyze individual performance or personal characteristics in depth. Contrarily, practitioners focused on personnel planning, selection, development, and performance often develop rich detail about individuals but overlook the workings of the broader organization.

The three chapters in this section offer perspectives on human talent that challenge such nearsightedness. Each in its own way positions individual issues within the organizational context. The authors demonstrate, moreover, how individuals and their performance are a window to organizational diagnosis.

ADDRESSING FUTURE STAFFING NEEDS

In Chapter 5, James Walker and Thomas Bechet introduce staffing as a lever for implementing organizational change and executing business strategy. They use long- and short-term linkages between business and human resource strategies as both prescriptions and diagnostic guides. Understanding the business context is thus the first step in their ambitious strategic staffing process, which goes on to define future staffing requirements and establish commitments.

Walker and Bechet alter their approach depending on whether organizations anticipate evolutionary or revolutionary changes. The latter situation makes staffing more difficult but diagnosis more valuable. Instead of extrapolating from the present, managers must engage in "what if" exercises, based on the presumed impact of *staffing drivers*. Individuals are sized up for fit to the future organization. If rapid change is likely, employees must be able to learn at an accelerated rate.

TRAINING NEEDS ASSESSMENT: THE BROADENING FOCUS OF A SIMPLE CONCEPT

As the title of Chapter 6 indicates, Ronald Zemke depicts training needs assessment today as more wide-ranging and complex than its early formulation—perhaps even an anachronism and oxymoron. Not only is training today a "critical, competitive, industrial weapon" for global competition, but it is increasingly used to combat social problems, such as substance abuse or sexual harassment. Thus, training needs assessment has necessarily become more intricate, siphoning conceptual foundations from broader fields, such as systems theory and I/O psychology.

In his colorful portrayals, Zemke identifies three situations, or scenarios, that prompt a training needs assessment: performance problems, market demands, and reorganization or reengineering. He does not necessarily assume a skill deficiency when performance problems are manifest, and he may investigate environmental and social conditions, such as reward systems and obstacles to performance. Like Walker and Bechet, he recognizes that reorganizations demand new learning and considers how to achieve that through training.

PERSONNEL-CENTERED ORGANIZATIONAL DIAGNOSIS

To observe the effects of the work environment, Douglas Bray, in Chapter 7, seemingly turns organizational diagnosis on its head with a penetrating evaluation of individuals. Because they are impinged upon by the organization, employees come to mirror its nature and style. To shape an integrated company image, Bray views a kaleidoscope of organizational influences within the same group or groups of individuals.

Bray illustrates personnel-centered organizational diagnosis with several studies he supervised in the former Bell System. Like Harry Levinson in Chapter 2, Bray is a detective, but his investigation begins not from the top but from the grass roots, using information gained from individual assessments to ferret out organizational problems. Most important, this inquisitive scientist–practitioner keeps asking why, probing in new directions along a path of logic, even into 10 organizations outside Bell for corroborative data.

Bray's serendipitous approach helps to avoid a problem identified by

Burke in Chapter 3, namely, that we can become trapped by a chosen model and end up not seeing variables beyond those we are directly pursuing. Although Bray recommends constructing an inventory of practices and intended influences, he cautions against "too tight a linkage between what is wanted and what is to be measured." He would retain the option, for example, of measuring "what values drive performance, not just whether a particular value the organization wants stressed is being served."

A NOTE ON VALUING HUMAN TALENT

Individuals populate each stage of the open systems paradigm. In the congruence model presented by Walton and Nadler in Part I, for example, people are resources (input), a subsystem of the organization as a transformational process (throughput), and via their performance, output. The chapters in Part II hint that there are darker ways of viewing human resources within the systems framework.

Efficient human resource planning, write Walker and Bechet, brings in a supply of people, like other inventory, "just in time." People are then transformed by the organization; in this sense, Bray calls people "products." And, he notes, the organization's treatment is not always nurture—it may be just the opposite. Or, as Zemke observes, organizations may "teach people to be perfectly competent in useless acts." What, then, becomes of these human products? Unfortunately, in the whirlpool of today's swift and often desperate organizational change, there is a danger of people being treated as damaged goods or outmoded tools. They are "decruited," in the euphemism of Walker and Bechet.

This is not to imply that the authors are coldhearted. In various ways, they subtly illuminate the potential of a careful diagnosis for avoiding callous treatment of individuals. A CEO described by Walker and Bechet urges his managers to develop a "stewardship for talent"; Zemke cautions that reducing head count precipitates constant training of the remaining staff for escalating levels of skill and responsibility; Bray deplores developmental neglect of new college recruits.

The gulf between softhearted behavioral scientists and coldhearted managers should not be overdrawn. Walker and Bechet describe an organization that is quite sensitive to issues of fairness and personal dignity and that purposefully adopted a goal of acting on performance problems. Too many organizations, afraid of being seen as mean-spirited (or sued), avoid such actions, and departments end up defending themselves by a practice I call "passing the turkey." This ends up benefiting neither the individual nor the organization. On the other hand, today's organizations would do well to recognize that there will be a price to pay if human resources talent is approached with the shortsighted attitude of "output the round pegs and input the square ones."

Through this next part of our diagnostic tour, think about the strengths, the shortcomings, and the feelings of the people who inhabit the increasingly demanding world of work. But also be prepared for some Humpty Dumpty diagnoses (explained in Chapter 6).

CHAPTER 5

Addressing Future
Staffing Needs

JAMES W. WALKER
THOMAS P. BECHET

Organizational effectiveness depends on having the right people in the right jobs at the right times to meet rapidly changing organizational requirements. Accordingly, identifying and addressing future staffing needs is an important element of organizational diagnosis and management of change. Effective staffing is a lever for implementing organizational change and for executing business strategy. Long-term staffing strategies are needed to help managers guide the recruitment, utilization, development, movement, and attrition of talent in the near term.

From the 1950s through 1970s many organizations applied "manpower planning" as a process for anticipating and meeting staffing requirements. In the typically stable, slow-changing environment of most business, military, and governmental organizations of the time, planning was based on extrapolation of current staffing patterns to meet future demands, taking into account attrition and internal movement.

In the 1980s and 1990s, "human resource planning" has been applied to help anticipate changing staffing requirements. More broadly, many companies address all aspects of managing human resources through planning, directly linking human resource actions to strategic business issues or priorities. Because human resource actions such as organization, staffing, development, performance management, and rewards address planned business changes, they are considered strategic. Human resource strategies are developed to establish these linkages.

Well-managed companies continuously define the competencies and levels of staffing needed to implement business strategies, usually based on assessment of business context changes. Through an iterative process, managers and human resource staff examine and improve staffing in relation to changing needs. Human resource planning provides a context for defining the actions needed to ensure staffing the future business.

Staffing actions typically include the following:

- Recruiting and developing the talent required to meet future capability requirements.
- Adjusting overall staffing and associated costs to match business requirements.
- Assigning talent in an organization to the highest value work they can perform (improving staff utilization).
- Enhancing the capacity of talent to perform higher value work through training, education, and job-related development.
- Retraining, redeploying, or "decruiting" (moving out) employees whose capabilities are not likely to fit future needs in a way that is fair and respectful.

Managing the overall supply and flow of talent, relative to changing organizational needs, is an integral element of organizational change. Accordingly, the analysis and planning process is an essential element of organizational diagnosis.

LINKAGE WITH BUSINESS PLANNING

Creating and implementing strategic staffing plans is easier in a more stable organization and more difficult in organizations experiencing rapidly changing conditions. However, planning is most valuable in organizations that are experiencing (or will experience) rapid change, because a context is needed to guide actions in the face of uncertainty. Human resource planning provides a guide to action, not a prediction of the future. In a changing environment, planning provides information that is understandable and useful to managers—different scenarios and contingencies that help them make better near-term staffing decisions.

Long Term, Short Term

The time frame for human resource planning should match the length of the business planning cycle. Business plans usually have both a long- and a short-term focus. Human resource planning typically has a short-term focus; for example, defining the necessary recruiting, movement, develop-

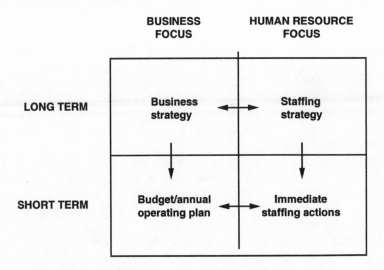

FIGURE 5.1. Linking human resource plans and business plans.

ment, and termination actions to be taken in the coming year. However, these short-term actions should be taken within the context of an overarching human resource strategy, that is, a plan for managing human resources over the longer term.

In well-managed companies both the business focus and the human resource focus include long- and short-term components, as illustrated in Figure 5.1. On the business side, a set of business strategies defines the direction in which the organization plans to move (and the actions that will be taken to do that) during the longer-term planning period (e.g., the coming 3 to 5 years). In the short term a budget or annual operating plan defines actions. Often, this annual plan is the first year of a long-term business strategy.

On the human resource side, immediate staffing actions (including recruiting, development, etc.) are defined annually, often as an integral part of the budgeting process. Many companies also prepare longer-term human resource strategies (defined as longer-term, directional plans of action) that support business strategies. These human resource strategies provide a context for defining and integrating short-term human resource activities and initiatives (such as training and development programs).

Direct linkages exist between business planning and human resource planning in both the long and the short term. As shown by the double-sided arrows in Figure 5.1, business strategies both influence and are influenced by human resource strategies.

Long-Term Linkages

Once business strategies are developed, it is possible to define human resource issues (gaps between desired and actual capabilities) that must be
addressed for effective implementation of the business strategies. These
gaps typically include shortages or surpluses in staffing levels, deficits in
employees with required competencies, and so forth. Staffing strategies to
address the gaps can then be developed (e.g., 3-year recruiting plans, ongoing executive development).

The human resource strategies can also impact the business strategies. Business strategies sometimes assume an adequate supply of appropriate talent that in reality cannot be recruited or developed in time. In
such cases business strategies must be modified in light of human resource
constraints. Numerous companies, for example, have slowed capital investment and business expansion plans because of assessed shortages of
managerial or technical talent.

Short-Term Linkages

Linkages must also be established in the short term. Annual budgets often
include head count projections, estimates of expenditures for training, and
other elements related to human resources. Short-term human resource
programs and activities must be consistent with these financial constraints. Similarly, the implementation of required short-term human resource initiatives influences short-term business plans.

Short-term human resource actions are thus influenced by short-term
business plans and by longer-term human resource strategies. Actions
must be consistent with (and help to implement) the longer-term human
resource strategies. Within this context, an organization identifies and implements the human resource actions that are most critical and best support longer-term business strategies. Human resource actions that do not
directly support business strategies must be reviewed carefully.

A Diagnostic Guide to Linkages

Logically, a company first develops a sound understanding of its long-
term business context and defines its long-range business plan. From this
base, management formulates both a reliable annual budget, including
staffing plans, and a long-range staffing strategy or human resource plan.
Management then determines and implements specific short-term actions
that meet immediate needs and also fit the longer-term requirements.

Some companies may find it necessary to begin the planning process
with short-term action planning. In these cases critical near-term issues or

management initiatives (e.g., controlling head count, assimilating an acquisition, improving utilization) must be addressed immediately. Over time, management shifts its focus to longer-term issues and strategies.

Managers and human resource staff may use the matrix in Figure 5.1 as a diagnostic guide to the linkage between human resource and business planning. First, identify all the initiatives currently undertaken in each cell of the matrix, paying careful attention to integration when several initiatives are identified in a single cell (e.g., companies that have several levels of business strategy or have separate efforts to develop visions and strategies). It may be necessary to augment current activities in one or more of the cells (e.g., strengthen the development of human resource strategies). Next, determine the extent to which linkages have been established between the various cells. Do linkages exist in both directions where appropriate? Are the linkages strong and well developed?

OVERVIEW OF THE STRATEGIC STAFFING PROCESS

Business planning is typically ongoing, with no clear beginning and end. Each year's planning cycle builds on the previous plan and base of information. Hence, the steps in developing a human resource plan or staffing strategy, presented in Figure 5.2, are not necessarily sequential. A company establishing a strategic staffing process from scratch, however, will find this to be a useful guide.

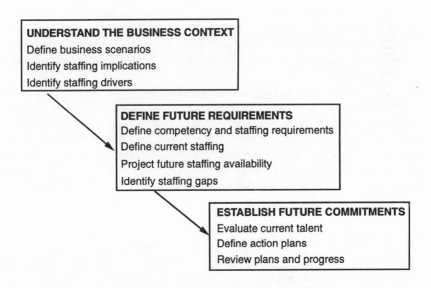

FIGURE 5.2. Planning for strategic staffing.

Understand the Business Context

Traditionally, staffing analysis and planning might have begun with examination of current staffing levels and mix (i.e., a staffing table or "manning chart" from which anticipated incremental changes could be planned). In today's changing business context, however, planning instead begins by looking several years into the future. Managers and human resource staff develop and evaluate alternative scenarios of future business conditions and demands. They identify staffing implications of the most likely scenarios and the factors that drive changes in staffing requirements (quantitatively and quantitatively).

The role of the human resource staff is to provide a framework for developing this understanding. They should guide the analysis by asking questions, examining business plans, and facilitating a dialogue with and among managers who are in the best position to anticipate future business changes.

Define Future Requirements

Once the future business context is defined, managers and human resource staff interpret anticipated changes in terms of competencies and staffing levels required. Again, the persons familiar with the business, technology, and work demands are best able to project requirements.

They also define current staffing, including both the head counts and the "head contents," that is, the capabilities currently represented in the work force. In some companies such information is available from automated systems or from regular management reporting; in most, even rudimentary information has to be amassed. Future staffing availability is determined by projecting attrition, transfers, promotions, and other staffing changes.

Rigorous data analysis and use of forecasting models is helpful in this step (and may be supported by human resource staff), but projections are ultimately management judgments. Based on their experience and knowledge, managers identify opportunities to improve job design, talent utilization, organization, and competency mix. Then they project available staffing supply relative to projected requirements and identify ways to bridge gaps, using analytic tools that enhance the rigor and speed of the process.

Establish Future Commitments

Action plans ideally are based on sound analysis of facts and alternatives. Near-term actions should not only address near-term staffing imbalances but anticipate longer-range needs. Because human resource staff are familiar with alternative actions, such as redeployment, outplacement, organization realignment, and recruitment, they play a key role in helping managers formulate suitable, realistic plans.

Commitments to action are specific and measurable. Managers define staffing objectives in ways that achievements may be tracked and evaluated. Where are we trying to go? How will we know if we are progressing? The more clearly future expectations are defined, the easier it will be to measure and evaluate the effects of management actions.

Roles in Planning

In most organizations line managers are ultimately responsible for defining staffing requirements, assessing current talent and performance, and making the selection and development decisions necessary to ensure that staffing supply will equal demand. Human resource staff play a key role in supporting this decision making by providing information, technical support, and consulting. They help managers who are unfamiliar with human resource planning to move up the learning curve.

In examining each component of the process, this chapter describes how human resource staff and line managers may together prepare effective strategic staffing plans. When human resource staff succumb to the temptation to develop staffing plans for their client organizations, such plans typically lose relevance, line management ownership, credibility, and, therefore, usefulness as guides to action.

Managers involved in planning need to apply enlightened, "out of the box" thinking for effective strategic staffing. Often, they and human resource staff raise more questions for consideration during the planning process than are answered. In a sense, planning is an educational exercise for participants in which framing the right questions is critical.

Human resource staff who have a grasp of business issues and a sound understanding of strategic staffing tools and techniques are in the best position to act as "internal consultants." Staff can provide value-added services, ensuring that managers identify critical staffing issues and prepare realistic plans for addressing those issues.

UNDERSTANDING THE BUSINESS CONTEXT

Strategic staffing analysis and planning is not merely a one-shot project or a product. It should never be a staff exercise with little impact on the business. It is a candid, focused, data-based process that enables managers to make near-term staffing decisions within a longer-range strategic context. By developing and implementing strategic staffing plans within the context of business planning, managers can ensure the "just in time" talent needed to meet changing needs and business objectives.

A long-term staffing plan considers the business context (e.g., business strategies or changes) that extends 3 to 5 years in the future. In this planning time frame more significant changes may be expected than can be addressed in a single year. At a minimum, it is necessary to consider changes in skill and staffing requirements needed to support future business requirements.

Define Business Scenarios

Because of the uncertainty of future requirements, the most difficult step is to define one or more scenarios of the business outlook. The answers to the following key diagnostic questions suggest what the business will be like:

- What changes in industry, competitive, and other external factors will affect the future of the business?
- What business strategies are to be implemented? What strategic objectives are to be met?
- What changes are called for in business, technology, and functional plans? What changes in capital investment or allocation are planned?
- What will be the impact of planned business changes and future objectives on the way the company is managed?
- How will customer requirements and expectations affect the business? What changes are anticipated based on inputs from key customers or perceptions of key managers regarding future customer requirements and expectations?
- What will be the necessary processes, organization, and functions to implement strategies and achieve objectives?

Identify Staffing Implications

Once business scenarios are defined, managers can identify the impacts those scenarios will have on required competencies and staffing levels. It is important to discern how different the business will be in the future—how radical future changes will be from the present situation. Where changes to the business will be evolutionary, managers project staffing requirements based on past experience and trends that may continue into the future. Such planning assumes that the current organization and job structure will continue into the future generally intact, providing the context for staffing needs. Further, planning may assume that future staffing changes will build on the current work force. This approach is also appropriate when the degree of change or the future state is uncertain (e.g., when an organization knows so little about what the future holds that it elects to plan using a "business as usual" scenario).

In contrast, other organizations expect radical, revolutionary change and therefore need fresh thinking about future conditions and requirements. Here, planning focuses on new initiatives and new thinking about what needs to be done and how work will be performed. Alternative visions define different future scenarios. Managers make various assumptions to guide planning, rather than basing assumptions on history; they may assume all factors are variables.

Because there is often less certainty regarding the extent of changes, it is helpful to develop one or more possible scenarios of the future business situation rather than rely on a direct relationship of business indicators and staffing requirements. A team of knowledgeable managers can develop such scenarios and select the ones most likely to occur. They should assume that organization and job structure will be different and that radical changes in the work force are likely.

With business scenarios as a context for planning, managers can define the nature of future work. Managers develop a feel for the type of work that must be done in order to implement business plans and strategies. In many cases human resource staff help managers to interpret business scenarios and identify such changes in required work. It is often useful to define, in broad terms, the primary activities that will engage people in the business.

The following questions should be addressed:

- What factors or changes in business plans will determine what work will get done or how that work will get done?
- How will changes in primary roles and relationships shape work?
- What kinds of work will people do?
- What will be the most difficult or challenging aspects of this work?
- How is this work different from what is being performed currently?
- What work will go away or be performed by others?

Alternatively, human resource staff may conduct an initial assessment of work changes, based on the inputs and concurrence from a team of knowledgeable managers. Once changes in work have been identified, managers should estimate the approximate volumes of that work. This brings business requirements a step closer to staffing requirements.

Identify Staffing Drivers

Finally, it is necessary to identify those changes in business plans that will specifically impact required competencies or staffing levels. Examples of staffing drivers include the following:

- Changing production volumes or mix.
- Changes in products or services; new products.
- Capital expenditures (e.g., new equipment, new facilities).
- Acquisitions or divestitures.
- Changes in current technology or implementation of new technology.
- Environmental demands (e.g., Environmental Protection Agency, Occupational Safety and Health Administration, Food and Drug Administration).
- Quality improvement efforts (e.g., technical or targeted training to support quality improvements, production innovation).
- Increased manufacturing flexibility.
- Changes in client demands and expectations (e.g., packaging, delivery speed).
- Cost containment.
- Management of work force changes.

Once drivers are identified, managers estimate how those drivers will change and the impact they will have on future staffing requirements. For example, if business activity in one area is expected to increase, the need for individuals with skills in that area will also increase.

DEFINING FUTURE REQUIREMENTS

Once the business context is understood, it is possible to begin the process of defining the competencies and staffing levels that will be required to effectively execute business strategies. Before such definition can begin, however, it is necessary to create a framework that can be used to structure the strategic staffing analysis and plan.

Define a Staffing Framework

A staffing plan includes a comparison of expected supply and demand in order to identify staffing gaps and surpluses. In order to compare supply and demand directly, a consistent format or framework must be used. This framework takes the form of a two-dimensional matrix, traditionally arraying function by salary grade (or some other estimate of level). Where business changes are minimal, the framework reflects current organization structure.

However, where business and work drivers indicate significant change, managers need to build a framework for planning that is different from the current organization structure or way of thinking about capabilities and staffing levels. This new framework may be unrelated to current organization structure, functions, job categories, salary levels or grades, or levels of employee capabilities.

It is sometimes helpful to define "levels of capabilities." For professionals, these levels may include entry, professional, advanced technical team leader, and project manager. For managers, levels may include managing workers, managing supervisors, and managing managers and executives. Roles will vary depending on the types of services, technology groups, functions, processes, and so forth.

As an example, four professional categories were defined in the information services unit of a large oil company. The framework reflects future skill requirements that are different from the traditional levels:

1. *Entry*: Employees who work under or require direct supervision.
2. *Advanced*: Individual contributors, including those with limited client contact.
3. *Technical team leader*: Employees who manage the technical aspects of projects, usually on a task force basis.
4. *Project manager*: Employees who have full-time responsibility and accountability for managing a group or major project.

Roles for this group were defined by function, including mainframe programming and applications, database administration, personal computer (PC) applications, and network applications. By combining the four levels with the four roles, a simple skills matrix was created that served as a framework for the human resource plan (see Table 5.1).

TABLE 5.1. Information Services Projected Staffing Availability

	Current head count				
	Entry level	Advanced	Team leader	Technical project manager	Total
Mainframe programming and applications	17	65	25	22	129
Database administration	1	11	8	0	20
PC applications	4	10	6	7	27
Network applications	4	4	5	0	13
Total	26	90	44	29	189

Define Competency and Staffing Requirements

The next step of the strategic staffing process is to forecast future staffing requirements. These are determined by examining the specific impact of each staffing driver on each needed category. Changes in both required competencies and staffing levels must be anticipated.

The analysis should provide answers to questions such as the following:

- What will be the primary categories/functions and levels of capabilities required in relation to the type of work required (skills matrix)?
- What staffing levels will be required in the cells of this matrix?
- What skills will these jobs require? (What are the specific skill requirements for each cell? What applications and abilities are needed to perform the various kinds of work?)
- How will these requirements change under future scenarios, given changes in staffing drivers?

The process must begin with a diagnosis of the competencies that will be required in each job category or "cell." Typically, only the most critical competencies (e.g., the ones that will truly differentiate effective performance) are defined. In most cases, 10 to 20 competencies are adequate for each category. Once competencies are defined, it is possible to define the number of individuals with those competencies that will be required to support business plans.

In some cases it is possible to define required competencies and staffing levels directly (e.g., starting with a blank sheet). In other cases, it is more effective to start with a definition of current competencies and staffing levels and have managers indicate how these will change in the future (e.g., fewer meter readers will be needed, but they will require more advanced customer service skills).

In the information services organization discussed earlier, a team of line managers inventoried current talent and defined the current skill set for individuals in each cell of the framework they developed. The managers also described how those skills needed to change for the information services function to meet client expectations in each of the coming 3 years. For example, the need for mainframe computer skills was decreasing, but the need for network administration and PC experience was increasing. The group then determined the number of employees that would be needed in each category in each of the next 3 years. The group allocated "whole positions"; that is, they did not deal with "full-time equivalents" (although the technique could still apply if such considerations were necessary).

Define Current Staffing

Once the demand side of the analysis has been completed, it is possible to define the supply side. Typically, managers use the strategic staffing framework to define the number of people currently in each job category. They then make assumptions regarding recruiting, movement, and turnover, and create a future supply that considers the effects of these staffing actions on the employee population being analyzed.

Some companies maintain current organization charts and tables of staffing. They have a position control system in which each position is identified, defined, and coded (numbered); all positions are authorized through the budgeting process. During the year replacements are selected as vacancies occur. Accordingly, management knows precisely the current staffing relative to planned and authorized staffing levels.

As organizations become more flexible and loosen controls on budgets, job evaluation, and hiring, there may no longer be reliable organization charts or staffing information. This information needs to be developed as a starting point in planning future changes.

Organization charts that display all positions (full-time and part-time) are often helpful in defining current staffing levels. These charts may be created and maintained by each manager (or provided by human resource staff) and cumulated to provide an overall organizational view. Charts may be graphic (e.g., a traditional box-and-line chart) or simply tabular (e.g., listing positions and incumbents in a line-by-line, indented format).

As planning evolves, companies often include contracted services as part of their resources. These indicate other people (e.g., data processing, security services, temporary clerical staff) who are essentially performing work for the company, either on-site or off-site.

Project Future Staffing Availability

The next step in the process is to project staffing levels and competencies into the future, based on the effects of movement, turnover, and retirements on the current population of employees. For current staffing in each category the following calculation steps are completed:

- The number of employees leaving the category (i.e., turnover, retirements, terminations) are subtracted out.
- The number of employees leaving that job to take other jobs are subtracted out.
- The number of employees coming to that job from other jobs are added in.
- The number of new hires are added in.

The planning time frame or horizon for these projections should match those of the demand/requirements analysis. Upon completion of this step an organization will have a realistic estimate of the numbers and types of employees that will be available at the end of the planning period.

Identify Staffing Gaps

The next step is to define specific shortages and surpluses between projected requirements (both skills and staffing levels) and projected available talent and to define the actions that would balance these. Once requirements have been defined and staff availability projected for the planning period, demand can be compared to supply for each category and various mismatches identified. In some cases demand will exceed supply. When this occurs, supply must be increased (e.g., through hiring or accelerated promotions). In other cases supply will exceed demand. Organizations may choose to reduce these surpluses through layoffs, or they may instead tolerate extra head count (e.g., to satisfy demand in a subsequent planning period).

In the information systems example, demand was compared to supply on a cell-by-cell basis. Overall, staffing had to be reduced by 50 positions (net) in order to meet corporate cost-reduction targets. However, the actual amount of required change was far greater. On the basis of an analysis of staffing drivers and the input from managers, the number of mainframe-related positions was expected to decrease by 70 while PC- and network-related positions each rose by 10. Thus, 90 "personnel actions" (i.e., 70 terminations in mainframe plus 10 additions each in PC and network) were required in order to reduce overall head count by the appropriate 50.

Computer-Based Models

Computer-based models can greatly facilitate the strategic staffing and analysis process, especially where populations are large and there are multiple business scenarios to be considered. These models can calculate demand for employees, project availability of employees (by "aging" the current work force through forecasted movement and attrition), and calculate staffing discrepancies by comparing demand to supply in each category.

Once shortages and surpluses are determined, managers can identify the staffing actions (e.g., movement, hiring, recruitment) needed to close gaps and eliminate excess. In some cases these movements can be discovered on an iterative, trial-and-error basis. In other cases "artificial intelligence" can be applied to the model, thus allowing the software to determine necessary staffing actions (based, of course, on management input). For example, a model may suggest recruitment needs and priorities based on analysis of the iterative effect of moves, promotions, and attrition.

Computer models vary greatly in complexity. Most models currently in use are PC based. Some are purpose-built human resource forecasting packages. Others are applications of "off the shelf" spreadsheet (e.g., Microsoft Excel) or database (e.g., Microsoft Access or FoxPro) packages. Either type provides a basis for simulating the effects of movement and allows management to test various staffing strategies.

ESTABLISHING FUTURE COMMITMENTS

Analysis must lead to action. Once an assessment of alternative actions to address anticipated staffing needs has been made, it is necessary to evaluate the current capabilities and development needs of talent, define action plans, and review progress as implementation evolves.

Evaluate Current Talent

To plan specific actions it is necessary to review current talent in light of required future capabilities, current performance, and potential for learning. For management employees, this is frequently included in an ongoing management succession and development planning process. In many organizations it is applied to all employees through a rigorous performance and development process (or through separate, linked processes).

In looking to the future, organizations must emphasize the capacity of talent to adopt required capabilities. Potential (defined in part as the capacity to learn) is often important because learning at an accelerated rate is necessary to implement organization change quickly. Development needs (i.e., the discrepancies between individuals' current competencies and those that must be mastered to perform effectively in the future) represent the gaps that learning individuals (and hence learning organizations) need to bridge.

Individuals who are assessed as having low potential and those who are poor or marginal performers are typically moved out; blocked performers are helped to bring performance up to par. High-potential employees are identified for participation in development actions.

Those in the information services function described earlier learned an important lesson in this regard. Initially, past performance was to be the sole criterion for identifying the employees who would be kept and those who would be let go. After completing the strategic staffing plan, the group was able to consider future required competencies as well. As a result, some individuals who were excellent performers in the past were asked to leave because they were deemed unable to learn and apply new technology. Similarly, some individuals whose performance was rated somewhat less than excellent were kept because their skills and experience directly supported future staffing requirements.

Define Action Plans

Specific staffing actions need to be defined to close gaps and reduce surpluses. These actions include recruiting, movement, turnover, and development necessary to meet these requirements. Action plans focus on outcomes. They address certain questions by identifying the actions required. For example:

- What external turnover/attrition is required?
  —Gradually reduce staffing levels/costs in a unit while strengthening capacity to perform.
  —Accelerate turnover in a group through voluntary or involuntary severance.
  —Remove blockages in positions by terminating or reassigning plateaued performers.
- What internal movement is necessary to achieve targeted staffing levels and mix?
  —Provide employment security through internal redeployment.
  —Manage movement strategically, whether upward, lateral, or diagonal.
  —Create broader career paths.
- What training and development will be needed?
  —Develop within the work force new required skills through focused training and reassignments.
- What changes in external recruitment are required?
  —Increase external hiring versus promotion from within to a proportion of 80/20 in order to infuse new thinking and approaches.
  —Shift the emphasis in external recruiting sources.
  —Shift the emphasis in skills and capabilities of recruits.

Specific objectives may be set in each of these action areas, based on the plan. The remaining work force is often reallocated according to the future requirements framework, that is, by addressing the question, How would our current talent fit into tomorrow's organization? In some organizations, this is done in "broad brush," reallocating whole groups of people to fit the future requirements framework. In other organizations, however, more specific allocations are made.

Review Plans and Progress

At least annually, and often more frequently, senior management reviews the implementation of staffing plans and discusses future plans so as to achieve agreement on them and commitment to them. This may be part of the annual budgeting review process. Alternatively, there may be separate reviews that focus on staffing, organization changes, and perhaps related topics such as quality and productivity improvement.

XELLENCE: A CASE STUDY

The following case example, although disguised, is based on the actual experience of a respected pharmaceutical company. The case generally follows the overall process described in this chapter; however, the company focused on staff utilization rather than longer-range strategic staffing. It illustrates how a company can begin to analyze and plan for its future staffing requirements by focusing on the work performed and then building toward a broader staffing strategy. It also demonstrates the value of employee and manager involvement in the process.

Xellence Inc. is a $2 billion revenue pharmaceutical company that emphasizes decentralized management and bottoms-up planning. Accordingly, managers in charge of 90 basic business units (cost or profit/loss centers) are responsible for their organizations. These business units are represented by division vice presidents, who constitute a company management committee. It was at a meeting of this committee that president Harvey Swartz raised the subject of future staffing.

Swartz commented that better planning is needed to avoid future layoffs. Xellence had experienced only one layoff in its history. In the early 1980s the company laid off 100 production workers, providing each with a generous severance package. Overwhelmed by feelings of guilt, Xellence rehired all 100 a month later, allowing the employees to keep the severance pay and providing the month's back pay as well. Said Swartz:

> *Only by planning ahead can we preserve job security. We can then make the best use of our talent as business needs change—and recruit externally only as a last resort, when clearly we don't have and can't develop the needed skills internally.*
>
> *For too long we have glided along, adding staff when we need them rather than planning for our staffing strategically. While profit margins were high, we allowed excess staffing. Now that competition has increased and margins have been cut drastically, we must reduce costs. The head count projections in our 5-year business plan anticipate hiring in excess of what we*

are likely to be able to afford. In our new strategic plan, we will call for zero net growth in head count.

This means we are going to be faced with difficult decisions on the allocation of head count throughout the company, and it is important that we look critically at our current situation, including staff levels and requirements. This will help us begin to establish a broader, more objective, and candid process for head count decisions and for planning future staffing changes.

While it is difficult for us to look ahead more than one or two years in our business, we need to define, as best we can, our future skill and staffing requirements. Our annual operating plan should include realistic, and justified, objectives for head count changes; our human resource plans should address ways we will better recruit, utilize, and develop talent in anticipation of our changing future needs.

We have churned more than three thousand people during these years— fifteen hundred have left the company and have been replaced through recruitment. This means that nearly one-third of our employees are new in the past 4 years. Maybe this is about right . . . I'm not sure. Some level of turnover is good for the organization. It allows new people with new ideas into the organization. But too much turnover means that we are losing valuable, experienced employees. I'm not convinced we have taken every opportunity to avoid replacing people or, when we do, to upgrade our technical skills. We need to manage our turnover very carefully.

After some discussion of ways to address these concerns, the management committee agreed that each division would conduct a diagnosis and prepare a human resource plan as the basis for the head count request in the next year's budget. It was also agreed that the human resource staff and an outside consultant would work with the division vice presidents to develop a suitable methodology for this.

Business Unit Analysis

First, senior human resource staff conducted interviews with each division vice president to gain a full understanding of the business planning process and to plant seeds regarding the strategic staffing process. On the basis of the results of these sessions, the director of human resources and his staff defined a staffing planning and analysis process. Each business unit manager would examine the current staffing situation and project staffing needs in the coming 3 years. The managers would submit with their head count budgets a brief human resource plan, using a form that asked the questions shown in Figure 5.3.

The director of human resources and an external consultant briefed

STAFFING DRIVERS

♦   What are the business changes that drive your work load or the demand for your services? Will new indicators become relevant in the future? Explain.

♦   How will these drivers change during the planning period? Will they increase or decrease? By how much?

♦   How will these changes in drivers affect your needs for staffing (both required skills and staffing levels)? Explain.

UTILIZATION

♦   What actions have you taken to improve utilization of current staff?

♦   What actions do you intend to take in the next year to further improve utilization of current staff?

♦   What organizational or structural changes do you anticipate? Explain their effect on staffing.

♦   Do others in the company duplicate what your unit does? Identify the activity and the duplication.

NET STAFFING REQUIREMENTS

♦   What will be the net effect of these changes on your staffing needs (both required skills and staffing levels)?

FIGURE 5.3. Xellence business unit plan.

each cost center manager on the format and content of the staffing planning process and described the linkages to the budgeting process. They met individually with managers requesting consulting assistance in preparing their human resource plans.

Analysis of Drivers

Managers in line organizations were asked to identify the business indicators affecting work load or the demand for their services. Some of the factors considered as business indicators are as follows:

• In the manufacturing and engineering division, staffing is affected by capital projects, new equipment, changes in technology applied, and changes in work processes. As an example, a new packaging and printing machine was being installed that significantly reduced the number of technicians needed to print and fill product boxes.

• In sales and marketing, staffing is affected by changing market focus, changing product mix, flattening and realignment of the sales organization, and a new emphasis on product management. As the product mix changed, the mix of customers also changed. This necessitated changes in marketing strategies and, in turn, marketing skills and staffing levels.

• In research, project requirements—the stages of ongoing research, changes in ongoing projects, new initiatives planned—drive staffing needs. Xellence was in the midst of an overall review of research priorities. In order to refill the product pipeline more quickly, Xellence sought an increased emphasis on applied research (rather than basic research) and product development.

Client Service Survey

In staff areas, staffing is based on client demands for services. To facilitate this diagnosis the director of human resources developed a questionnaire with inputs from managers in each staff unit. He sent the questionnaire survey to all business unit managers to obtain their perceptions of services being provided to them by the staff functions. For each key service provided by each staff function, users were asked to answer the questions shown in Figure 5.4. The results of the survey were used by staff groups to define services to be provided and desired levels of activity. This information was then used to define required competencies and staffing levels for staff functions.

Planning by Managers

During the initial implementation of the staffing planning process, the director of human resources challenged managers to apply critical thinking to their units' changing roles, job priorities, performance expectations, and cost-effective alternatives for achieving objectives. Specifically, they were asked to identify actions taken to improve utilization and plans to do so in the next year. This emphasized the responsibility for managing the people they already had—their stewardship for talent. Asking the questions clearly communicated to managers in each business that they should be taking actions of this nature.

The identification of staffing drivers and consideration of how changes will affect future staffing provided a useful frame of reference for formulating the human resource plans. Few managers at Xellence had ever been asked to describe explicitly a vision of how work would be different in the future because of changes in the business. In some cases, for example, similar work done in different units was combined and placed in a single unit in order to increase efficiency. In other cases, teams were created to perform activities that in the past had been done by a disjointed

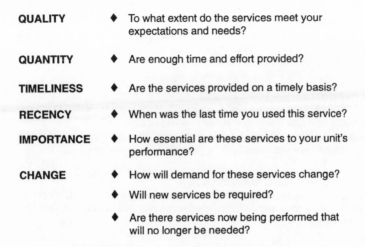

QUALITY	◆ To what extent do the services meet your expectations and needs?
QUANTITY	◆ Are enough time and effort provided?
TIMELINESS	◆ Are the services provided on a timely basis?
RECENCY	◆ When was the last time you used this service?
IMPORTANCE	◆ How essential are these services to your unit's performance?
CHANGE	◆ How will demand for these services change?
	◆ Will new services be required?
	◆ Are there services now being performed that will no longer be needed?

FIGURE 5.4. Xellence staff services diagnosis.

group of individuals. Having this framework in mind facilitated the definition of the skills and staffing levels that would be required to support business plans and strategies.

Activity Profiles

Employees provided a rich source of information and ideas that supported staffing analysis and planning. The involvement of employees also created an expectation that something would be done, that needed changes would occur.

To facilitate employee participation in the process, the consultant and the human resource manager developed a questionnaire (Figure 5.5) to help managers obtain relevant information directly from their subordinates. With these activity profile questionnaires data were collected on primary job activities and ways talent could be utilized more effectively.

First-level managers were encouraged to distribute this questionnaire to their employees and to discuss the results with them. Most found that it provided a valuable basis for considering job design changes and for planning future performance. It was, for many employees and managers, the first time they had openly talked about the work being done and ways to change it. In some cases human resource staff worked closely with individual managers to gather and analyze this information.

In the absence of a continuous quality improvement process, the activity profiles provided a focus for employee involvement and actions on changing work design.

♦♦ PRIMARY JOB ACTIVITIES
What are the most time-consuming parts of your job? Identify all activities that take
at least 10% of your time and estimate the percentage of time required.
Rank order the importance of the activities.

♦♦ OPPORTUNITIES FOR CHANGE
If you suddenly had an extra day a week (20% more time) to devote to your job, on
what major activities (existing and new) would you spend it?
If you had one less day a week to devote to your job, what major activities that you
now perform would you scale back or eliminate?

♦♦ TIME-CONSUMING IMPEDIMENTS
What impediments add to the time needed to do your job (e.g., getting approvals,
lack of clerical or other support, lack of effective information systems, lack of
clear priorities)?

♦♦ DUPLICATION
Do others in the company perform activities that duplicate what you do or what
your department does?
What opportunities exist to remove duplication of effort?

♦♦ ORGANIZATION
Do you perform any activities that should be performed by someone else?
    Automated?
    Contracted out?
    Centralized or coordinated with similar activities?
    Eliminated?
    Reduced in scope or frequency?
    Simplified or streamlined?

♦♦ ONE CHANGE
If you were to make one change in your job to increase its value to the company,
what would it be?

FIGURE 5.5. Xellence Activity Profile Questionnaire.

Utilization Improvement

Using the information from employees, as well as their own knowledge
and analysis of the situation in their units, managers examined ways to improve utilization. Their plans included actions to accomplish the following:

- Redefine work in current positions.
    —Reduce lower-value work by simplifying or eliminating it in or-
      der to replace it with higher-value work.
    —Reassign work among positions, resulting in changes in position
      responsibilities and requirements.

—Eliminate duplications and unneeded steps or work among positions (i.e., reengineer processes).
—Redesign positions to better match work with the available talent and to develop or challenge available talent.
- Realign the organization structure.
  —Adapt the structure to better fit markets, customers, functions, and so forth.
  —Consolidate work groups to improve utilization and results.
  —Flatten the structure; eliminate management levels by combining levels and widening spans.
  —Explicitly identify and emphasize teams (rather than hierarchy).
- Implement staffing alternatives.
  —Shift employees to part-time or independent contractor status (e.g., consultants).
  —Contract ("outsource") services to vendors.
  —Share services with other companies; establish joint ventures.

Managers were encouraged to examine and redefine work whenever a position became vacant. As the human resource planning manager explained: "Even though our attrition is low, we can achieve a lot of change simply by reexamining every job when it becomes vacant. And there's often a chain of vacancies when jobs are filled from within the company. Too often we simply fill a position without asking whether the work is really needed and reexamining the best way to perform the work."

Roll Up and Review Plans

The business unit human resource plans were consolidated at each management level, culminating in the preparation of an overall plan for each division. In the process, managers evaluated alternatives and incorporated choices into the consolidated plans. Some units proposed staff additions that were deleted as plans evolved. The senior managers taking such actions went back to the units to explain these decisions.

The human resource planning manager and the external consultant met with each business unit head to review his or her submitted plan and consider ways it could be improved. Later, they also met with each division vice president to similarly review and consolidate business unit plans into divisional human resource plans. They summarized the outcomes of the plans for review with Harvey Swartz and discussion at the management committee. This summary included a review of the objectives and the process followed and of the net staffing changes resulting from the plans and identified the duplications of effort across divisions.

In the first planning cycle, divisions requested 162 additional new positions (based on an employee population of 5,200), including 112 for research, 14 for manufacturing, 22 for sales and marketing, and 14 for staff units. Many of these changes, assuming a "business as usual" strategy, did not apply directly to the new strategy that emphasized increased product development. Swartz reacted swiftly: "If there are to be any new positions, they should be where it counts most—in research and new product development. There are some justified needs in other areas, but we should keep our priorities straight." In most cases, managers got the message and revised their head count estimates accordingly. Some divisions reported that new positions were being added in business units but only by eliminating or consolidating other positions. In some instances head count was reduced by contracting services out. Swartz observed, "I think we have begun to manage our staffing more objectively. I think we've clearly accepted accountability for head count planning, improving utilization, and sorting out duplications of work. Also, we're beginning to apply strategic thinking in our staffing."

As a result of the process, it was agreed that managers would no longer need to prepare special justifications for new positions during the year, special job requisitions and specifications, and authorizations to hire staff for any positions already included in the human resource plan. The personnel and budget approval procedures were thereby streamlined, and unit managers empowered to move forward on hiring when the actions were part of the approved annual plan.

Next Steps

In the next 2 years refinements were made in the process. Units were asked to address total dollar costs, not simply the number of positions. This required accounting and planning for temporaries and contracted services as well as employee head count. Also, more emphasis was given to improved management of current staff, with even more stringent demands for justifying new positions. As a result, the sales and marketing departments made significant shifts in the deployment of talent, realigning the organization to focus on the highest value-added roles and market segments. At the same time, more emphasis was given to individual and team development.

With the support of the human resource staff, several programs were developed to aid managers in implementing required staffing changes. A more intensive performance review process was aimed at identifying and acting on marginal talent. The normal performance appraisal process did not adequately differentiate good and bad performers and did not consider the competencies that would be required in the future. A more specific set of criteria, based on required future competencies, was created and used as a yardstick to assess individuals and identify development needs. Employees whose skills and development were not keeping up with requirements were identified, and in some cases these individuals were "encouraged" to leave. A special performance incentive program now provides cash payments to individuals and teams for special achievements that specifically support the implementation of business plans and strategies.

Special provisions were also adopted to facilitate voluntary early retirements and separations. The intent was to generate more movement in the organization, to create vacancies so as to allow redesign of work for improved utilization and staffing. Employees were encouraged to think in terms of change rather than stability and to look at utilization opportunities as ways to tap their highest capabilities, further their development, and add the greatest value to the company.

As staffing analysis became accepted as necessary, managers also adopted more rigorous forecasting of staffing requirements. The manufacturing and engineering unit took the lead, initiating a 5-year forecast of staffing requirements (numbers and mix) by level and area. Others followed the example, adapting the framework and forecasts to fit their planning contexts.

Concern for Employees

Xellence is striving to manage staffing changes in ways that minimize disruption (e.g., gradual attrition, early retirements, focused hiring, performance-related terminations). The company seeks to respect current employees, be fair, and make every effort to provide employment continuity, while implementing needed business change.

Obtaining employee participation and maintaining open communications about the human resource planning process were intended, in part, to foster a positive perception of staffing actions. Employees would be more likely to accept the results of a plan they understood and in which they had participated. Several articles in the company's employee magazine described the process and its effects on jobs and people, along with the importance of change to the company's success. It was repeatedly emphasized that human resource planning was intended to help preserve jobs, not eliminate them.

In some companies primary attention (and resources) are focused on the employees who are leaving the organization. Xellence discovered that it was more important to focus on the "survivors," that is, to retain, motivate, and develop talented employees during times of change.

Planning for staffing at Xellence is gradually shifting from a focus on staffing levels toward a broader assessment of staffing needs based on both changing demand and changing supply. Both are necessary to define long-term staffing requirements of the business and how they will be met.

Together, these steps resulted in more dynamic human resource planning each year. The detailed, unit-by-unit review of each job, of the work being done, of opportunities for improvement, and of staffing resulted in continuous change. As Swartz is prone to say, "There are no givens. Every year we must plan as if there were no yesterday!"

SUGGESTED READINGS

London, M., Bassman, E. S., & Fernandez, J. P. (1990). *Human resource forecasting and strategy development*. New York: Quorum Books.
Walker, J. W. (1992). *Human resource strategy*. New York: McGraw-Hill.

CHAPTER 6

Training Needs Assessment: The Broadening Focus of a Simple Concept

RONALD E. ZEMKE

In Lewis Carroll's (1872) *Through the Looking Glass*, Humpty Dumpty tells Alice, "When I use a word it means just what I choose it to mean—neither more nor less" (p. 124). In organizational diagnosis work in general, but most certainly in the subset focused on human resource development, *needs assessment* is very much a Humpty Dumpty sort of phrase, often—if not usually—meaning neither more nor less than a given declarer means for it to mean. And rightly so!

In broad general terms, the idea of a training needs assessment is obvious, reasonable, and straightforward. According to Dugan Laird (1978), one of training and development's patron saints of reasonableness and pragmatism:

> Before people can perform their tasks properly, they must master the special technology used by their organizations. This means acquisition of knowledge and skill. Sometimes this acquisition is needed when the employee is new to the organization; sometimes it is needed because the organization changes its technology; sometimes it is necessary if an individual is to change places within the organization. . . .
>
> A training need exists when an employee lacks the knowledge or skill to perform an assigned task satisfactorily. (p. 9)

Laird's straightforward, pragmatic 1978 description of needs assessment was very much in tune with the work and the times of McGehee and Thayer (1961), who were among the first, if not the first, to address the need for training needs assessment in more than a cursory fashion:

The use of training to achieve organizational goals requires careful assessment of the training needs within a company: A determination of the goals which can be served by training, the people who require training and for what purposes, and the content of training. . . .

Training in industry is not an end but a means to an end; it exists only to help achieve organizational goals and objectives. To be effective, this management tool must be used when and where it is needed and not as window dressing to impress visiting firemen. (p. 24)

In those simpler times, when jobs were mostly manufacturing based, tasks and procedures could be completely and accurately defined and described, and jobs remained largely stable and unchanging for long periods of time, such guidance was sufficient. That was then; it certainly isn't now.

Today, employee training is seen as a critical, competitive industrial weapon in an unstable and constantly shifting global marketplace. In the United States the 1992 presidential race saw two of the three major candidates compete, in part, on their views of the role of industrial training in the revival of the American economy and world competitive standing (Zemke, 1992).

Training today is called upon to address—if not redress—social problems that would never in simpler times have been thought of as mentionable, much less addressable, in the workplace. In a 1992 survey of 1,600 U.S. companies with 100 or more employees, *Training* magazine found that 50% or more routinely offered employees instruction in such once unlikely topics as substance abuse, writing skills, public speaking, sexual harassment, time management, listening, and interpersonal skills. In addition, a substantial minority (20 to 50%) reported routinely offering instruction in reading skills, workplace diversity, creativity, ethics, and smoking cessation. That curriculum, plus 31 other commonly offered topics, was delivered to 41 million Americans at an estimated direct cost of $45 billion. That is more dollars than were spent on all postsecondary education in the United States in the same time period (Filipczak, 1992).

TRAINING NEEDS ASSESSMENT: THE NEW VIEW

Just as that which rests routinely under the umbrella of industrial training has become more varied and complex, so too has the practice of training needs assessment. In fact, the phrase *training needs assessment* has come to be viewed as somewhat anachronistic, if not something of an oxymoron: If training is the solution, why do you conduct a needs assessment (Stolovitch, 1988)?

Where training needs assessment was once considered a simple process of asking straightforward questions about relatively mundane workplace tasks and activities, it has in recent times been recast and reconceptualized as an integral part of a broadly focused *human performance technology* (Geis, 1986). This technology, as variously described by Geis (1986), Odiorne and Rummler (1988), and Kaufman (1986), takes its conceptual framework at least as much from cybernetics, systems theory, organizational behavior, industrial/organizational psychology, and cognitive psychology as it does from educational psychology, pedagogy, and instructional practice and theory.

Within this systems or holistic approach it is de rigueur to speak of a training problem or training needs assessment or analysis. Training or instruction is considered but a single solution out of a vast array of possible solutions to an organizationally significant human performance problem. Some writers (Kaufman, 1982) even expand the charter of needs assessment beyond organizational concerns and human performance problems to inquiries of the societal impact of organizational problems and possible interventions.

According to Kaufman (1986):

> Linking organizational efforts, organizational results, and organizational payoff in and for society will allow any organization to do the following:
> • Determine gaps between current and desired internal and external results.
> • Determine where in the organization the needs exist.
> • Place priorities among these needs.
> • Select the gaps of highest priority to close.
> • Prepare objectives for closing the priority needs.
> • Identify causes and origin of the needs.
> • Identify and select the best methods and means to close the gaps.
> • Determine the effectiveness and efficiency of the methods and means selected to meet the needs. (pp. 25–59)

This is clearly a much broader stage than McGehee and Thayer had in mind in 1961 when they boldly suggested that a needs assessment look not only at the "skills, knowledge or attitudes an individual employee must develop if he is to perform the tasks which constitute his job in the organization" but also at the operations in which the performance must be done and at the organization's "objectives, its resources and the allocation of those resources as they relate to the organizational objectives" (pp. 24–25).

Inevitably, perhaps, this vigorous expansion of the charter of training needs assessment to "human performance problem analysis" (to coin yet another phrase) has led to a veritable Babel of terminology and questionable definitional nuances. Rossett (1987) puts the situation into clear and needed perspective:

Needs assessment. Front-end analysis. Problem analysis. Needs analysis. Goal analysis. Task analysis. Discrepancy analysis. Needs sensing. Quasi-needs assessment. We are awash in a sea of words, phrases, and idiosyncrasies which fail to guide performance technologists as they attempt to conduct useful whatchamacallits.

The performance technologist who is charged with the problem of correcting limp french fries in retail sales outlets across the nation isn't interested in the fine distinctions between needs, task, problems, and front-end analysis. This performance technologist wants to know what to do first, next, and last, what to ask and observe in person and through surveys, that will lead to confident understanding of the situation. (p. 60)

Our preference has been to mind Rossett's warning and keep our defining and hair splitting to a minimum. Perhaps the most functionally flexible and utilitarian approach to understanding the focus of needs assessment in the performance technology era is offered by Kaufman and Valentine (1989):

If we use *need* to mean a gap in results, then a *needs assessment* is the identification, prioritization, and selection of gaps in results. Following from that, needs analysis is the process for identifying the causes of the needs. After you have selected the needs (needs assessment), identified the causes (needs analysis), identified possible ways and means to meet the objectives, and selected training as a viable avenue, then you may use a *training requirements analysis*. (p. 14)

The contemporary practice of training needs assessment, as opposed to contemporary academic discussion of needs assessment, is largely situationally dictated. There are at least three distinct situations that require—or at least call out for—a training needs assessment:

1. *Performance problem scenario*: When a significant organizational performance problem exists, is considered by someone in authority to be in need of amelioration, *and* is suspected to have a substantial human performance component.
2. *Market forces scenario*: When the organization is, in general, growing—or contracting—quickly, a single function or group is expanding and needs to add employees quickly, or current employees need to be qualified for other responsibilities within the organization or unit.
3. *Reorganization/reengineering scenario*: When the organization is contemplating (or has decided to make) a substantial change in the way work is organized, performed, or structured and it is anticipated that substantial changes in performer skills or group interactions will be required.

TACTICAL APPROACHES TO NEEDS ASSESSMENT

"Pure" instances of the aforementioned three situations exist and surface in every organization, but, by and large, today's practitioner is most frequently faced with a combination. For instance, the organization has, through a divination unknown to the human resources development (HRD) practitioner, decided to embrace Total Quality Management (TQM) *and* the organization is expanding into new markets *and* there is a persistent problem with errors made in client accounts. The practitioner is contacted by someone in this mishmash of problems, plans, and fancies and instructed to figure out what training is needed. That said, there is still merit in looking at approaches to these basic situations in their pure form.

Scenario 1: The Performance Problem (or "Help! We've Got a *Problem*")

In actual fact, if a training and development practitioner were ever contacted by a line manager or line personnel officer to "consult on a human performance problem," he or she would faint dead away! Though we pretend otherwise, and work mightily to enlighten them to the contrary, line managers most frequently view support staff functions as poultices waiting to be applied to their problems. The actual content of queries to a training/HRD practitioner is more in line with "I want you to come down here and train X to do Y [or stop doing Y]." The textbook prescription to such queries—commands actually—is to deliver a lecturette about doctors, aspirins, and the difference between symptoms, causes, and cures. In practice, we've found that line managers don't actually care to be so lectured to and, as often as not, *have* ruled out a good number of nontraining causes to the presenting problem. That does not, however, obviate the practitioner's responsibility to verify that there is indeed a reasonable case to be made for an instructional intervention. Typically, this verification takes place in two steps.

Step 1. Skill Deficiency Verification

A skill deficiency assumes that the request for an instructional intervention may well be valid. Mager and Pipe (1970, p. 11) suggest that the following questions need to be answered in this step or stage of the assessment.

What Is the Performance Discrepancy?
- Why does the client think there is a training problem?
- What is the difference between what is being done and what is supposed to be done?
- What is the event that caused the client to say things aren't right?
- Why is the client dissatisfied?

Typically, a glaring or expensive error has been made, or a significant customer has raised a fuss about a problem or situation. While problems with a frequency of one are hardly the cause for an intervention, they *can* be significant indicators of a more systemic problem and should be treated with due gravity. The seasoned practitioner knows how to use such opportunities without overreacting to them or inducing others to overreact.

Is the Performance Discrepancy Important? Related questions are the following:
- Why is the discrepancy important?
- What would happen if the client left the discrepancy alone?
- Could doing something to resolve the discrepancy have any worthwhile result?

In *gap analysis* parlance, a difference between the real and the ideal that doesn't make a perceptible difference in outcomes is not a difference; that is, it isn't important enough to respond to with an intervention. Conversely, a difference between real and ideal situations that makes a difference in results is important regardless of how small that gap may appear. For example, asked to "fix" a sales force composed of salespeople who had been selected the same way and trained very similarly but who were achieving very different results, analysts studied a wide variety of possible variables—age, sex, selling presentation, territory assignments, and so on. The most significant difference turned out to be number of sales calls, specifically, one half of a sales call a day. This seemingly small difference, magnified by a 50-week, 280-day work year, indeed subsequently proved to be an important performance gap.

Is It a Skill Deficiency?
- Could employees perform the task if they really wanted to?
- Could they do it if their lives depended on it?
- Are their present skills adequate for the desired performance?

For example, observations of a team of three telephone service representatives quickly revealed that as a team, and individually, their pace of work was well below the standard for the job; that is, they were handling fewer calls per hour than the organization considered appropriate. When queried on their results, the phone reps were well aware of the shortfall. And when challenged, they had no problem demonstrating performance that easily exceeded the standard. When asked to explain, they argued that the standard could be met but, in their view, only at a significant cost to customer satisfaction and long-term customer retention. Thus, the gap was not a skill deficiency but a difference in goal interpretation. From this point, the assessment can veer in one of two directions, neither of which is to begin to fill the request the client initially made for healing the problem.

Is It a Skill Problem? If the practitioner is convinced that the problem is based on a skill deficiency, there are still four more questions from Mager and Pipe (1970, pp. 33–57) that need to be answered before instructional intervention is proffered:

1. *Was the skill present and used in the past, and is it used seldom now?* The object of this question is to determine if the skill is used so seldom that it will almost always be deficient despite training. Frequently, one finds that instruction was provided in the past but that the skill is not now available though it *was* at the end of training. The assumption is that any amount of reinstruction will have a dubious impact on the problem because call for the skill is so infrequent that any amount of training—that is, reinstruction—will be inefficient, if not plainly ineffective.

2. *Is the skill used often?* The heart of this query is directed at discerning whether practice and/or feedback may be a better alternative than instruction. The majority of law enforcement officers, for example, never have cause to discharge a side arm in the course of active duty. As a result, law enforcement agencies have commonly instituted stringent practice and range qualification standards for officers. Training per se would likely be an ineffective solution to deficiencies in this skill, but practice with augmented feedback is likely to have a positive effect.

3. *Is there a simpler solution than training?* This exploration is to assess whether job aids, checklists, written instruction, behavior models, or task simplification might not be more cost-effective—and a more reliable solution—than instruction.

4. *Does the employee have what it takes?* If, indeed, instruction seems the most viable solution but has not "taken" in the past, it is—as a last option—appropriate to question the person–job match.

Step 2. If It Isn't Skill or Practice, What Is It?

The second group of questions is to be asked if there is not a clear skill or practice deficiency. If the employees can indeed pass the "if their lives depended on it" performance test, the practitioner must widen his or her scope of inquiry and look at the environmental and social conditions surrounding the performance. Again following Mager and Pipe's (1970, p. 105) protocols, there are four major questions to be pursued to ferret out causes of human performance problems that are not related to a lack of skill or infrequent skill demand.

1. *Is the desired performance punished?* This avenue of questioning looks for both physical and social punishers for performance. Job site working

conditions can, for instance, interfere with tests and tasks that are easily and successfully performed at desks or in the laboratory. Likewise, job tasks that in isolation can be performed at a high rate and to high standards may create social conditions intolerable to the performer. If performing a job extremely well can lead to the unemployment of a colleague, the employee can experience considerable pressure to back off from that attainable standard.

2. *Is nonperformance rewarding?* The focus of this inquiry is on both nonperforming and performing in a nonstandard fashion. To determine the consequences that accrue for nonperformance one might ask the following questions:

- What is the result of performing the employee's way instead of the prescribed way?
- Does the employee get more attention for misbehaving than behaving?
- What is it that rewards his or her present way of doing things?
- Is it mentally or physically less troublesome for the employee to do it his or her own way?

3. *Does performing really matter?* The operant parallel to this avenue of inquiry is extinction. The search is for nonconsequences, that is, few or no consequences accruing for performance of the required behavior, thus obviating any motivation to perform.

- Does performing as desired matter to the performer?
- Is there a favorable outcome for performing?
- Is there an undesirable outcome for not performing?
- Is there a source of satisfaction for performing?
- Is the performer able to take pride in his or her performance as an individual or as a member of a group?
- Does the performer get satisfaction of his or her needs from the job?

4. *Are there obstacles to performing?* All forms of stimulus or response interference—task interference, conflicting demands, lack of authority, physical barriers—are candidates for querying in this category of performance problem causation. Under Mager and Pipe's (1970) scheme, appropriate subquestions in this category are the following:

- What prevents employees from performing?
- Do they know what is expected of them?
- Do they know when to do what is expected?
- Are there conflicting demands on their time?
- Do they lack the authority to perform the task? The time? The tools?
- Are they restricted by policies or by a "right way of doing it" or "way we've always done it" attitude that ought to be changed?

Culmination of the Performance Problem Scenario

The Performance Problem Scenario, or Performance Problem Analysis, culminates with (1) a map of the variables looked at by using a variety of tools (observations, interviews, performance data, etc.); (2) the analyst's assessment of probable causation of the problem based on his or her analysis of the data; and (3) an intervention recommendation. Characteristically, the intervention recommendation will have multiple facets. For instance, the telephone customer service example mentioned earlier resulted in calls for (1) reexamination of phone call standards, including time expectations, content, and outcomes; (2) development of a series of service rep team meetings focused on developing more effective ways of handling customers; and (3) new ways of coding calls and assessing performance.

Scenario 2: Market Forces
(or "Build Me Ten More Salespeople Stat!")

Though 1993, the time of this writing, may not be a high point for job creation, history has taught us that business invariably cycles between contraction and expansion; thus, the need to find, train, and retain a variety of workers—and do it quickly—will most likely be upon us again before the end of the decade. Likewise, when one sector, segment, or size of organization is downsizing or belt-tightening, another is experiencing growth. Sometimes the same organization that is downsizing in one division or department is expanding, and even aggressively recruiting and training, in another area.

Whatever the case may be, the training needs assessment challenge is the same, namely, to determine what successful performers need to know and need to be able to do and to communicate this information in a way that enables someone to create a training intervention based on that assessment. By and large, this process of creating a description of the knowledge, skills, and abilities of a successful performer is referred to as *competency mapping* or *competency modeling* (Blank, 1982).

While there are almost as many approaches to competency model development as there are competency model advocates (Zemke, 1988), there is a general practices schema (Odiorne & Rummler, 1988):

1. *Select an expert panel to profile the job.* Select a group of experts to articulate a model or profile of the job to be captured and eventually trained. If, say, Axcel Software, Inc. is in need of a large number of new field sales representatives, the expert panel or team would most likely be composed of sales managers and directors with sales and sales supervision experience, as well as a smattering of successful senior sales representatives.

2. *Identify skills, knowledge, and abilities for success.* The expert panel articulate their views and recollections of the skills, knowledge, and abilities a successful incumbent must possess. This information, plus whatever

other data the needs analyst has been able to ferret out, is used to create an opinion survey, usually paper-and-pencil, that is used to tap a still broader body of experts. Respondents are asked to agree or disagree with the assembled list of behaviors and characteristics and to rate and rank their importance to job success.

3. *Review survey results and develop examples.* The surveys are assembled and the results reviewed by the initial panel. The expert panel will, at this stage, frequently be asked to generate examples of appropriate performance for each agreed-upon competency.

4. *Sort and prioritize competencies.* The expert panel sort the knowledge and skills into like groups and then prioritize them by importance or criticality to job success.

5. *Identify learning priorities.* The final expert panel task is to decide which competencies or knowledge/skill groups must be mastered immediately by new employees and which can be considered advanced competencies to be learned at a later time.

A frequent variation to competency model development is to add a more direct assessment of the actual performers. For instance, the needs analyst may conduct interviews with and on-job observations of high- and low- performing employees and include data from those observations and interviews along with the survey results.

Odiorne and Rummler (1988) suggest five cautions to the competency building approach to training needs assessment:

1. It is difficult to relate competencies and the resulting knowledge and skill requirements to job output and organizational performance. Therefore validation and evaluation are difficult. You might teach people to be perfectly competent in useless acts.
2. It is difficult to assess relative importance of competencies and therefore difficult to set priorities for the knowledge and skills input.
3. The consensus of experts, even if arrived at, will not necessarily identify the critical differences between exemplary and average performance, which is key to identifying training input that will affect job output.
4. The findings tend to be general, identifying topics such as "financial planning" versus "skill in preparing annual requests for capital appropriations using form 10."
5. It does not specifically address other factors influencing the performance of the job in question. The individual may be "competent" as defined by the knowledge/skill input, but we will not necessarily see the desired job output because of the lack of specific performance factors such as feedback and consequences. (p. 159)

While competency models have been popular for describing, and creating training plans for, managerial and professional jobs, they are less helpful for assessing and prescribing training for technical jobs. Odiorne and Rummler (1988) contrast the strengths and weaknesses: "This approach is more appropriate for managerial and professional jobs with broad, difficult-to-define job responsibilities such as 'organize, plan, control' than for jobs with specific, well-defined outputs" (p. 159).

Scenario 3: The Reorganization
(or "We're Changing All the Jobs, Do Some Training")

Organizations are constantly tinkering with their structure, their technology, and the construction of departments, functions, and jobs. It's been called simplification, reorganization, continuous improvement, and, most recently, reengineering. Formerly, such efforts to improve productivity, access, and/or cost structure have had minimal impact on day-to-day work activities. And even when they did substantially change operational aspects of the organization, the retraining involved was relatively minor. Today that is no longer the case. Almost all contemporary reorganization efforts look for ways of eliminating tasks, if not whole jobs, combining functions, and generally doing more with less overhead—which generally translates to "with fewer people."

The human resource impact is that remaining staff are frequently confronted with, at minimum, an imperative to learn new systems, procedures, and technology. More importantly, these new jobs generally carry more responsibility and, consequently, more organizational impact than the old jobs. On top of all that, these new reengineered jobs require more independence, decision-making skill, judgment, and initiative than any of the old jobs they were synthesized from.

The needs assessment necessitated by contemporary reorganization and process reengineering is likewise a synthesized form of performance problem assessment and competency model creation. In addition to being comfortable with both of these approaches, the needs analyst must be able to work within a volatile environment of changing task specifications and responsibilities.

Suppose Axcel Software decides to recreate its sales and marketing approach rather than simply add to its field sales force. Specifically, Axcel decides to eliminate its field sales force and replace it with a direct marketing staff. As a part of this reinvention, two telemarketing centers—one dealing directly with retail buyers, one with software store retailers—will be established. The ensuing needs assessment will have to be a hybrid of the performance problem analysis and the competency model development approaches. The onset of the assessment would look very much like the competency development process with two modifications. First, one or more telemarketing experts, outsiders to the organization, would need to be added to the expert panel. Second, a subgroup of the expert panel would need to be assigned to benchmark telemarketing operations similar to the centers Axcel is going to establish. It is critical that the HRD practitioner be a member of this team. As part of the ensuing benchmarking visits, the needs analyst would use a template like the Mager and Pipe (1970) protocols to anticipate performance problems through the experiences of managers and salespeople in the benchmark organization. For instance, the needs analyst can create questions or information need criteria around issues such as good and bad feedback experiences and metrics, successful and unsuccessful reward and recognition programs, and good and bad training models. Insight from these questions would greatly inform both the training intervention for the new Axcel sales and marketing model *and* critical call center management tools.

Just as important, the needs analyst can put on his or her performance problem analyst hat during the "shakedown" of the call centers and add valuable insights. The performance problem analyst viewpoint can be helpful, for instance, for interpreting performance data, debriefing front-line performers, and observationally assessing interactions between supervisors and frontliners. In addition, the needs analyst can be adjusting the telemarketing training on the basis of the frontliners' real-time experiences.

A CONTINUING EVOLUTION

As an investigatory discipline, the practice of training needs assessment is, in relative terms, young and evolving. As it matures and moves from its narrow foundations, it takes on characteristics of other, older, disciplines. Industrial/organizational psychology, educational psychology, operations research, systems science, and market research are but a few of the most obvious contributors to the growing conceptual and operational tool kit of the needs analyst.

Whether training needs assessment as an independent entity will continue is a moot point. More importantly, as long as human beings must be in the business of learning new skills to survive and thrive in the workplace, there will be a need for tools, techniques, and approaches to effectively and efficiently capture those critical knowledge, skill, and attitude performance elements.

REFERENCES

Blank, W. E. (1982). *Handbook for developing competency-based training programs*. Englewood Cliffs, NJ: Prentice-Hall.
Carroll, L. (1872). *Through the looking glass*. New York: Morrow.

Filipczak, B. (1992). What employers teach. *Training: The Human Side of Business,* 29(10), 43–55.

Geis, G. L. (1986). Human performance technology. In National Society for Performance and Instruction, *Introduction to performance technology* (Vol. 1, pp. 1–20). Washington, DC: National Society for Performance and Instruction.

Kaufman, R. (1982). *Identifying and solving problems: A systems approach.* San Diego: University Associates.

Kaufman, R. (1986). Assessing needs. In National Society for Performance and Instruction, *Introduction to performance technology* (Vol. 1, pp. 25–59). Washington, DC: National Society for Performance and Instruction.

Kaufman, R., & Valentine, G. (1989). Relating needs assessment and needs analysis. *Performance and Instruction,* 28(10), 10–14.

Laird, D. (1978). *Approaches to training and development.* Reading, MA: Addison-Wesley.

Mager, R., & Pipe, P. (1970). *Analyzing performance problems, or you really oughta wanna.* Belmont, CA: Fearon.

McGehee, W., & Thayer, P. W. (1961). *Training in business and industry.* New York: Wiley.

Odiorne, G. S., & Rummler, G. A. (1988). *Training and developing: A guide for professionals.* Chicago: Commerce Clearing House.

Rossett, A. (1987). *Training needs assessment.* Englewood Cliffs, NJ: Educational Technology Publications.

Stolovitch, H. (1988). Curriculum development for business and industry. *Performance Improvement Quarterly,* 1(3), 43–45.

Zemke, R. (1988). Job competencies: Can they help you design better training? In J. Gordon, R. Zemke, & P. Jones (Eds.), *Designing and delivering cost effective training* (pp. 109–112). Minneapolis: Lakewood Publications.

Zemke, R. (1992). Training in Campaign '92. *Training: The Human Side Of Business,* 29(10), 67–72.

CHAPTER 7

Personnel-Centered Organizational Diagnosis

DOUGLAS W. BRAY

Concerns about organizations' human resources have intensified and pro-liferated to a degree that could not have been imagined even a few years ago. The struggles of American business in the global economy, far from reducing the attention given to personnel matters, have highlighted the role of an organization's people as critical to business survival and suc-cess. Programs to encourage participative management, empowerment, or total quality or to encompass diversity or reduce stress are ubiquitous.

Much as human resources practitioners may revel in being sum-moned closer to center stage, it is unlikely that such programs are always adopted because of pressing organizational needs. Faddishness is ram-pant (not a new phenomenon), and both managers and personnel practi-tioners may be swept along by current fashions. The focus of this volume on organizational diagnosis underlines the importance of sophisticated problem analysis in guiding human resources interventions.

Those seeking to improve organizational functioning often focus on one type of human resources process. Some look at selection, placement, and appraisal; others are concerned with training and development; still others explore the structure and functioning of the organization as a whole. Each of these three areas of investigation may provide information of value, but they are rarely interrelated. Yet the ultimate payoff of these processes is the effect of the totality of them on the performance and po-tential of employees.

THE NATURE OF PERSONNEL-CENTERED DIAGNOSIS

Personnel-centered diagnosis aims to avoid the one-sidedness of other methods by focusing on the organization's human resources themselves.

They are seen as *products* of the organization's nature and the way things are done in it. A comprehensive evaluation of the same individuals can reveal much about how the organization's various influences play out in employees' work lives. The goal is "to see a world in a grain of sand" (Blake, 1803).

Those who make up an organization's human resources have characteristics important to their contributions and potential contributions. These include knowledge and skills, aptitudes, motives, interests, values and attitudes, and aspects of personality. At any particular point in work lives these characteristics are a combination of what employees brought with them and their experiences since they were hired.

Organizations are not responsible for the makeup of individuals they consider for employment. This is the result of complex life processes, starting with genetic factors and moving through family, educational, and other experiences, including, for some, having worked elsewhere. Organizations do, however, choose those they hire. They are gratified when strengths existing at employment underpin success and chagrined when weaknesses lead to failure.

It is remarkable how little most organizations know about those they employ to become their managers.[1] Many companies hiring college graduates at entry level are concerned merely with credentials, such as a degree testifying to ability to do a specialized job such as accounting or engineering. Management potential is not evaluated, since it is thought that enough of those taken on as specialists will turn out to have such potential. Even in organizations where most college recruits are expected to advance in management, employment decisions are routinely based mainly on the possession of a bachelor's or master's degree from a well-thought-of school and on favorable impressions made in interviews.

Each of the individuals the organization employs has a unique combination of abilities, motivations, and personality traits. If one thinks of mature managers as being the product of "nature" and "nurture" (Bray, 1989), this combination is the nature side of the process. These natures are impinged upon by the organizational environment from the first day of employment. The outcomes determine the character of the managerial work force.

The organizational environment is made up of a myriad of factors that affect managers as their careers unfold. Some of these are deliberate efforts to develop knowledge and skills by formal training, job rotation,

[1]Although personnel-centered organizational diagnosis can start at any employee level, this chapter will be concerned only with exempt levels since all the cases to be discussed involve managers. The term *manager* is used to include those who supervise or lead others as well as technical/professional employees at comparable levels who may not be supervisors or leaders.

and coaching. Others have to do with job challenge, incentives and rewards, and opportunity for advancement. Then there is the whole area of how one is led, stretching from micromanagement to true empowerment. Work pace, the necessity for overtime, and travel demands are important. This list, incomplete as it is, is convincing that "nurture" or the lack of it will play a strong role in shaping managers.

The personnel-centered diagnostic approach holds that much can be learned about an organization by studying job incumbents. A first question may be the extent to which they possess the abilities needed to do their jobs. In today's world this inquiry would encompass far more than specific aptitudes and narrow job skills. Skills such as those needed to function as a team member and to lead and empower others must be added to the more familiar ones of fact-finding, analysis, and decision making.

A second critical question has to do with job motivation: At a broad level, how do the nature of the work and the rewards for doing it accord with life goals? What are the rewards sought—money, recognition, challenge, autonomy, advancement? How satisfied are incumbents with the rewards offered and how equitably do they feel they are given?

Many organizations now aspire to be value driven, involving, for example, the goal of superlative customer service. They hope that associates will, insofar as possible, act consistently and even proactively toward such goals. So it is important to ask, What values really drive job behavior? and Are these are the ones envisioned by top management?

Personnel-centered diagnosis seeks data in all the aforementioned areas and more, gained by evaluating comprehensively the same individuals. The ambitiousness of the approach means that the number of individuals evaluated must be modest. Only a sample of managers can be included in even the moderate-sized organization. Furthermore, such a sample cannot be drawn from all types and levels of jobs. All focus would be lost. A first investigation should, instead, be limited to incumbents in a critically important job or to a defined class of employees, such as recently employed management trainees or those managers in the pool from which promotions to executive levels will be made. Although a few of the diagnostic findings may be relevant only to the job or group sampled, it is likely that much will be learned that can be generalized to other parts of the organization.

MEANS OF MEASUREMENT

Evaluation of the many components outlined requires a varied array of instruments. Behavioral simulations will be needed to measure interpersonal and administrative skills. The nature of the skills sought will depend on the culture of the organization but might include, among others, communicating, leading, coaching, delegating, fact-finding, analyzing, and decision making. In any case, an adequate evaluation of these skills will call for simulations. These simulations will often be individual, but in this era of work teaming, simulations involving groups may well be needed. The areas of motivation, perceptions, and attitudes would seem to require at least one targeted interview, and focus groups would also be useful. Paper-and-pencil methods can serve to measure general mental ability and the specific knowledge required for job performance. Questionnaires can provide wide coverage of perceptions and attitudes and serve as a lead-in for interviews as well as a supplement to them.

The idea of combining several of these methods suggests assessment center methodology. In an assessment center, the characteristics to be evaluated are commonly conceptualized as "dimensions"—clusters of behavior, motivation, attitudes, and so forth. Exercises are designed to produce data relevant to these dimensions. The assessment staff observes and shares this information, rates assessees on the dimensions, and makes overall evaluations and recommendations (Thornton & Byham, 1982).

There is a difference between a full-fledged assessment center and using methods that assessment centers employ (Task Force on Assessment Center Guidelines, 1989). Also, an assessment center is a process and not necessarily a place. An off-site facility has advantages such as insulating assessees from job demands and interruptions, identifying the activity as distinct and important, and having a defined start and finish. However, such a center is not necessary. Evaluative exercises can be incorporated into regular business activities (Bray & Byham, 1991). Participants are told the sessions they will attend and the duration of each. They then arrange appointments with the assessors, whether in-house or consultants, scheduling these meetings around their usual activities so that the process is completed within a few weeks. Company offices and conference rooms are used. Whether or not a complete assessment center is launched, methodological rigor is still called for. The characteristics to be evaluated must be clearly specified, the simulations and other methods must be clearly related to these characteristics, and evaluators must be thoroughly trained.

The validity of the evaluative process will be greatly influenced by the openness of the participants. The congruence between participants' life goals and current job, as well as future job possibilities; their perceptions of the organization; their relationships with supervisors—all are sensitive matters. In addition, some people are threatened by the examination of their abilities and potential. It is highly advisable, therefore, to guarantee participants complete individual confidentiality. They should, however, be promised individual feedback if they so choose.

The personnel-centered approach is intended to reveal symptoms of difficulties or opportunities for improvement in the way the organization is functioning. It will not always definitively identify the causes of the problems it points to. The approach provides clues that will suggest directions for further investigation. This means that the evaluation of a relatively small sample, perhaps 50, will suffice. However, this sample must be restricted to those in a particular job in one division or department. The participants should be those who are subject to the same organizational influences, such as type of leadership, climate, reward systems, and so forth. Comparisons of those, for example, in the same job in different divisions can be highly revealing but would require multiple samples of comparable size.

Follow-up investigation after the personnel assessment phase would seek answers to such questions as the following: Are the predominant perceptions of organizational culture and values misperceptions? Are opportunities for advancement as limited as believed? Are deficiencies in team leadership due to a lack of effective training? Offhand answers will not do. A later section of this chapter will offer guidelines for supplementing assessment results.

CASE EXAMPLES

Evaluating College Recruits into Management

Personnel-centered diagnosis, as proposed in this chapter, has never been carried out completely. Assessment center methodology has, of course, been widely used for selection and development and has demonstrated its usefulness in revealing a range of individual characteristics. However, little attention has been paid to what those assessed might tell us about the organization. Few assessment centers have included exercises to get at perceptions and feelings about the organization, its incentive systems, supervisory practices, values, stability, or other critical matters. We have been looking at people primarily to find out about them, which is certainly of great importance, but not about how the organization affects them.

In light of this, it is surprising that the research from which all the diagnostic investigations described later in this chapter were derived was initially undertaken to answer a question about the effects of organizational life. The Management Progress Study (MPS) was set in motion at AT&T in the mid-1950s. This was a time when the supposed negative effects of a career in management in large corporate enterprises were commanding the attention of sociologists and writers in the popular literature (e.g.,Whyte, 1956). It was asserted that striving for success in a big business smothered individuality, resulting in a legion of indistinguishable "organization men" with uniform personalities and values.

Although most executives ignored these charges, Robert K. Greenleaf, the director of management development at AT&T, felt that the company had a social obligation to look into the issue. Tens of thousands worked as managers in the vast Bell System, and although the enterprise was naturally most interested in the results of their work, what was happening to the managers was surely important. Even from a narrow company point of view, the stifling of individuality would be a strong negative for corporate vitality. AT&T decided to launch a research investigation, and I was employed to design and direct it.

It was decided that the questions to be asked would be answered most definitively by a longitudinal design to reveal if managers changed over time and, if so, how. It was further decided that the first group of participants in the study would be new college graduates hired as management trainees. They would be evaluated as soon as possible after employment to minimize any effects on them of exposure to the organization. Then they would be followed for several years to detail their experiences and their reactions to them.

The nature of the questions being asked required that a very wide net be cast. Abilities, goals, personality, attitudes, and off-the-job relationships and pursuits were to be evaluated. The method chosen was that of an assessment center including behavioral simulations, depth interviews, cognitive tests, projective tests, and personality and motivational questionnaires (Howard & Bray, 1988). Such inclusiveness would usually be required in personnel-centered organizational diagnosis.

It is noteworthy that Greenleaf's interest was in the effects of organizational culture rather than in personnel selection. He declared early that he didn't believe there was much room for improvement in college employment methods, no doubt because the Bell System was considered a leader in this area. This prediction proved to be so much in error that the fallout caused the MPS to be thought of primarily as a selection study.

While evaluating the first groups of MPS participants, in two of the operating telephone companies, the assessment center staff was startled by the significant percentage among them with low management potential. The assessors had been led to believe that graduating in the top third of one's college class was weighted heavily in the hiring process, but now this was not credible. Investigation revealed that although this standard, based on early research (Bridgman, 1930), had been recommended for years, it was not being effectively implemented. The employment forms of many of the recruits showed that they had incorrectly indicated the third of the class they had attained, and there was a strong upward bias; it turned out that many college seniors did not know where they stood in their class and that recruiters had accepted their estimates too readily.

The data obtained by the assessment center that had raised suspicions about the accuracy of the rank-in-class information most directly was performance on the cognitive tests. Many more recruits than would have been expected scored below average on the published test norms and below the average attained by Bell System middle managers who had taken the tests in management development programs. Class rank, cognitive test data, and the judgment of the assessment staff based on recruit performance over the $3^1/_2$-day assessment period, indicated that only half of those evaluated had the managerial potential the company was seeking. This shattered whatever complacency top AT&T managers may have had about the pool of future middle and upper managers they were assembling. If this was the case in the two companies that led off the MPS, what was going on in the rest of the System?

Using an assessment center to find out was impossible because the total number of recent college graduates employed by Bell companies totaled 1,000 or more a year. It was, nevertheless, decided that the AT&T personnel research group would initiate a Bell System-wide study of the graduates hired in the current recruiting year. This study would, among other things, secure verified rank-in-class data and provide for the administration of several tests. Cooperation of all but one of the 19 operating telephone companies was obtained, providing data on 653 recently employed college recruits.

The overall Bell System results were not disastrous. Rank-in-class data were somewhat disquieting; 17% of recruits had been in the lowest third of their classes. However, about two-thirds of those tested scored above the 50th percentile of the Educational Testing Service's norms on the School and College Ability Test (SCAT). Nevertheless, there was a long-standing conviction in the Bell System that they were looking for more than the average college graduate, and one-third of the newly hired graduates earned less than an average score.

Far more striking were the differences among telephone companies. Several of the companies had a high percentage of scorers in the top quartile on the SCAT (e.g., 69%, 53%) whereas others had few in the top quartile (e.g., 4%, 9%, and 12%). These data surprised and so disturbed Greenleaf that he nonchalantly leapfrogged two levels of management (something rarely done in the hierarchical organizations of the time) and called them to the attention of an executive vice president who had previously been his supervisor. This gentleman, who was to reach the presidency of AT&T only a short time later, presented the findings to a Bell System presidents' conference that took place the following week.

It must not be inferred that anybody equated general mental ability or scholarly achievement with management potential. Leadership qualities, interpersonal and communication skills, motivation, and other characteristics were, of course, recognized as essential. Cognitive ability was, however, readily accepted as necessary although not sufficient. Few doubted that the great differences among the Bell System companies were a matter of concern.

The presentation by the executive vice president communicated clearly that he expected action, but he issued no orders. Management employment methods at that time were ultimately the choice of each telephone company. The role of AT&T was to provide information, leadership, and recommendations. In this instance, the companies initially reacted in different ways. Since most had accepted the importance of rank in class of recruits for some time, they took steps to determine this more accurately, even defraying clerical costs in registrars' offices where this was necessary. A few companies decided to add the SCAT to their college employment methods. One of these was a company whose results had been decidedly poor.

Over the next several years a more uniform approach developed, strongly promoted by a new AT&T director of management employment. All the companies eventually adopted the SCAT, and a "top half, top half" policy prevailed, that is, that college employment people were, with rare exceptions, to make job offers only to those in the top half of their classes and in the top half on the SCAT. Since the Bell System was an attractive employer, recruiters still had many applicants from which to choose.

We learned many other things about the recruits. Too many were deficient in interpersonal and administrative skills and appeared unlikely to develop them simply on the basis of job experience. Their expectations about their future quality of life as a Bell System manager were so favorable as to be clearly unrealistic. Perhaps because of their youth and the times, many were strongly motivated to gain approval from their bosses and their colleagues, a dependency that militated against decisive management.

Active data collection from and about the MPS participants continued for more than 25 years. Much more could be said, and has been said (Howard & Bray, 1988), about the study, and this is not the place to repeat it. However, comment is called for on the findings relevant to one of the original MPS aims, namely, to discover whether life in a large bureaucracy produced uniformity in those who led it. The answer is a resounding "No." A comparison of the many scores and ratings at the 20th year of the study with those at the beginning showed significantly greater variance at year 20 for a great many of the variables and almost no cases of less variance. "Clearly, with few exceptions, the men became more different from each other with age, more their own men. Their development edged not toward conformity but toward individuation" (Howard & Bray, 1988, p. 163).

An Evaluation of Engineering Managers

During the years that followed the early assessments in the MPS, the use of the assessment center method for management selection and development spread throughout the Bell System (and to many other organizations as well). The uses to which the method was put provide illustrations of its value as a diagnostic tool.

The first of these is a study of engineering management, which took place 15 years after the first MPS assessment. The chief engineers in several Bell companies were convinced that many third- and fourth-level managers in their engineering departments were significantly lacking in managerial skills. They requested that AT&T's human resources group develop a training program to remedy these supposed deficiencies. The human resources staff resisted this proposal for several reasons. One was that there was no hard evidence that the third- and fourth-level engineers lacked the required skills. Secondly, even if they did, it was necessary to identify specific deficiencies before remedial training could be developed.

Because AT&T had a management assessment center in regular operation, it was suggested that a sample of engineering managers be put through it to evaluate their management capabilities and define any areas of weakness. This assessment was organized around 18 dimensions, including such characteristics as mental ability, leadership, organizing and planning ability, work standards, and motivation for advancement. Implementation of the plan was delayed when the chief engineers proposed that assessment be expanded to encompass dimensions representing the special requirements of engineering management. This required defining such dimensions and designing additional assessment exercises. After extensive discussions with the chief engineers, 14 additional dimensions were decided upon. Among them were fact-finding, economic judgment, technical translation (the ability to communicate technical material to those without technical expertise), and technical development (motivation to increase one's technical expertise).

This expanded assessment required 3 days of the participants' time— 2 days for the general management portion and 1 day for the new engineering management segment, dubbed "T-MAP" (Technical Management Assessment Program). Participants underwent the process in groups of five or six. The total sample included 40 assessees, drawn at random from 11 Bell System companies. Participants were guaranteed that individual results would be available to no one but the researchers.

The findings were dramatic. In the general management assessment 40% of the sample were rated less than acceptable, while in T-MAP 50% were judged this poorly. When the results for the two assessment phases were combined, 65% earned a less-than-acceptable rating in one or both of them. These findings bore out the suspicions of the chief engineers that all was not well. The question of whether a significant number of middle-management engineers did, in fact, lack adequate management skills and motivation was definitively answered. Note, however, that a wider diagnostic effort would have been generated if the question of managerial performance had been formulated more generally. We would still have wanted to evaluate skills and motivation as we did, but we would also have wanted to get clues to causality. Some of the time at the assessment center might have been spent in learning about the participants' perception of and attitudes toward the leadership of their organizations, opportunities for achievement in their jobs, the reward system, and many other organizational influences on them. Questionnaires and targeted interviews would have been appropriate, as would focus groups (inasmuch as the participants came to the center five or six at a time).

The assessment that was conducted raised some interesting questions. Seventy-five percent of the participants scored above average on the mental ability test (Bell System college graduate norms). They were clearly trainable on at least the cognitive aspects of managing. Whether they had been given any such training during their careers would have been a painfully obvious question.

Assessment dimension ratings suggested that motivation was an important problem. Only 17.5% of those assessed were seen as above average in motivation for advancement while 57.5% were below average. Equally surprising was the fact that 52.5% were rated below average in interest in technically oriented subjects. Thus, two motives important in job performance and satisfaction appeared to have been lacking for many.

There is strong evidence that motivation for advancement dissipates over time when opportunities are perceived as scarce (Howard & Bray, 1988). One would have wanted to find out what the reality was for these engineering managers. If promotions were, in fact, hard to come by, what alternative rewards, such as recognition or more challenging assignments, existed? The observed lack of interest in technical matters would make one want to discover whether there had been efforts to promote such interests, such as inviting guest speakers or forming clubs, and whether bosses provided any leadership or stimulation in this area.

Finally, for this case example, *all* the participants in this study were rated as adequate by their bosses. In fact, 70% were judged to be completely satisfactory or better. Unless both the chief engineers and the assessment center were dead wrong, the standards of these bosses needed examination. Leniency may have blinded them to training needs or motivational problems. They themselves may have needed training in performance management. At a more speculative level, an unstimulating organizational culture in the department may have affected both those assessed *and* their bosses.

The evaluation of engineering managers did not result in remedial action, although such was called for. The engineering executive who had been most instrumental in initiating the effort retired, and the human resources group reorganized, with those who inherited the project more interested in other things. Such abandonment of human resources initiatives is, unfortunately, reported all too frequently.

Studies of Generational Differences

Just as the 20th-year assessment of the participants in the MPS was getting under way, Bell System human resources executives suggested a parallel assessment of current college graduate management recruits. They felt that these young managers might be significantly different from those of the previous generation and that the differences would have important implications for selection and development methods. This proposal received unexpectedly strong support, and the Management Continuity Study (MCS) was initiated. In the period 1977–1982, 391 new college hires were assessed. The assessment, like the original MPS assessment center, involved behavioral simulations, intensive interviews, and paper-and-pencil and projective tests. The characteristics evaluated included abilities, motives, personality, and attitudes.

The suspicion that recruits of the late 1970s and early 1980s might be unlike those of earlier years in important ways proved to be true. Although, in general, no differences in abilities appeared, motivation and attitudes did show some marked discrepancies. Among these were significantly less interest in rising toward high levels of management, less motivation to act as leaders, and a far less optimistic view of life as a manager (Howard & Bray, 1988).

Because the Bell System had always been highly concerned with the potential of management recruits, these findings called for further investigation. It was deemed possible that the telephone companies were no longer considered as attractive as employers as they had once been and that the more motivated college graduates were going elsewhere. On the other hand, it was possible that there was a general change in the motivation and attitudes of the new generation. It was important to review the experience of other organizations.

Few, if any, organizations had directly comparable data, so it was decided to try to persuade some to evaluate a sample of their college recruits with instruments used in the MCS. Since a full assessment was out of the question for financial and logistical reasons, paper-and-pencil tests and questionnaires had to be relied on. The ones selected required a half day of each participant's time. Although this seemed a modest request, it was too much for many organizations contacted. As a matter of fact, even though

AT&T was to provide all the materials, data analysis, and reports at no cost to the other organizations and had promised confidentiality, fruitless contacts were made with scores of companies before a sufficient number could be persuaded to participate.

To gain the greatest value from this undertaking, which was titled the Inter-Organizational Testing Study (ITS), it was decided to sample not only recently employed college graduates but college graduates of an age comparable to that of the subjects in the MPS sample at the time of their 20th-year assessment. Thus, for each organization two generations of managers would be represented. This would afford a parallel to the MPS–MCS comparison and would also yield data relevant to the changes in characteristics with age observed in the MPS group (Howard & Bray, 1988).

The ITS was carried out in 1981–1982 with 10 outside organizations. They varied in size from a few thousand employees to over 25,000. They included, among others, a railroad, a bank, an engineering consulting firm, a news organization, and two government agencies. In total, 380 young managers and 386 managers approximately 20 years older were tested.

The results clearly negated the hypothesis that the Bell System was attracting recruits who were less motivated for managerial careers than those who joined other organizations. This is revealed by a comparison of data for the young managers in the MCS and ITS in Figure 7.1 on three important characteristics: leadership motivation (the Dominance scale of the Edwards Personal Preference Schedule), ambition (advancement motiva-

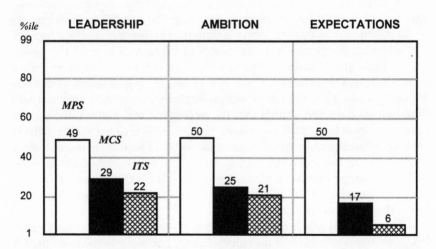

FIGURE 7.1. Percentile ranks of three samples of young managers evaluated on measures of leadership motivation, ambition, and expectations about a management career.

tion on the Sarnoff Survey of Attitudes Toward Life), and expectations (an inventory of expectations about a management career, developed in the Bell System). The average score for the ITS sample was lower than that for the MCS group in all three cases.

Figure 7.1 also shows for comparative purposes average percentile scores on the three characteristics for the original MPS group when they were young managers in the 1950s. These scores are sharply higher, supporting the belief that the college graduates of the late 1970s and early 1980s were not as motivated for managerial careers as those of the previous generation (Howard & Wilson, 1982; Miner & Smith, 1982). Average scores on the leadership motivation measure were no higher than the 30th percentile in any ITS organization, and one organization showed an 8th percentile result.

Although the Bell System could be assured that it was doing as well as, and even a little better than, others in recruiting college graduates, some ITS results were disquieting. Among the scores on an attitude survey were one for job satisfaction and another reflecting feelings about a number of aspects of life in the organization (called "general management attitude"). Although all except one of the ITS samples of young managers scored lower on job satisfaction than the MPS group had scored 20 years earlier, the Bell System, at the 32nd percentile, ranked 6th out of the 11 ITS companies. The Bell System also ranked 6th on general management attitude with an average score at the 18th percentile. A complete presentation of the MCS assessment results is in Howard and Bray (1988).

A striking piece of data for one of the ITS participants, Organization F, was a significantly lower average score on the cognitive measure, the SCAT, for their middle managers as compared to their new college recruits. Organization F's young managers scored highest of any of the young groups in the study, at the 50th percentile of the original Bell System college recruit norms. The same organization's middle managers scored only at the 38th percentile. This difference was particularly noteworthy because MPS longitudinal data had shown that the average SCAT score of the participants rose from the 49th percentile at the start of their careers to the 64th after 8 years and to the 69th after an additional 12 years (Howard & Bray, 1988). Three of the seven ITS organizations that administered the SCAT to both the younger and older managers showed large differences in favor of the older groups, and none but Organization F showed the older group lower than the younger group.

This unusual result for Organization F's middle management group led to an inspection of their inventory scores, particularly those on the Edwards Personal Preference Schedule. On leadership motivation (the Dominance scale on the Edwards) Organization F's participants were the second lowest among the ITS middle managers, scoring at the 43rd percentile. This compared to a 76th percentile for the highest-scoring ITS organization. Organization F's middle managers were the second highest on motivation for succorance (to receive understanding and help) at the 77th percentile; they were second highest on the need for order and lowest on the need for change (to be interested in variety).

These indicators conjured up a picture of a middle management that was unimaginative, noncreative, and not very sharp cognitively, and that lacked leadership characteristics. Such a picture might have been expected to motivate higher management to take further diagnostic steps to investigate a seemingly serious problem, and they did request and receive a more detailed report. Whether anything further was done in Organization F is not known.

What further steps would have been appropriate? On the basis of the test results one might have suspected that the management skills (not evaluated in the ITS) of Organization F's managers were deficient. This question would have been answered in the full assessment approach to diagnosis outlined at the beginning of this chapter. Lacking this, one might be tempted to review bosses' ratings of middle-aged managers at this level, but given that supervisors rarely say any of their direct reports are unsatisfactory or even below average, hard facts might not be gained. One could develop managerial simulations and put a sample through them, but this might not be the best use of resources.

In diagnosis, as in other human resources procedures, there have to be some judgment calls. In the present case the clues are strong enough to conclude that the middle managers of Organization F are not as strong as those in several other ITS organizations. One might then move on to the question of how this came about. The reason for wanting to know is not to write history but to make sure that the causative factors are addressed.

Although all the possibilities cannot be explored here, selective attrition is a prime suspect. If the organization's personnel records were good enough, one might develop a list, or at least a representative sample, of college graduates employed contemporaneously in Organization F with those tested in the ITS. Employment qualifications of those no longer with the organization could be compared with data on those who stayed. If the information was adequate and there were no differences between the leavers and stayers, poor employment screening might be indicated and certainly would be if, at least on paper, many of those hired had presented mediocre qualifications.

Suppose, however, that comparisons—possibly even supported by managers recalling that some excellent people had left—were convincing enough to lead to the conclusion that the typical middle manager might not have reached that level had more of the better candidates stayed. The question, Why did they leave? leads to a whole set of issues. Among them are matters of pay, opportunities for advancement, job challenge, nature of supervision, identification with the organization, and so forth.

Most organizations do not do effective exit interviewing, and even if they try, they often receive socially acceptable answers rather than the blunt truth. It is unlikely that existing data within Organization F could have reconstructed the past accurately. It would be more productive to turn one's attention to young managers of the present to identify sources of dissatisfaction that might lead to the departure of those employees the organization would dearly like to retain.

The Career Motivation Study

The ITS was not the only effort stimulated by the MCS. Because of its importance in the development of future management, AT&T launched an intensive investigation of the career motivation of recent college hires. Although this was initially intended to be limited to an intensive study of such motivation, the findings led to a second step, a diagnostic investigation of the relationship of career attitudes to the climate of the two telephone companies participating in the study.

The first step was to develop a career motivation assessment center (London & Bray, 1983). Although a lengthy description of this center would be inappropriate here, enough must be presented for an understanding of the findings it produced and related diagnostic research. The dimensions around which assessment was organized derived from two sources: One was the experience gained from the MPS and MCS, the other a theoretical conceptualization of managerial career motivation.

Such motivation was seen as involving three domains: career identity, career insight, and career resilience. Career identity (how central career is to one's identity) included the subdomains of work involvement, particularly in managerial work, and desire for upward mobility. Career insight concerned perceptions of the self and the organization as they related to career goals. Career resilience addressed resistance to career disruption in a less-than-optimal organizational environment. Over 30 dimensions were thus derived, and a 2-day assessment center designed. The exercises included behavioral simulations, in-depth interviews, standardized personality and interest questionnaires, and projective tests. London has provided a complete description of this assessment program (London, 1985; London & Bray, 1984).

Each of two Bell System operating telephone companies agreed to provide 24 recent college recruits to be evaluated. No information on the performance of individuals would be available to the companies, but participants were to receive feedback on their own performance. Participants were assessed in groups of six. The assessors were psychologists assisted by a graduate student test administrator. The purpose of the study was to deepen understanding of career motivation through an analysis of assessment results, including the many interrelationships among dimensions, domains, and the assessment exercises.

A broadened investigation into company climate was triggered by significantly different assessment findings for the young people from the two companies. Among these were stronger motivation for advancement, more inclination toward ascendancy in group situations, and greater commitment to managerial work on the part of those from company B. Although the possibility of a difference in employment standards in the two companies could not be completely ruled out, it was not the whole explanation for these differences. Available background data on the two groups showed no substantial differences except for a slightly higher grade-point average for those in company B. Interviews with bosses, one of the early steps in the follow-up work, showed no differences in their judgments of the managerial abilities of the two groups of participants.

The assessment results were not given to the companies until the feedback interviews with the participants were completed. The findings were then presented to the two human resources vice presidents in a joint meeting and resulted in a request for additional work to illuminate the factors underlying the results (London, 1985). This eventually included reinterviewing the study participants, as well as their bosses, $1^1/2$ years after the original assessment. In addition, focus group sessions were held with other young managers not in the study group, and existing company attitude survey data were analyzed.

Attention turned first to the developmental programs, or lack thereof, for college recruits in the two companies. Company A did not really have a development program other than learning one's first-level management job. Although those who did well could expect advancement some day, promotional opportunities were hard to come by, and, in light of a turndown in business conditions, there would be much competition for them. Nor did organizational rigidities allow for many transfers into other departments for developmental purposes. In any case, college recruits were seen as a means of serving current business needs rather than as corporate resources for the future.

Because of the absence of a program, opportunities—and even information—were in the hands of the recruits' second-level supervisors. In many cases these bosses were not college graduates, and few saw their role as one of developing future higher-level management. Many of the recruits had resigned themselves to a bleak future or were contemplating leaving the company.

Company B had had an ambitious development plan for college recruits for many years. This plan called for challenging assignments right from the start, one purpose of which was to determine whether the recruit indeed had potential for middle management. Rotation among departments was facilitated. The young managers were seen as important resources for the future, and early advancement was anticipated. Unfortunately, as in Company A, business conditions seriously limited opportunities for promotion, and many of the recruits found themselves languishing in first-level jobs. They too had second-level bosses who were not always particularly sympathetic. However, the organizational climate was more open. Higher management communicated the facts of the situation and was openly regretful that promising futures were being delayed. Recruits were also free to discuss their feelings with the director of the management development program.

Other evidence of the difference in climate between the two companies came from presidents' letters included in annual reports to stockholders over the previous 5 years. A noteworthy difference was that references to employees in Company A amounted to a sentence or two in the concluding remarks, thanking employees for their work and loyalty. In sharp contrast, the letters in Company B were replete with information about how changing conditions were impacting the work force, what the company was doing about this, how steps were taken to see that all employees had the opportunity to speak their minds, and so forth.

This is where this diagnostic effort came to an end. Both companies were seen to have encountered the problem of limited opportunities for their college hires. One might guess that Company B's development program, with its implication of early advancement, made matters worse. In some ways it did. Those on the program complained loudly. Nevertheless, they remained more ambitious and more achievement oriented and had higher expectations for a favorable career than those in Company A or in other Bell System companies. It appeared that the continued expressed interest in them on the part of top management and the open climate of their organization militated against despair.

Comments on the Cases

The examples that have been presented illustrate that thorough evaluation of defined groups of employees can yield information of significant value. None of them, however, fully represents personnel-centered organizational diagnosis as I conceive it. That approach has at its start the goal of finding out everything of significance about a sample of employees-their abilities and motivation *and* their perceptions and attitudes about important aspects of life in the organization.

The assessment of engineering managers, as a case in point, asked the important question of whether there was a widespread lack of managerial skills and motivation in that group of employees. That question was conclusively answered, but no systematic data were gathered about the leadership they were experiencing, the effect on them of the reward system, their autonomy, the departmental climate, or other organizational factors. The assessment programs in the MPS and MCS could not have profitably examined such organizational factors because the great majority of the participants were short-service college recruits with little exposure to the organization. The long-term follow-up in the MPS did, however, produce many unique findings, such as the relationship between advancement, or lack thereof, and personality and motivational development. The focus, however, was always more on exploring the nature of managers than on the functioning of the organization. The research into the structure of career motivation was also initially focused on individuals but led unexpectedly into an exploration of the influence of organizational climate.

One other ambitious Bell System study that utilized a specially designed assessment center was the AT&T Managerial Stress Research Project. This study paid much attention to organizational factors, particularly the turmoil in the company prior to the dissolution of the System and the reorientation to a highly competitive stance. This study was covered in detail in a previous book in this series (Bunker, 1994).

GATHERING FURTHER INFORMATION

The evaluation of job incumbents is not a stand-alone diagnostic method. Findings must be examined in the context of the practices and influences intended by the organization to affect the performance, motivation, and attitudes of those holding a particular job. A detailed and comprehensive inventory of these practices and intended influences should be developed for comparison with the assessment findings.

Some items in this inventory will have been specified in preparation for the assessment phase. For example, the knowledge and skills held necessary for successful performance must be set forth in order to devise instruments for measuring them. In other areas, however, too tight a linkage between what is wanted and what is to be measured should be avoided. We want to know, for instance, what values drive performance, not just whether a particular value the organization wants stressed is being served. The following are some of the questions the inventory might address:

- What knowledge and skills are necessary for successful performance? Do incumbents function as part of a team or as individual contributors? Are team member or team leader skills needed? What aptitudes would indicate potential for greater responsibilities?

- How are people selected for this job? Who makes the selections, and what criteria are used?
- What training or development do incumbents receive?
- What type of leadership do incumbents experience?
- What rewards are available for good performance? What are the financial incentives? How are they administered? How are selections made for promotion?
- What organizational values are expected to guide performance?

The assessment phase of the diagnostic process yields data on the capabilities and motivation of incumbents and on their perceptions of the organization as it impinges on them and on their work. A comparison of these data with the organization's perspective, as reflected in the job inventory, will reveal any significant disjunctures. Their causes will sometimes be readily apparent. In other cases, some further digging may be necessary to arrive at root causes.

The personnel-centered approach has a number of advantages. In the first place, it encourages—in fact, demands—a comprehensive specification of all the systems that are believed to affect those in a particular job category. It then further requires the identification of the abilities, motivations, attitudes, and values important in the job and thought to be affected by these organizational systems. This rigorous first step in the process may in itself yield valuable insights.

It is important to appreciate that these personnel-centered activities are highly compatible with more global diagnostic strategies. For example, many OD models include characteristics of organization members as significant data. Yet, although this information is included conceptually, there is often no follow-through. The plan being presented in this chapter can be adapted to different approaches while producing information for one of their critical ingredients.

Evaluating the relevant characteristics of a group of individuals offers the advantage of greater insight into the nature of problems and possible interventions. For instance, training needs, potential for training, and motivation for training can be looked at all at once.

As indicated earlier, it is likely that the results of studying one important job can be generalized. If selection is poorly done, if training is inadequate, if pay and advancement decisions are seen as unfair, or if stated organizational values are not adopted in the target position, it is likely that there is trouble elsewhere. In any case, it is preferable to really learn about one key job than to have a smattering of information about many.

This chapter began with a mention of organizational fads. A program often attracts much attention in a short time and is widely adopted without any evidence that it is really needed in a particular organization. The suspicion that it was only a fad grows as the program fails in many applications. The failures, however, may spring as much from a lack of sound information about the organization itself as from the particulars of the program. Bergholz (1992) has traced the frequent disappointments with total quality programs and similar efforts to a lack of data on all the factors that make for success or failure and to a concern with process rather than results. Data are needed about such factors as the organizational environment, suppliers, customers, organizational values, and particularly the employees who are to carry out the program. Viewing employees as reflections of the organization is a good place to start.

REFERENCES

Bergholz, H. (1992, December). *TQM: Tough questions for management: Why most total quality efforts fail.* Paper presented at a meeting of the Metropolitan New York Association for Applied Psychology, New York.

Blake, W. (1803). Augeries of innocence. In A. H. Munson (Ed.), *Poems of William Blake* (p. 83). New York: Thomas Y. Crowell, 1964.

Bray, D. W. (1989). *Management careers: Their nature and nurture* (Monograph No. 10). Pittsburgh: Development Dimensions International.

Bray, D. W., & Byham, W. C. (1991). Assessment centers and their derivatives. *Journal of Continuing Higher Education, 39*(1), 8–11.

Bridgman, D. W. (1930). Success in college and business. *The Personnel Journal, 9*(1), 1–19.

Bunker, K. A. (1994). Coping with total life stress. In A. K. Korman & Associates, *Human dilemmas in work organizations* (pp. 58–92). New York: Guilford Press.

Howard, A., & Bray, D. W. (1988). *Managerial lives in transition: Advancing age and changing times.* New York: Guilford Press.

Howard, A., & Wilson, J. A. (1982). Leadership in a declining work ethic. *California Management Review, 23*(4), 33–46.

London, M. (1985). *Developing managers.* San Francisco: Jossey-Bass.

London, M., & Bray, D. W. (1983). An assessment center to study career motivation. *Career Center Bulletin, 4*(1), 8–13.

London, M., & Bray, D. W. (1984). Measuring and developing young managers' career motivation. *Journal of Management Development, 3*(3), 3–25.

Miner, J. B., & Smith, N. R. (1982). Decline and stabilization of managerial motivation over a 20-year period. *Journal of Applied Psychology, 67*, 297–305.

Task Force on Assessment Center Guidelines. (1989). *Guidelines and ethical considerations for assessment center operations* (Monograph No. 16). Endorsed by the Seventeenth International Congress on the Assessment Center Method. Pittsburgh: Development Dimensions International.

Thornton, G. C. III, & Byham, W. C. (1982). *Assessment centers and managerial performance.* New York: Academic Press.

Whyte, W. H. Jr. (1956). *The organization man.* New York: Simon & Schuster.

PART III

PERSPECTIVES ON THE HIGH-INVOLVEMENT WORKPLACE

Introduction

The chapters in this section delve into three more aspects of organizational functioning: culture, reward systems, and teams. These topics, mentioned but unexplored in earlier chapters, relate to management and motivation of employees. All are deeply significant in a psychological sense—culture as the collective unconscious, rewards as a key to motivation, teams as a source of interpersonal identity and satisfaction.

These three chapters have something more in common: All give special attention to the high-involvement workplace. Increasingly, organizations rely on some form of worker empowerment to enhance productivity, quality, customer service, and other competitive advantages. But as Robert Rogers and William Byham caution in Chapter 8, empowerment is "not something to be taken lightly." They underscore, as does Kimball Fisher in Chapter 10, the formidable energy and effort that must be summoned to change organizations toward high worker involvement. It is what Burke (Chapter 3) would call a transformational change. This is precisely why an initial diagnosis is essential; organizations must know what they are getting into, if it will meet their needs, and how painful it may be before launching such a major effort.

High involvement invades many corners of an organization, and the authors emphasize the importance of systems alignment. A concern raised in the introduction to Part I was that congruence and alignment could lull organizations into resistance to change. If we follow Kotter's (1978) argument, systems should be aligned in the moderate run, but it is the state of system elements—whether or not they are inherently constraining—that determines long-run adaptation. As will be seen, the authors' prescriptions for high-involvement systems are nonconstraining, which should leave the system open to change.

DIAGNOSING ORGANIZATION
CULTURES FOR REALIGNMENT

Chapter 8, by Robert Rogers and William Byham, is a comprehensive guide to diagnosing organization cultures. To check an organization's focus, they first identify the "barometers of an organization's success" with a creative combination of external and internal scans. Meeting with the organization's executives off-site, they help them formulate the organization's "ideal future state" or vision—a tough assignment if it is to be a driving force rather than impotent platitudes. To achieve the vision, the executives must hammer out a discrete set of organizational values and link them to behavior.

Rogers and Byham use a high-involvement culture to illustrate how to diagnose the alignment of organizational systems. After orienting executives to empowerment, they investigate how far and fast to take it. But effective implementation requires an analysis of the many systems that must support, reinforce, and measure the newly adopted culture.

Of special interest is their diagnosis of communication systems. Like Levinson in Part I, they search for meaning in written documents and other signs and symbols. But they also home in on meetings, "the stage on which corporate values are played out," and leader behavior, "the most powerful symbolic message in an organization." Their examples here are vivid and enlightening.

EFFECTIVE REWARD SYSTEMS:
STRATEGY, DIAGNOSIS, AND DESIGN

One system that Rogers and Byham seek to align with organization culture is that of rewards. Edward Lawler demonstrates in Chapter 9 not only how to do that but why we should. Multiple objectives can be achieved with rewards: "A good reward system design consultant often spends as much or more time clarifying the intent of the reward system as she does working with the organization to design it." Motivation is often a goal, but reward systems can also affect attraction and retention, skills and knowledge, culture, structure, and costs.

Lawler gives special attention to diagnosing the structure of reward systems. Are they, for example, based on performance? His discussion of the process of administering rewards reminds us of how much organizations are changing—employees and peers are becoming involved in this sensitive area in ways they have never been before. His diagnosis of the gap between the actual impact of reward policies and practices and the desired impact forms the guts of redesign.

To illustrate pay system design, Lawler uses alignment with high involvement, consistent with the approach of Rogers and Byham in Chapter

8. In his well-reasoned manner, he explains how the pay system of an organization using employee involvement should differ starkly from one using traditional management.

DIAGNOSTIC ISSUES FOR WORK TEAMS

What does Procter & Gamble have in common with the Seattle Metro and the San Diego Zoo? The answer is *teams*—the semi-autonomous, empowered type of teams. And what makes these teams special? Kimball Fisher launches Chapter 10 by straightening us out on what makes a team, how teams relate to empowerment, the nature of self-directed teams and their roots in sociotechnical systems, and the different types of teams, which vary by duration and scope of activities.

Fisher illustrates how to determine when teams are and are not appropriate. Surprisingly, it doesn't seem to matter that much if the work is boring or the fields are brown. Leadership is critical, though, and he shows us how to evaluate leader readiness for such a radical transformation.

Although Fisher's vast experience has let him witness the awesome power of team-based organizations, he warns that many applications fail. Accordingly, he shows how to diagnose team effectiveness and reasons for team dysfunction. When teams falter, chances are good that management is not sufficiently committed to this difficult change process.

A NOTE OF CAUTIOUS ENTHUSIASM

Reading the chapters in this section carries the risk of catching the authors' contagious enthusiasm for high involvement. Whether using Fisher's arrow or Byham's dial, you may feel an urge to push the organization toward the high end of the empowerment continuum. Pay attention, then, not just to the success stories but to the caveats—and the need for a careful diagnosis ahead of time to determine if management has the hunger and the stomach for high involvement.

To begin this last set of explorations into organizational diagnosis, join Robert Rogers and William Byham for a cultural tour. Just beware of being *Zapp'*d by the lightning of the empowerment concept (Byham, 1990).

REFERENCES

Byham, W. C. (1990). *Zapp! The lightning of empowerment*. New York: Harmony Books.

Kotter, J. P. (1978). *Organizational dynamics: Diagnosis and intervention*. Reading, MA: Addison-Wesley.

CHAPTER 8

Diagnosing Organization Cultures for Realignment

ROBERT W. ROGERS
WILLIAM C. BYHAM

The need for organizational change or realignment to better (or more flexibly) satisfy customers' needs is clearly evident in today's global marketplace. Given that an organization's culture is the sum of its salient values, the challenge for senior leaders is how to create or develop a set of values that gains the commitment and energy of all employees toward a strategically viable direction—whether that be enhancing customer loyalty, improving product quality, or obtaining greater market share by reducing the cycle time for new products. Such realignment, however, cannot occur successfully without a precise and detailed diagnosis of organizational factors, processes, and systems that through the years have created barriers to change. Three broad areas require diagnosis:

1. *Focus*: Where should the organization be going? What does it want to be?
2. *Employee involvement*: Are employees at all levels motivated to adopt a new direction and the new behaviors required by the new direction? This usually involves some application of a high-involvement strategy.
3. *Systems alignment*: Are organizational systems aligned such that they support and reinforce behavior that contributes to the achievement of the new direction?

Data for a diagnosis come from a variety of sources, including one-on-one interviews, focus groups, opinion or climate surveys, training impact audits, and direct observation. The outcome of such an analysis is a clear picture of major barriers that are retarding or will retard a change effort, as well as clear indications of the remedial interventions that need to occur.

CHECKING THE FOCUS

To assure direction or focus, an organization needs to identify three inter-related components:

1. *Critical success factors*: Clearly identified, measurable make-or-break factors that must be achieved if the organization is to be successful.
2. *Vision*: A defined and articulated sense of direction for the organization's future. Typically, this appears in a vision or purpose statement that spells out the senior leaders' hopes and dreams for the organization.
3. *Values*: A set of shared values that communicates how the vision is to be achieved.

Critical Success Factors

Critical success factors are those paramount issues that are going to make or break a company in the next 3 to 5 years. They can be identified by considering marketplace and customer demands, competitors' successes, or technological advances. For example, an organization's difficulty in getting new products conceived, designed, developed, and to market may be dramatically hindering its competitiveness. Or an organization's selling costs may be higher than the competition's. Critical success factors describe the current situation and provide a focus for change. They are the barometers of an organization's success.

Some common critical success factors we have observed in organizations include the following:

- Global expansion
- Customer satisfaction levels
- Costs as a percentage of revenue
- Client retention rates
- Short process times
- Flexibility in responding to customer needs
- Retention of high-caliber employees

Most organizations can focus on no more than four or five factors at a time; any more creates a diffusion of priorities. When, for example, senior leaders of a large industrial products manufacturer identified 16 factors, they confused their employees, who scrambled to address all the issues that senior management stated were critical.

To define their critical success factors, senior leaders need to consider data from a variety of sources. An *external scan* involves gathering customer opinions and feedback as well as analyzing market conditions and the competition. Customer surveys, market research reports, project reviews for major customers, complaint tracking data, lost sales analyses, and service audits (such as mystery shoppers) all furnish important information. One of the best external scans we've seen was a survey that asked customers to rank suppliers on numerous categories, such as product quality, professionalism of the sales force, complaint resolution, pricing, and so forth. The comparison helped the sponsoring company to pinpoint where it was stronger and weaker than its competition. Informal feedback from one-to-one discussions between customers and the organization's executives, sales force, or field service people is also important.

An *internal scan* involves gathering opinions from employees about the organizational barriers to their success. It uses data from employee surveys, cultural and quality audits, exit interviews, and focus group meetings. Many progressive senior leaders now hold informal meetings with exempt and nonexempt employees to solicit ideas for improving the company. Informal information comes mainly from impromptu discussions between employees and executives.

It is important to combine data from internal and external scans to identify critical success factors. For example, a Georgia bank faced with a declining market share discovered from surveys that a high percentage of customers were dissatisfied with the way they were treated by tellers. Customer interviews distinguished three areas where the bank's tellers were lacking: acknowledgement, courtesy and respect, and friendliness. Although many customers were comfortable with the bank's convenient locations (numerous branch offices) and its security, the lack of friendliness was so critical that more than 15% of the customers were seriously considering switching banks.

The bank's internal scan pinpointed why the tellers were not treating customers as expected:

- Tellers had no training in customer interaction.
- Numerous organizational systems clearly communicated higher priorities than customer satisfaction.
- Management's treatment of employees produced a domino effect of disrespect. Because tellers felt that management did not treat them with friendliness and respect, this attitude trickled down to teller–customer interactions.

Diagnosis of both the internal and external environments clearly indicated the deficiencies in bank operations critical to success. The bank was able to determine the aspects of its culture that required change, and it successfully implemented a change process.

In another service organization an external customer scan revealed a client retention rate of only 62% for each of the previous 3 years. This was significantly lower than industry averages of 80 to 85%. The organization's low retention rate was seen as a major cause of its relatively high selling costs, which in turn led to missed profit goals. During the internal scan, employees indicated that established organizational systems rewarded salespeople for bringing in new clients but provided no rewards or recognition for those who took care of existing clients, thus failing to reinforce the benefits of long-term partnerships.

The final determination of critical success factors usually takes place in an off-site meeting of senior leaders. The leaders review the data produced by the internal and external scans and add their considerable knowledge of the marketplace, the competition, and internal processes and problems. After a great deal of discussion they pinpoint the four or five critical success factors for their company's future.

Creating a Vision

Throughout history great leaders have focused the energies of groups of people by articulating a compelling vision of the future. Clearly defining the direction toward which their organization needs to strive serves the same purpose for senior executives.

Some organizations have clear and appropriate vision statements; most don't. Articulation of a vision can be accomplished in a separate meeting of senior leaders, or the task can be combined with the delineation of critical success factors. We usually do these together. Both can be accomplished in one day if adequate prework is done.

In the off-site meeting we ask the following questions to help senior leaders visualize the ideal future state of their organizations:

1. *What will your organization's market position be?* The vision must highlight whether the organization is to be the leader or a dominant player in a market, or only a viable competitor.

2. *What will your customers say about your organization?* Here we are looking for possible competitive advantages, that is, things customers might see as the major benefits of this company over others. Whereas the first question focused on a target or goal, this question helps to identify a means to reach it.

3. *What will your competition say about your organization?* This question also tries to identify competitive advantages for the future. For example,

responses may be "They are always out with new products first," "Their service responsiveness is extraordinary," or "Their costs of sales and manufacturing are much lower than ours." The advantages become part of the vision for the future and also may pinpoint a critical success factor.

4. *What will your employees say about the organization?* This question is similar to the internal scan mentioned earlier, but the response indicates senior leaders' perceptions of how well employees will be in alignment with the vision or goal for the future. For example, if "successful long-term partnerships with customers" is part of the response to Question 2, employees would say their company focuses on customer loyalty and enhanced levels of customer satisfaction. They would clearly understand the value of the customer to everyone in the organization.

5. *How will the organization operate with regard to decision making, structure, communications, and so forth?* The response to this question quickly identifies leaders who understand how empowerment and high involvement relate to customer service, quality, productivity, faster cycle time, and other needs. Senior leaders need to see that for most cultural transformations to work, the typical bureaucratic nature of hierarchical organizations must change and decision making must shift to frontline levels of the organization.

6. *Why should employees want to work here?* This question helps senior leaders focus on the key role employees will play in the attainment of the organization's aspirations for the future. Although most senior leaders acknowledge people as their most important component, not many have a clear picture of how meeting employee needs and developing loyalty and commitment are directly related to the future state the leaders are trying to create.

By leading the senior executives through such a series of questions, we avoid getting the typical responses that focus on profitability or size. Financial objectives and numerical goals are more appropriately included as part of a business plan for a specific time frame or in a mission statement.

The difficulty in creating a vision stems mainly from leaders' tendency to think of all the things they want for the organization rather than view the vision statement as a means of focusing the energy of employees. Many organizations have a vision statement, but few are effective in focusing energy. In diagnosing an organization's vision statement, we typically look for four components that help make it a driving force for the organization rather than a list of platitudes or senior leaders' dreams:

1. *Is there a nonfinancial/nonquantifiable goal with which most employees will want to be associated?* Examples of such a goal are being the industry leader or the most respected, admired worldwide provider.

2. *Does the vision statement express the major strategic advantage the com-*

pany now enjoys or hopes to obtain by achieving the vision? This may be, for example, innovation at 3M, service at L. L. Bean, or technological leadership at Microsoft.

3. *Does the vision provide some inspiration to employees in the company?* People want to be associated with a world leader. People want to work for an organization committed to empowerment, collaboration, concern for people, and so forth.

4. *Is the vision aligned appropriately for the business and the marketplace in which the organization competes?* This strategic alignment can make or break the company. A vision to be the lowest-cost provider when customers' main concern is quality or service can be a disaster!

Vision statements must be tied to solid business realities; they must be customer driven, people focused, and value based. When Jack Welch became CEO of General Electric, he espoused the vision of being number one or number two in any business the company was in. He liquidated or sold the businesses that did not or probably would not fit. The vision remains clear and attainable: GE is first or second in all 13 current businesses.

Another organization that created and accomplished a clear vision is Scandinavian Airline Systems. In the mid-1980s, Scandinavian created the vision of being the number one on-time carrier for business travelers in Europe within a year. At the time this was articulated, the company's on-time record was last in the industry, resulting in a low market share. Scandinavian's vision described its goal and the strategic marketplace advantage it would create. One year later, Scandinavian had the best on-time record of any carrier in the industry, and it was on its way to becoming a favorite of business travelers.

However, simply having a vision doesn't ensure success. In the 1980s, Eastern Airlines and Sears Roebuck promulgated visions of being low-cost providers. But one of Eastern's competitors, Delta, had the vision of being the best service provider in the airline business in North America and drew business customers from Eastern. Sears's vision prompted numerous actions (such as more part-time staff and fewer full-time salespeople) that subsequently led to decreased customer satisfaction and retention. On the other hand, Wal-Mart's low-cost-provider vision was aligned with systems and actions that didn't detract from customer satisfaction, and the company was able to retain a sufficient level of service to meet customer needs.

Creating a vision is a special challenge that is essential for a successful change. While critical success factors identify the key areas that need to be focused on to achieve results, the vision provides the goal posts or the direction toward which the organization will head. The next step is to determine how the organization is going to get there, that is, guidelines for the decisions the associates will make and actions they will take to achieve the vision. The values that exist within an organization determine the *hows* of achieving an organization's vision.

Values

Every organization has a set of values. Values are the attitudes, mind-sets, and beliefs that determine how work is accomplished and how employees interact with each other and with customers. They are the subtle control mechanisms that informally sanction or prohibit behavior. The total culture is based on these shared values, which are reflected in the behaviors of not only the leaders but all employees at every level.

Three aspects of an organization's values must be diagnosed to determine readiness for a cultural shift:

1. *What are the current commonly shared values that influence behaviors on a daily basis?* Regardless of whether the organization has consciously established and communicated a set of values, they do exist, for leaders' actions influence what employees fear as well as what gets rewarded.

2. *Are the current values the ones the leaders really want in the organization's culture of the future?* If the culture supports "shooting the messenger," for example, very few customer complaints will ever reach the top, even though senior leaders might want and need that information.

3. *Are the organizationally espoused values linked to behavior?* Too often we find lofty values such as trust, integrity, respect, or open communication, but the organization fails to define precisely how each value translates into day-to-day behaviors. In this case, the values don't mean much to employees.

Diagnosing Current Values

The methodology to collect and analyze the necessary data about values can vary, depending on the size of the organization and the willingness of employees to share their feelings honestly. For larger organizations, in which the fear factor tends to be higher, anonymous questionnaires provide the best vehicle for collecting large amounts of data that help identify patterns or trends in employee perceptions. Typically, the questions on the survey ask employees to rate agreement on statements such as the following:

- This organization's priority is always profit.
- The customers come first when we are trying to make decisions.
- It doesn't do any good to complain to senior management; nothing ever changes around here.
- Management won't address conflict; it usually festers until a major battle occurs.
- In making decisions, management frequently tries to balance quality of life for employees with costs.
- There are too many levels involved in the approval process, which slows down our response to customers.

The questions can focus on a wide range of values, but those most commonly evaluated include the following:

- Teamwork/collaboration
- Empowerment/involvement
- Innovation
- Quality
- Sense of urgency
- Risk taking
- Meeting customer needs (customer service)
- Continuous improvement
- Trust
- Cost consciousness
- Concern for people
- Quality of life

Note that profit does not appear on the list. Profit is a measure, not a value. By communicating profit as a value, senior management is, in essence, promoting short-term thinking.

Questionnaires can provide volumes of data, but they don't provide specific examples of what really drives behavior in the organization. Focus groups can be an effective mechanism for understanding the values guiding action in an organization, provided the employees in the group are free to express their opinions and give examples without fear that they will be chastised for their views. The questions asked are similar to those on a values survey, except the facilitator asks the participants to give specific examples of when or how behavior was controlled, influenced, directed, rewarded, or punished. Focus groups can help define items for the written survey, but they are best used after survey results have been analyzed. Questions to the group can then solicit more information on the questions that received the lowest ratings or probe why particular items received a wide range of responses.

A third methodology, which works well for midlevel managers and above, is to question leaders on how they make decisions. As they discuss alternatives or provide rationales for their decisions, the practitioner often can determine what drives their behavior, what they value, and what they are communicating to others. The following examples of decision-making rationale illustrate some contrasts:

- A micromanagement approach, in which senior leaders make decisions dealing with specific details, versus an empowering approach, in which decisions on details are clearly left to lower-level managers or employees.

- An emphasis on customer satisfaction versus an emphasis on costs, where senior leaders will go only so far to meet or exceed customer needs.
- A concern for employees' quality of life versus meeting deadlines or objectives no matter what the price.
- A propensity to find and punish the guilty party who made an error versus a more systematic approach to finding the causes of problems and eliminating them.
- A "turf-protection" and "cover-your-butt" mind-set versus a process orientation to continuously improve.
- A belief that people want to do a good job and will do so if properly led and coached versus a belief that people need to be pushed, cajoled, and controlled or they will loaf.

Obviously, the best way to diagnose the values that currently exist in an organization is to combine all three methods—surveys, focus groups, and decision-making analyses.

Defining Desired Values

Once the existing values are determined and understood, the desired values for the future need to be identified and agreed upon. This typically is guided by a survey instrument that asks large numbers of employees and managers to rate (1) values currently driving behavior and (2) values that should drive behavior in the future. The data are analyzed by organizational level and, where appropriate, by department or other client groups. The differences among groups, and between what exists now compared to what should exist, help the organization's leaders visualize the direction and depth of the change effort needed.

A consultant/facilitator shares the results of this survey with the senior management team in an off-site 2-day session. The role of the consultant is to help the senior leaders refine the definitions and consider the implications of the selected values for moving the organization toward the defined vision. The consultant must ensure that in finalizing the values the executives do the following:

- Define each value clearly and precisely so as to illustrate its importance to the future success of the company.
- Develop six to ten specific measures that demonstrate how the value affects behavior in the organization. For example, responding to customer complaints immediately is a behavior that illustrates the importance of the value *customer satisfaction.*
- Agree on one value as a driving value that will take precedence when values conflict. For example, *quality of life* for associates might

at times conflict with *meeting customer needs*, or *teamwork* might conflict at times with a *sense of urgency*.

- Fully commit to changing their own behavior to support each of the new values selected. For example, if *bias for action* or *sense of urgency* becomes a value, executives then can't berate subordinates for making mistakes in haste.

Linking Values and Behavior

Regardless of which values an organization selects, everyone in the organization needs to understand how the values affect—and should guide—behavior. When the link between values and organizational practices is evident, the values become more concrete and practical. People know how to use the values as guides to their decisions, and the behavioral change process can begin.

As an example, when sales of Gillette Corporation's Sensor razor took off shortly after its introduction, top management in the Latin American division anticipated rapid growth that would put strains on its available management force. A focus on the value *developing organizational talent* was clearly needed. Not only did the senior executives in that division quickly communicate the new focus to all managers, but they emphasized it in the performance management system. Line managers became accountable for setting objectives that defined specific activities to further develop existing talent. Senior leaders trained managers to establish developmental plans and implement activities for achieving those plans. Gillette effectively used the value *developing organizational talent* to help achieve the critical success factor of having enough management talent available to support the growth caused by the success of a new product.

In a recent annual report (General Electric, 1992), CEO John F. Welch clearly communicated his behavioral expectations for senior leaders relative to GE's values. He categorized managers into four groups:

1. Those who hit their numbers and lived by GE's values.
2. Those who did not hit their numbers but lived by the values.
3. Those who did not hit the numbers and did not live by the values.
4. Those who hit the numbers but did not live by the values.

The first group he deemed promotable. Welch would give people in the second group another chance. The combination of not hitting the numbers and not living the values was grounds for dismissal. The fourth group proved to be the most difficult, but Welch's communication was clear: GE no longer would allow continued employment of managers who hit the numbers but did not manage and live by the company's values. Welch's requirement that all senior leaders in the company operate, model, and live by its values is the strongest message we have seen of a CEO's support of a set of values.

DEFINING A HIGH-INVOLVEMENT STRATEGY

High involvement, or empowerment, is frequently chosen today as an organizational value. There are at least three reasons for this:

1. High involvement puts decision making lower in the organization, where decisions can be made more rapidly and, hopefully, more accurately.
2. Employees are increasingly seeking empowered positions in which they can make a difference and measure their own successes.
3. The job ownership that is associated with empowerment creates an energy that drives continuous improvement in a broad variety of areas.

Thus, high involvement is both a value that many organizations are seeking and a means for the achievement of other values. It can be a potent strategy for influencing employees to adopt the organization's new vision and values and change their behavior.

Whether high involvement is to be a value or a strategy, top management must be certain that their interpretation of the concept is understood throughout the organization. Often, this is difficult because top managers themselves disagree on the meaning of high involvement and how best to implement it. Thus, before launching such an organizational change effort, an important diagnostic step is to help senior management define what degree of involvement is desired and how fast the organization will achieve it.

What Is High Involvement?

High involvement means creating a sense of ownership of jobs or projects by providing clear performance expectations, methods of measuring success, control of resources, coaching, and decision-making responsibility and authority. A high-involvement strategy pushes responsibility and decision-making authority to lower levels—to those nearest the customer or product. Having the ability to make meaningful decisions about one's job, being asked for input on other job-related areas, and being treated as a meaningful, contributing adult lead to strong job commitment.

Byham (1993) has described empowerment as a source of energy that drives continuous improvement behavior in critical success areas, such as quality, productivity, customer service, or cycle time reduction. He hypothesized a relationship between the amount of authority and responsibility provided and the amount of energy created. He pictured involvement along a continuum (see Figure 8.1) with four key levels:

1. *No involvement*: Autocratic, dictatorial management.

2. *Low involvement (organizational identification)*: Organizations share operating information with all levels, seek ideas relative to new products or services, celebrate achievements organization-wide (not just by a few executives at the top), and encourage people to identify with the organization. This in turn creates energy to work hard and innovate. People who identify with the organization believe their personal success is tied to organizational success.

3. *Involvement (consultation/participation)*: In participative cultures, leaders actively seek employee input and employees feel a sense of involvement in all major decisions affecting them. Consultation produces job identification, which creates pride and concern. This translates into concern for quality, acceptance of new ideas, and so forth.

4. *High involvement/empowerment (responsibility and authority)*: Employees have decision-making responsibility. They can measure their outputs. Job success is their success.

Figure 8.1 shows these sources of energy as a dial to illustrate that they

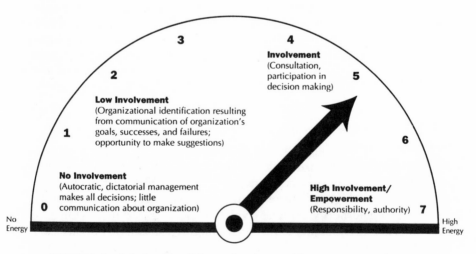

FIGURE 8.1. Relationship of degree involvement to empowerment energy.

are cumulative. That is, almost all organizations that reach a high level of involvement must provide considerable information about the successes and problems of the organization to build organizational identification, elicit participation where appropriate, and provide opportunities for empowerment. A dial is also an appropriate metaphor because effective leaders use all four levels at different times, depending on the situation and people involved.

Employee experimentation, innovation, and a commitment to continuously improve are what organizations need to effect organizational realignment, no matter what the focus of the realignment. Total quality and process reengineering efforts often are strategies to achieve critical success factors. Yet a survey of a large number of organizations involved in change processes found that success was related to simultaneous implementation of a high-involvement strategy (Lawler, Mohrman, & Ledford, 1992): "The implementation of quality practices appears to be very synergistic with the implementation of employee involvement.... Companies that integrate or coordinate the two initiatives experience considerably more positive changes than do those that run separate total quality and employee-involvement programs" (pp. 111–112).

A high-involvement/empowerment strategy often is associated with the use of teams in an organization. Natural work teams or cross-functional teams provide opportunities for decision-making authority and responsibility that are impossible to give individuals. Also, performance may be more easily measured at the team level than at the individual level, and without the ability to measure success no empowerment is possible. Further, teams can be given responsibility for their own self-governance in addition to job responsibilities. This greatly increases team members' sense of control over their own environment and their identification with and ownership of the outcome of the team.

Exploring High Involvement: Should We?

High involvement is not something to be taken lightly. It often involves eliminating layers of management, breaking up "organizational silos," changing reward and compensation systems, physically redesigning how work is accomplished, and committing to large expenditures on training.

We have found that in order to make meaningful investment decisions that commit time and money to the process, management needs considerable orientation. They must understand that high involvement is not an end in itself but a means to achieving critical success factors. That link must be clear to senior management, or they will not provide the long-term attention and support needed to make the strategy work. To decide whether to move an organization down the road to high involvement, top management must understand what empowerment is and its value to the organization.

Managers can be oriented appropriately through three activities:

1. *Reading about applications of high involvement.* Many books (e.g., Byham, 1990; Lawler, 1992) provide an overview of what high involvement is and present various methods of implementing it. Case histories are particularly useful because they communicate the continuing effort that must be made by the organization to achieve high levels of involvement. Managers must learn that high involvement is not something they just start and then forget; they must apply continual effort to make it stick in their organization.

2. *Visiting other organizations that are using high involvement successfully.* "Seeing is believing" is an old saying that still holds true. No books, videos, or other means can capture the impact of a visit to a high-involvement organization. There is an electricity in the air. Little energy is wasted. People are excited about their work and eager to share their accomplishments with visitors. Managers and employees work as a team and share both the positives and negatives they face.

3. *Attending a workshop on empowerment.* Even after reading and visiting, most leaders still need to meet with an expert on empowerment and discuss the various options open to the organization. These discussions can be done one-on-one or in a workshop.

We have found that a 1-day workshop for leaders is a cost-effective means of helping them make a decision about whether or not to move ahead with high involvement. Some of the questions discussed in the workshop are the following:

• *What is the meaning of high involvement/empowerment?* Many leaders find it difficult to differentiate empowerment from "good management" or personnel practices that have been popular over the years. There is often a feeling that empowerment is just the same old personnel concepts warmed over.

• *What specific, measurable impacts on the critical success factors can be expected from a high-involvement strategy?* Managers need to develop a realistic understanding of the measurable impacts of high involvement on the organization, in both the short term and the long term. It is fully appropriate to expect some substantial short-term benefits from high involvement because most organizations have "low-hanging fruit" that can be plucked fairly easily by a truly involved work force. However, the real benefits take longer, and the organization must be willing to stay the course to achieve major organizational change.

• *Will the organization's performance management system support a high-involvement strategy?* In addition to vision and values, employees will need a clear understanding of what they're responsible for, the goals they are attempting to achieve, and how success will be measured. Without this, individuals can't feel empowered.

• *Will teams be used?* If so, leaders must decide such issues as what types of teams will be formed, to what extent jobs will be redesigned, and how much reliance will be placed on cross-functional teams. Many executives mistakenly think of establishing teams as an end in itself as opposed to a means of creating empowerment.

• *Is the organization prepared to make the necessary training commitments?* A key to understanding the cost of implementing an empowerment strategy is an appreciation of the considerable training needs for both those who will be empowered and those who must become empowering.

• *How willing are senior leaders to communicate and share critical information about the company with associates on a regular basis?* They must be prepared to reveal results, successes, failures, problems, and future plans.

• *How does this strategy fit with other organizational design strategies, such as eliminating layers of management?*

• *How are senior leaders going to change their own behavior so that they will model the newly desired culture?*

• *How much pressure will they put on middle managers to change their practices?*

High-Involvement Strategy Workshop: How Far, How Fast?

Once an executive group decides to invest in a high-involvement strategy and defines an appropriate site for its first application, important decisions remain. Many of these are difficult and bring out misunderstandings about the nature of empowerment and the organization's commitment to it.

We have found that it takes 2 days of intensive discussion by top management to make these strategy decisions. In a workshop setting, participants complete eight questionnaires that force them to define the amount of empowerment appropriate for the target organization and to estimate the speed of movement toward full achievement of their new responsibilities. For example, to define the amount of job empowerment, a questionnaire presents a series of responsibility areas. Each participant defines whether the responsibility should remain with the supervisor, whether the supervisor should share responsibility by seeking inputs from subordinates, or whether it is appropriate to empower an individual or team to handle it. If the latter is chosen, the timing of the assumption of that responsibility is defined (now, in 6 months, in 12 months, or in 2 years).

The participants' decisions are posted on a large chart and discussed until a consensus is achieved on each area of responsibility. The result is a fleshing out of the organization's commitment to empowerment. What had been a rather abstract commitment now solidifies, as specifics of execution are defined.

We stress in the workshop that it is not appropriate for all organizations to be at extremely high levels of empowerment. Many effective organizations have chosen, for good reasons, not to be at high levels. These include almost all Japanese organizations operating in America, many of which are extremely effective in terms of quality, productivity, and customer service. Also, it must be understood that an organization can achieve high levels of empowerment in one part of the organization without having a total organizational commitment.

The importance of defining the desired level of empowerment cannot be overemphasized. If an organization has a vision of providing much more empowerment than it will actually deliver, systems will be set up to accomplish that vision. This means that the organization will hire individuals for jobs that don't exist and that people will understandably be upset and will probably leave. It means that the organization will be wasting money training people on things they won't be empowered to do and giving them skills they won't be empowered to use. It means sending mixed messages throughout the organization.

The output of the strategy workshop is a road map of the organization's plans for empowerment and its expectations on timing. This road map is vital for the guidance of committees charged with implementing empowerment. Planning should be based on a 3- to 5-year time frame, after which the organization may develop a new plan and move to higher levels of empowerment if appropriate.

ALIGNING ORGANIZATIONAL SYSTEMS

The third critical area to be diagnosed to determine readiness for culture change is alignment of organizational systems. The critical success factors, vision, and values (including empowerment) must be supported, reinforced, and measured to increase the likelihood that they will become reality. Organization systems that perform these functions fall within four primary domains: communications, accountability, skills, and rewards. Most of our examples of systems alignment will concern implementing high involvement, but the same domains are important for any culture change.

Communication Systems

Every event or action in an organization communicates something. When actions run parallel to what the leadership is saying, trust and credibility typically build. However, when actions and speech making are disconnected or incongruent, trust and credibility are weakened significantly. This simple formula is the basis for the cliché "walking the talk."

Communication systems are simple to understand but difficult to manage. In our experience, senior leaders almost always believe they do an excellent job of communicating to the organization. But we have yet to find an organization that has fully succeeded in getting its messages across to all employees.

Communications take many forms. They include formal and informal communications, meetings, rituals and symbols, and—the most powerful form—the behavior of leaders.

Formal Communications

Formal communications include official releases of information, which offer opportunities to diagnose organization culture and include the following:

• *Corporate pamphlets or brochures.* Most organizations have some pamphlet or brochure that describes their vision, total quality efforts, or some other major focus for the organization. Do these communication devices define the meaning of the vision and values in behavioral terms? Many we have seen are carefully worded, idealistic statements about how important quality or service or innovation is to the company, but few actually define each value so an associate can identify it and say, "So that's what I'm supposed to do to help make this value come alive." For example, many preach *customer service* as a critical value for the company, but few define the value with specific behavior, such as "confirming satisfaction with each customer in every interaction." Without examples of expected behaviors, most brochures or pamphlets proposing a new focus for the company are seen as merely another dream of the senior leaders.

• *Corporate newsletters, newspapers, and magazines.* Is the corporate newsletter or newspaper used to help articulate company direction, vision, and values? Most important, is it a continuous reminder of how employees are helping to achieve them? TRW's newsletter, for example, spotlights individuals and groups that "find a better way," thus recognizing those employees who support the company's continuous improvement value.

• *Corporate videos.* How well does the organization use videos to communicate and reinforce its vision and values? The Buick Motor Division regularly uses videos to communicate effectively its customer service vision and how the organization is progressing in making that vision come alive.

Often, formal communications are used as a precursor of values change (an advertising vehicle) rather than as reinforcement and encouragement for employees to change. This can actually hinder the change. Advertising a value change without actually implementing it can come across as just another program of the month. We witnessed this in one large Fortune 500 company, where the quality department eagerly told us about the Quality Day of the previous week. There were banners, pins, hats, shirts, speeches by senior management, and numerous other communication vehicles to try to gain individuals' enthusiasm for and commitment to the value *total quality*. The problem was in the message: People interpreted the communication vehicles as part of a gimmicky new program, not something that was going to change the way work was being done. When we asked people at different levels in the organization what they were going to do differently the next day at work, they answered, "Nothing." They had seen this before. They would wear the buttons, use the new coffee cups, wear their hats for a while, and this endeavor, just like previous "new" programs, would fade away.

Communication Channels

The channels for communication can be dissected also:

• How open are the communication channels in both directions, that is, from senior management down to frontline employees and, perhaps more important, from frontline employees up to senior management?

• How well do the communication channels work from corporate to field personnel? Because in most organizations field units are closer to the customer, we would look at how well market and competitive data get to corporate personnel on those factors (such as technological advances) that dramatically affect critical success factors.

• How effectively are communication channels and systems (e.g., voice mail, electronic mail, faxes) used to clarify priorities and directions and to reinforce positive behaviors in support of the new direction?

Meetings

The first thing we examine is whether senior leaders hold meetings with employees. If they do, we next determine what gets discussed and how much the senior leaders talk versus listen at these sessions. In the turnaround of Chrysler, CEO Lee Iacocca made extremely effective use of "town talks": He addressed all issues, listened to his employees, and rebuilt the trust of Chrysler associates and their commitment to a new direction. Eschewing top-down communication also has proved beneficial at GE, where groups of employees and managers meet to explore and discuss issues while senior managers listen.

Meetings are the stage on which corporate values are played out. They send important symbolic messages. The practitioner can check the communication of values in meetings by considering the following questions:

• *How is conflict dealt with?* Are diverse opinions actively sought, listened to, and discussed rationally, or are disagreements and conflicts stifled or avoided? If an organization values trust and teamwork, that value can be readily observed in meetings throughout the organization.

• *How open are senior managers to arguments about their policies or ideas?* Do people disagree with, even challenge, the power brokers in the group? If so, a clear message is sent that it's okay to disagree with senior leaders and that they really do value and want the involvement and input of others.

• *Are decisions acted upon?* A critical indicator of commitment to any issue is the follow-up that occurs after the meeting. If there is further action, the value and importance of the meeting is enhanced; if not, the senior leaders lose credibility and communicate a lack of commitment to decisions reached. More important, they show how little they value the time and ideas of others.

• *How are decisions reached?* Do senior leaders try to reach a consensus of all participants, which would show high levels of involvement, or do they simply try to coerce the group into their way of thinking? The latter is actually manipulation that destroys most positive values an organization may be trying to create.

• *How often are the vision and values and critical success factors discussed or addressed during corporate meetings?* A telling indicator of senior leaders' commitment to a new direction and culture is the number of times the organization's visions, values, and critical success factors are used as decision-making criteria in meetings. For example, the former CEO of AT&T Global Business Systems, Jerry Stead, had a meeting policy that emphasized customer needs and ways to improve customer satisfaction. If a meeting lasted more than 15 minutes without a discussion of customer issues, everyone was allowed to leave the meeting.

When Motorola started its total quality journey in the early 1980s, chairman Bob Galvin changed the order of topics at monthly executive meetings. Previously, the first 2 hours of every meeting had been spent reviewing financial results. Once the organizational focus switched to total quality, Galvin reordered the agenda; reviewing quality improvement results the first 2 hours and covering financial results last sent an important message throughout the organization regarding priorities.

Rituals and Symbols

Organizational rituals and symbols include subtle—and not so subtle—messages about the way things are done. They are strong communicators of what senior leaders truly mean and believe in. Many examples can illustrate the point. Who is called by first names and who is not? Who needs a medical excuse to visit a doctor during work hours? Who gets to eat in the executive dining room? Who gets an office? Who gets a metal desk and who gets a wooden desk? Who gets assigned parking? Who has country club memberships and gets to play golf during the workday? At what level do perks stop?

An organization must examine the messages sent by these symbols to determine if they are aligned with the vision and values that are being put into place. Often they are not.

Behavior of Leaders

The most powerful symbolic message in an organization is the behavior of leaders. This includes every aspect of the behavior of all leaders in an organization, from the CEO through management to supervisors and team leaders. This is the area of "walking the talk" that either establishes or destroys trust and credibility.

A diagnosis of an organization's ability to change its culture must start with the behavior of its executives. Do they live the values? Are they too focused on the bottom line to make decisions to increase customer satisfaction and loyalty? Do they act as a team with other executives, or is teamwork something they expect only from lower levels? Do they involve employees in making and implementing decisions, or do they think decision making is their prerogative?

Leaders must recognize how the vision and values come alive in the organization and reinforce the process. For example, at Milliken & Company, a Malcolm Baldridge National Quality Award winner, CEO Roger Milliken always began visits to field sites with the same question: "What have you done lately to improve quality?" People at all levels of the organization heard the message and quickly began finding answers by taking actions that they thought would satisfy the CEO. The message he was sending was clear, consistent, and understood by all.

The behavior of an organization's leaders communicates most powerfully which values they truly hold for themselves and others. If those behaviors are communicating a message different from the organization's formal communications, the credibility of the leaders diminishes quickly. Alignment with a high-involvement culture, for example, requires eight key leader behaviors:

1. Maintaining or enhancing the employees' self-esteem.
2. Listening and responding with empathy to employees' issues and concerns.

3. Asking for help and encouraging involvement when resolving organizational issues.
4. Offering help without removing responsibility for action.
5. Sharing information with lower levels in the organization.
6. Acting as a coach, facilitator, and encourager, rather than as a controller or director.
7. Providing situational controls according to the task delegated and the person being empowered.
8. Establishing clear goals and objectives so employees can monitor their own performance.

Only by demonstrating these eight critical behaviors can senior leaders show they are genuinely committed to high involvement. Their example inspires leaders throughout the organization to likewise provide an environment in which employees feel a sense of ownership of their jobs and a higher level of commitment to the organization.

There are numerous ways to determine if leaders are "walking the talk" of high involvement. Probably the most effective is to ask associates, either through focus groups or questionnaires, to rate their managers in each of these behaviors. Often an effective tool is some form of 360-degree feedback instrument, where leaders are evaluated by subordinates, supervisors, and peers.

Informal Communications

Finally, there is the informal communication process. Commonly called the grapevine or rumor mill, it is extremely active in organizations in which any or all of the other methods break down or are nonexistent. Something always fills the void created by insufficient communication in an organization—usually inaccurate or inappropriate information.

Authority and Accountability Systems

If an organization wants to change, it must clarify the roles, responsibilities, and expectations of all associates. Authority and accountability must be aligned with the organization's vision and values.

Roles and Responsibilities

We look at three areas to determine alignment of roles and responsibilities:
1. *Job design.* For empowerment to occur, meaningful authority and accountability must be built into jobs. Do job responsibilities include broad-based, decision-making authority with clear roles, or are jobs designed to meet the needs of senior leaders? Examining job design requires

looking at the responsibilities of particular jobs from both a technical and behavioral point of view. For example, an organization that has restructured into teams might determine that responsibility for purchasing supplies will shift from the purchasing department to a member of each team. The function of the purchasing manager's job obviously has changed from one of actually handling purchases to one of coaching those who now have that responsibility.

2. *Organizational structures.* Just as job design can affect empowerment and involvement, so too can the broader organizational structure. How hierarchical and traditional is the structure compared to one designed to maximize organizational flexibility and responsiveness to customers? Traditional bureaucratic hierarchies often are not flexible enough to adapt to industry changes and cannot reduce cycle time or improve processes to remain competitive. The problem is that no one feels accountable. Decisions can always be pushed up the organization. Is management willing to eliminate organizational silos and focus on horizontal processes directed toward customer satisfaction or some other critical success factor?

3. *Teams.* How much does the organization use teams of all types—functional and cross-functional—to achieve empowerment and continuous improvement? Do they have clear key result areas, measurement methods, and goals? Many organizations are finding that self-directed teams provide a tremendous boost to the transformation of an organization and directly address critical success factors. (For a more detailed examination of teams, see Chapter 10, this volume; Fisher, 1993; and Wellins, Byham, & Wilson, 1991.)

Performance Management System

Many organizations use their performance management system primarily to determine compensation. A more effective approach is to make it a system of accountability and a driver of organizational change. The performance management (not appraisal) system acts like a funnel that takes macro goals (business strategy) down to individual jobs and behaviors. The diagnostician must determine if the system focuses on the achievements that address critical business issues or if it exists simply to make compensation decisions easier for senior management. Even worse, does the system exist because someone at an upper level thinks there should be a system?

Senior leaders at one Midwest retailer complained, for example, that a strategy to shift the organization's merchandising efforts was not working. Our investigation revealed that the macro goal had never been translated into new purchasing goals, promotional campaigns, or shelving ideas. Breaking down the strategic initiative into specific activities and objectives for the units corrected the problem and helped the organization realize its strategy (Rogers & Ferketish, 1992).

Similarly, a European chemical firm implemented a total quality management program that included a massive corporate advertising campaign around the firm's quality initiatives. Yet when we examined the performance management system, we found that no quality initiatives had been translated into goals or objectives for senior leaders. And, as expected, the goals and objectives never were communicated to the rest of the organization. Therefore employees' activities, which would support the quality initiatives, never came about.

The key diagnostic question is, "Does the performance management system link individuals to the strategic business plan?" Strategic initiatives must be broken down into clearly defined accountabilities and responsibilities and then integrated into the performance objectives of all associates who are responsible for turning them into actions. For lasting change to occur, employees at every level of the organization need to know what they are responsible for (key result areas), how success will be measured, and what is expected (goal). They also need feedback on their progress toward their goals, help where appropriate, and reinforcement when goals are met.

A performance management system should clarify expectations and provide feedback on both quantifiable objectives (the *whats*) and behavioral objectives (the *hows*). These objectives must align with the strategic initiatives, critical business issues, and the organization's values. For example, Table 8.1 shows how the need to get products to market fast (sense of urgency) can be translated into key result areas and quantifiable objectives (the *whats*).

TABLE 8.1. How Values Translate into Objectives

Value	Key result areas	Objectives
	Speed of product development	Product A will be available for by April 1
		Product B will be approved by the development team by January 20
Sense of urgency		Product development will reduce the current average time to market (68 weeks) by 12 weeks before the end of the year.
	Staffing	All open positions will be filled within 2 months by contract resources or full-time hires.

The *how* objectives, although more difficult to measure, are equally as important as the *whats*. Just as employees need to be held accountable for achieving quantifiable objectives, they likewise need to be held accountable for living and exhibiting behaviors that are consistent with the organization's values. Table 8.2 illustrates how the values of customer service and teamwork can be translated into behavioral expectations.

We also look for the responsibility and ownership employees have for the operation of the performance management system itself. Employees need to be actively involved in generating and setting objectives and expectations, tracking performance by using available resources, soliciting feedback and assistance, participating in the review process, and planning developmental activities. If the process is top-down only, with management in complete control, we typically observe a system that's not working. Without employee involvement and commitment, the performance management system will revert to simply a paper process that drives merit pay increases.

Measuring and Communicating Business Performance

Employees in a high-involvement organization need information about the performance of the business as well as about their own contribution to it. There must be systems to collect the appropriate information and to disseminate it to associates. There are several important diagnostic issues here, identified by the following questions:

TABLE 8.2. How Values Translate into Behavioral Expectations

Value	Behavioral expectations	Tracking method
Customer service	In all interactions with customers, employees will use the confirming satisfaction behavior.	Supervisor monitoring Team feedback sessions
	For customer complaints, employees will accept responsibility for resolving complaint and getting back to the customer in a short period of time.	Customer complaint tracking Self-report
Teamwork	In conflicts, issues will be addressed directly and immediately before they escalate to supervisor.	Supervisor monitoring Project reports
	Team members' expectations will be obtained at team formation stage.	Team feedback sessions

• How often and how clearly is financial information on the company's results provided to all employees in the organization? Is it clear how employees contribute to bottom-line results so that everyone can feel a sense of involvement in the outcomes?

• Does the measurement system include a comparison level or benchmark to the best in the industry?

• Are the critical success factors measured in depth? For example, customer retention may be a critical success factor, yet many organizations we've seen haven't clearly defined what a retained customer is in terms of revenue or longevity.

• Are customer satisfaction data and customer results easily accessible to *all* employees? We have seen few, if any, effective total quality efforts that don't provide continuous and comprehensive data on customers to employees who interact with them. In addition, many other employees need customer data as they make decisions on products, processes, and even people.

• Does the measurement system include internal as well as external customer satisfaction? If so, the partnership chain to the external customer is dramatically strengthened. Although some of these measurements may be hard to quantify, they are better than no measurement at all.

• Are the organizational measurement systems easy to use and easy to understand?

• Are there too many measures that add only confusion and lack of focus? Many statistical process control advocates can overdo the necessity for measurement systems. Florida Power and Light, after winning the Deming Award, dismantled a large portion of their measurement system because of the bureaucracy it had created.

Skills Development and Selection Systems

In any cultural transformation, people will be asked to take on new responsibilities and demonstrate new behaviors. Systems for training, career planning, and employee selection must all be consistent with the new vision and values.

Training Systems

Without proper training, many people are going to be set up for failure. Nothing is more frustrating than being excited about an opportunity to grow and experience new challenges and then failing because of a lack of competency and coaching.

Training performs two critical functions for an organization: It develops skills so people can perform better in the newly created culture, and it communicates clear expectations of how people are to behave in the future. Therefore, alignment with the vision and values as well as the critical success factors is an important consideration as we diagnose an organization's training system. In particular, we ask the following questions:

• *Is training linked strategically to the organizational change effort?* For example, if *long-term relationships with clients* is a critical success factor, then teaching salespeople manipulative trial-closing techniques is counterfunctional. If building customer rapport is critical to customer satisfaction but no training is offered in rapport-building skills, the organization is missing an opportunity to reinforce a value.

• *Do the senior leaders view training as an expense or an investment?* Too often senior leaders require proof that training affects the bottom line. Many organizations who see training as an investment, such as Federal Express, Corning, Xerox, and Texas Instruments annually allocate specific amounts of resources and time (such as 3 to 5% of salaries or 40 hours) for training.

• *Are managers and others in the organization reinforced for developing organizational talent, and are employees reinforced for developing their own talent?*

• *Do they have the necessary skills to diagnose needs and select developmental opportunities?*

• *Are training assignments based on individual and unit training needs assessments?* If organizations are to spend 3 to 5% of payroll on training, they should make sure the training is needed and targeted to the appropriate areas. This can be accomplished with interviews, focus group discussions, and critical incident methodology. The assessment center method offers an especially comprehensive way to determine strengths and areas in need of development across levels in the organization.

Five training areas are critical for organizations participating in a cultural change, especially one that is grounded in high involvement:

1. *Business knowledge.* Measuring and communicating information on the organization's strategies, market position, competition, profit margins, or other factors will not be worthwhile if employees don't understand how the organization works and what makes it successful. Typically, organizations making a cultural change share more information than in the past about both customer needs and complaints and their competitors' activities and major strengths and weaknesses, and employees at all levels must be able to comprehend and use this information. Business knowledge gives associates a better understanding of how their specific responsibilities fit into the organization, how their jobs are related to the larger goals of the organization, why improvement is needed, and how the new shared values will drive the change. Business knowledge can be conveyed through several different mechanisms, including awareness sessions, training programs, or regular communication channels. It is most powerful as an ongoing process, not a special event at the start of a change process.

2. *Technical skills*. These skills enable employees to perform the basic tasks of their jobs, such as assembling parts, using a computer, or cooking a hamburger. When employees are asked to take on new responsibilities, additional needed skills must be defined and additional training provided. For example, when becoming members of a self-managed team, production employees usually need to perform all the functions of the team (multiskilling) and may need management skills such as scheduling or budgeting. Engineers concerned about profit margins may require skills in price calculations. Salespeople may require skills in writing contracts. Developing technical skills also builds employees' confidence and emphasizes the importance of their new roles.

3. *Interactive skills*. This is a training area that many organizations overlook during a transformation. These skills enable interactions to occur in such a way that the values are supported, whether the interaction is one-to-one or in groups and whether it is with peers, subordinates, superiors, customers, or suppliers. Interactive skills provide a direct link for turning new values into behaviors. They are particularly critical when an organization is trying to create a high-involvement culture because of the need for frequent meetings around processes. As involvement with others to get a job done increases, so does the need for interactive skills.

4. *Continuous improvement skills*. These skills enable employees to look at their inputs, job processes, and outputs and systematically analyze ways to improve them. The steps of continuous improvement usually include assessing the situation, looking for causes, targeting ideas and solutions, implementing actions, and making the actions ongoing. The skills also include using tools such as cause-and-effect diagrams, run charts, and solution-impact diagrams.

5. *Leadership skills*. As organizations move to high involvement, the need increases for leaders at all levels to develop appropriate leadership behaviors. In their new roles as coaches, encouragers, facilitators, and reinforcers, leaders need higher skill levels in all these areas as well as in delegation and gathering information. Seeking, not telling, is the cornerstone of empowerment. This behavior clearly communicates that leaders understand their new role as coach rather than director.

The role of leader no longer belongs to just those people in traditional management positions. As employees become members of task forces, cross-functional teams, or self-managed teams, the need for skills in leading meetings, reaching consensus, resolving conflict, and gaining commitment for ideas falls on everyone. For example, organizations that operate with cross-functional, process action, or self-managed teams often train all team members in leadership skills. If shared leadership responsibility is the goal, then everyone needs the skills.

In addition to diagnosing an organization's needs relative to each training area, the practitioner must determine the organization's readiness and commitment to increasing the quality and quantity of training. The following questions help diagnose the strength of the skills thrust in an organization:

• *Does the organization offer training in each of the five critical areas?* Meeting with training directors or reviewing curriculum catalogs tells us at least whether the subjects are covered.

• *Do training programs give participants maximum practice opportunities to build competence and confidence in their skills?* Unfortunately, many organizations perceive skill development simply as awareness building. Consequently, they do not concentrate on developing employees' confidence in performing the new skill. This is comparable to watching a training videotape on skiing or golfing and expecting to perform well. Watching a tape might create an awareness of the behaviors or actions needed, but the viewer won't develop skills or confidence. The best way to develop the skills is to take lessons—hands-on experience—from someone who plays the game.

• *Do managers get involved in the training?* Can they model, coach, and reinforce newly taught skills?

• *Are there mechanisms on the job for the newly trained employee to use the new skills and get periodic feedback and reinforcement?* These might be special assignments, job rotation, task force membership, or other special on-the-job activities.

Career Planning System

Career planning, too, a sister system to training, can have a substantial impact on an organization's culture. Here we look for how the organization balances organizational needs with the individual career ambitions of its people. This is a much harder task today given the amount of downsizing and flattening that organizations have gone through in the last few years.

We examine three key aspects of a career development or planning system by asking the following questions:

1. Does the organization have specified career tracks that allow individuals who are viable candidates to advance within an appropriate time frame?
2. Are "learning paths" in place to assure continuing learning in a flat organization? Can people move laterally to improve their skills and knowledge?
3. Is the system perfunctory, or do managers spend time honestly and openly helping associates map out realistic learning and career paths?

Selection Systems

Selection systems need to identify people whose behavior on the job will demonstrate the desired values. It is simply a huge waste of time and effort to build a high-involvement culture and then let anyone into it. Finding the right people can take much of the risk out of a culture change effort.

In reviewing an organization's selection system we ask the following questions:

• *Has the core set of skills and motivations needed to fit into the new culture been identified?* For example, a high-involvement, continuous improvement culture will require vastly different skills and motivations than a typical controlled, hierarchical bureaucracy.

• *Do the criteria for selection go beyond experience, education, and work history to get at key behaviors and motivations that are aligned with the new culture?*

• *Are various methods used to collect comprehensive data on applicants?* Interviews and application forms are fine, but if we want to assess behaviors, the best techniques require an actual demonstration of them. Simulations, for example, allow applicants to show their skills at needed levels.

• *Does the selection system examine both motivation for the targeted job and fit with the organization's culture?* For example, does the applicant best fit a culture that is involving/empowering versus hierarchical, flexible versus static, constantly changing versus stable?

Reward Systems

Reward systems, such as compensation, promotions, and recognition, play a critical role in helping organizations modify their culture. As with other systems, rewards should help shape or drive behavior in the desired direction.

Promotion System

Very few, if any, executive decisions communicate more about values and beliefs than promotion decisions. A promotion announcement sends a strong message about what management *really* sees as important. It either reinforces the values espoused by senior leaders or illustrates for all the hypocrisy of the leaders.

It's important to discover how senior leaders make promotional decisions and how much the decisions are linked to organizational values and future needs. Certainly, performance results of candidates should be a major factor in promotion decisions, but results alone never tell the complete story. Senior leaders can't ignore the *how* part of the performance equation, which shows if a candidate is fundamentally in line with the vision and values for the future.

Recognition System

Many organizations going through change or anticipating the need to change their cultures do not have the luxury of being able to offer promotions, or even enhanced compensation, as rewards. Consequently, an organization's use of appropriate recognition opportunities can be a viable reinforcement system and can also send a message relative to vision and values. Unfortunately, we have found that few organizations use opportunities effectively.

To diagnose recognition practices, we pose the following questions:

- Do senior leaders see recognition and reinforcement of positive behaviors as one of their key roles?
- Is time allocated for recognition events or even for senior leaders to show their appreciation for individual efforts in support of the desired direction?
- Do recognition events take into consideration the motivations of individuals or teams, or are they the same for all?
- Is the recognition provided specific and timely?

Compensation System

Compensation is often a difficult system to align with a new organizational direction and focus. In examining this system in organizations, we seek responses to the following questions:

- If an organization is attempting a cultural transformation, how does the compensation system for senior leaders reinforce short-term thinking versus a long-term view of success?
- How well does the compensation system involve all employees by sharing the benefits or gains realized by the change? If frontline employees don't see the benefit of their commitment to the transformation, change will be hard to maintain.
- Are outputs other than profits and revenues incorporated into compensation systems? Compensation can be used equally as well as or even better than other systems to reinforce quality, service, customer retention, development of people, teamwork, reduced turnover, and so forth.
- If total quality and self-directed teams are in place, have the compensation systems been modified to reinforce key behaviors that contribute to team success?

SUMMARY

Culture realignment is necessary for many organizations if they are to remain competitive. This requires changing the everyday behavior of employees. Yet because people prefer to do things in ways that have become comfortable, they tend to resist behavior change. They need strong reasons to change, which are readily provided by a high-involvement strategy. Critical success factors, vision, and values focus in a common direction the employee energy created by high involvement. This concentration of energy is vital to organizational success. But the effectiveness of efforts to create high involvement and to gain acceptance of an organization's vision and values is strongly affected by the alignment, or lack of alignment, of various organizational systems.

Organizations considering culture change or transformation can begin by diagnosing three areas: focus, employee involvement, and systems alignment. The results of such a diagnosis will determine where they need to begin and where lie the largest gaps that need to be closed.

REFERENCES

Byham, W. C. (1990). *Zapp! The lightning of empowerment*. New York: Harmony Books.

Byham, W. C. (1993). *A guide to implementation of a high-involvement (empowerment) strategy* (Monograph No. 19). Pittsburgh: Development Dimensions International.

Fisher, K. (1993). *Leading self-directed work teams: A guide to developing new team leadership skills*. New York: McGraw-Hill.

General Electric Company. (1992). *1991 annual report*. Fairfield, CT: Author.

Lawler, E. E. III. (1992). *The ultimate advantage: Creating the high-involvement organization*. San Francisco: Jossey-Bass.

Lawler, E. E. III, Mohrman, S., & Ledford, G. E. Jr. (1992). *Employee involvement and total quality management: Practices and results in Fortune 1000 companies*. San Francisco: Jossey-Bass.

Rogers, R. W., & Ferketish, B. J. (1992). *Creating a high-involvement culture through a value-driven change process* (Monograph No. 18). Pittsburgh: Development Dimensions International.

Wellins, R. S., Byham, W. C., & Wilson, J. M. (1991). *Empowered teams: Creating self-directed work groups that improve quality, productivity, and participation*. San Francisco: Jossey-Bass.

CHAPTER 9

Effective Reward Systems: Strategy, Diagnosis, and Design

EDWARD E. LAWLER III

Reward systems are a critical part of any organization's design. Their fit with other systems impacts the organization's effectiveness and the employees' quality of life. In line with important changes over the past decade in the way organizations are designed and managed, new reward systems are surfacing. How to diagnose the functioning of current reward systems and design more compatible ones is thus an emerging challenge for human resources practice (Lawler, 1990; Schuster & Zingheim, 1992).

This chapter begins by considering the role of rewards in an organization. It then describes the diagnostic steps in evaluating reward systems and critical design factors. Finally, it focuses on the fit between reward systems and the high-involvement management approaches that are becoming increasingly popular. Although the chapter focuses on financial reward systems, much of what is discussed is relevant to other rewards, such as recognition and promotion.

REWARD SYSTEMS AND BUSINESS STRATEGY

The overriding principle guiding this discussion is that to be effective, organizations must have congruence among their various operating systems. Systems are neither good nor bad in the abstract. They must be evaluated in the context of the organization's other systems and its business strategy.

An organization's business strategy indicates what it is supposed to

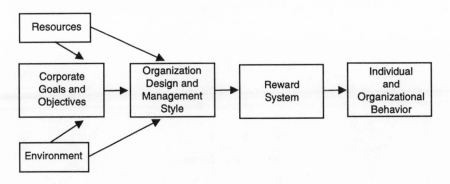

FIGURE 9.1. Role of reward system.

accomplish and how it is supposed to behave. It specifies the kinds of performance and performance levels the organization must demonstrate to be effective. Thus, it is a critical guide for the design of its structure as well as its systems, such as those concerned with information, human resource management, and, of course, rewards.

Figure 9.1 depicts one way of thinking about the reward system in an organization. It shows that its design should be driven by the basic organization design and the management style of the organization, which in turn should be strongly influenced by the organization's strategy. The reward system in combination with the organization's design drives the performance of the organization because it influences critical individual and organizational behaviors.

Figure 9.2 makes essentially the same point as Figure 9.1, except with a slightly different flow. It depicts the design process an organization should use in creating a reward system and in testing its effectiveness. Business strategy should be the foundation for identifying the critical behaviors that the organization needs to demonstrate. This, in turn, drives the design of the reward system. The challenge is to correctly identify those features of a reward system that will produce the individual and organizational behavior needed to make the strategy come alive. Three critical elements of reward systems are identified in Figure 9.2. The first is the core principles or values about reward systems that the organization holds. These may be stated or simply be implicit in the way the organization operates. Core principles are the fundamental, relatively long-term commitments that organizations make about reward systems, such as a belief in pay for performance and a belief in secrecy about pay.

The reward system is composed of process and structural features. Process features include such things as communication policies and decision-making practices. These are critical. Not only do they reflect the over-

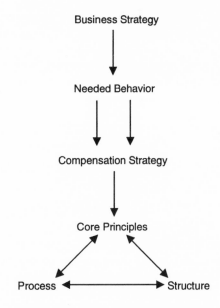

FIGURE 9.2.   Reward system design model.

all management style of the organization, but they influence how well reward system practices will be accepted and understood and how much
commitment they will engender. Finally, reward systems include actual
practices and structures. These are the features of reward systems that get
the most attention. They include pay delivery systems, such as gain-sharing plans and profit-sharing plans, as well as administrative policies and a
host of other specific organizational programs.

Reward systems are assumed to be effective to the degree that the
core principles, processes, and structures are in alignment. This is depicted in Figure 9.2 by the arrows among the three elements. The fit here is
critical, because organizations need to be consistent in what they say and
what they do. Violations of this consistency inevitability lead to misunder-
standing about how the reward system works and failure to motivate the
proper or needed behavior.

DIAGNOSING ORGANIZATIONAL REWARD SYSTEMS

The organizational diagnosis must take into account how reward systems
in general, and pay systems in particular, can actually affect individual
and organizational behavior. There are five key diagnostic questions that
must be answered:

1. What are the objectives of the reward system?
2. How does the reward system fit with other operating systems?
3. How does the current reward system operate? What are its practices and structures, and what processes are in effect?
4. What is the impact of the reward policies and practices?
5. How does the actual impact of the reward system compare with the desired impact?

The following discussion reviews the basic design dimensions of reward systems that are related to each of these questions.

What Are the Objectives of the Reward System?

Within limits, it is true that if an organization can specify what it wants a reward system to do, an appropriate reward system can be designed. The problem in many organizational diagnosis and design situations is that management cannot specify the behaviors that it wants the reward system to produce. There are a variety of reasons for this, ranging from an unclear organizational strategy to a failure to understand the potential array of organization design elements that can influence behavior.

Good reward system design consultants often spend as much or more time clarifying the intent of the reward system as they do working with the organization to design it. This identification must go beyond such simple responses as "to attract and retain the best employees" or "to motivate effective performance." The strategy should identify the kind of people to be attracted and retained, how long they need to be retained, what kind of skills the people should have, and so forth. Similarly, it needs to be clear about what kind of performance is to be motivated and how much emphasis is to be placed on group and team performance. Attention also needs to be given to the issue of organizational structure and the desired degree of integration and differentiation.

In questioning an organization's management about their objectives for a reward system, the diagnostician must keep in mind what outcomes can reasonably be expected. The research on reward systems suggests that potentially they can influence six factors that in turn impact organization effectiveness.

Attraction and Retention

Research on job choice, career choice, and turnover clearly shows that the kind and level of rewards an organization offers influence who is attracted to work for it and who will continue to work for it (see Lawler, 1973; Mobley, 1982). Generally, organizations that give the most rewards tend to attract and retain the most people (Gerhart & Milkovich, 1992). This seems to occur because high reward levels lead to high satisfaction, which in turn leads to lower turnover. Individuals who are presently satisfied with their jobs expect continued satisfaction and, as a result, want to stay with the same organization.

The objective of a reward system should be the retention of the most valuable employees. To accomplish this, rewards must be distributed such that the more valuable employees feel satisfied when comparing their rewards with those that they can receive in other organizations. The emphasis here is on external comparisons because turnover means leaving an organization for a better situation elsewhere.

One method is to reward everyone at a level above that in other organizations. This strategy has two drawbacks: For some rewards, such as money, it is very costly; in addition, it can cause feelings of intraorganizational inequity inasmuch as the better performers are likely to feel unfairly treated when their rewards are comparable to those of poor performers in their organization, even though external comparisons are favorable (Lawler & Jenkins, 1992). Faced with this situation, the better performers may not quit, but they are likely to be dissatisfied and to complain, look for internal transfers, and mistrust the organization.

What, then, is the best solution? For most organizations the answer lies in having competitive reward levels and basing rewards on performance. This should serve both to encourage the satisfaction and retention of the better performers and to attract achievement-oriented individuals, who prefer environments where their performance is rewarded. But the better performers must receive not just more rewards but *significantly* more rewards, because they feel they deserve more (Adams, 1965). Slight differences in rewards may do little more than make the better and poorer performers equally dissatisfied.

Reward systems are one of the several ways to influence absenteeism. Research has shown that absenteeism and satisfaction are related, although the relationship is not as strong as the one between satisfaction and turnover (Mobley, 1982). When the workplace is pleasant and satisfying, individuals come to work regularly; when it isn't, they don't. Thus, one way to reduce absenteeism is to administer pay in ways that maximize satisfaction.

Absenteeism can also be reduced by tying pay bonuses and other rewards to attendance (Lawler, 1981, 1990). This is easier to do than tying rewards to performance because attendance is more measurable. This approach is costly, but sometimes less costly than absenteeism. It is a particularly useful strategy when both the work content and working conditions are poor and do not lend themselves to meaningful improvements that deal with absenteeism directly.

Motivation of Performance

When certain specifiable conditions exist, reward systems have been demonstrated to motivate performance (Gerhart & Milkovich, 1992; Lawler, 1971, 1990; Vroom 1964). People are inherently neither motivated nor unmotivated to perform effectively; performance motivation depends on the situation, how it is perceived, and individual needs. The approach that can best help us understand what motivates performance is called expectancy theory (Vroom, 1964; Lawler, 1973). Three concepts serve as the key building blocks of the theory.

1. *Performance–outcome expectancy.* Every behavior has associated with it, in an individual's mind, certain outcomes (rewards or punishments). In other words, individuals believe or expect that if they behave in a certain way, they will get certain things. For example, individuals may expect that if they produce 10 units, they will receive their normal hourly rate, whereas if they produce 15 units, they will receive their hourly pay rate plus a bonus. Each performance level can be seen as leading to a number of different kinds of outcomes.

2. *Attractiveness.* Each outcome has an attractiveness to the individual. This attractiveness varies for different individuals because it results from the needs and perceptions derived from other factors in an individual's life. For example, some individuals may value an opportunity for promotion or advancement because of their needs for achievement or power whereas others may not want to be promoted and leave their current work group because of a need for affiliation with others. Similarly, recognition, such as a picture in the company newspaper, may have great value to some but little for others.

3. *Effort–performance expectancy.* Also associated with each behavior is a certain expectancy or probability of success. This expectancy represents the individual's perception of how hard it will be to achieve such behavior. For example, employees may have a strong expectancy (e.g., a 90% chance) that if they put forth the effort they can produce 10 units an hour but only a weak expectancy (e.g., a 25% chance) of producing 15 units an hour.

Putting these concepts together, the motivation to behave in a certain way is greatest when an individual

- Believes that the behavior will lead to certain outcomes (performance–outcome expectancy).
- Feels that these outcomes are attractive.
- Believes that performance at a desired level is possible (effort–performance expectancy).

Given a number of alternative levels of behavior (e.g., 10, 15, or 20 units of production per hour), an individual will choose the level of performance that has the greatest motivational force from a combination of the relevant expectancies, outcomes, and values.

On the basis of these concepts, it is possible to construct a general model of behavior in organizational settings (see Figure 9.3). Working from left to right in the model, motivation is seen as the force on an individual to expend effort. Performance results from a combination of the effort put forth and the level of ability. Ability, in turn, reflects the individual's skills, training, information, and talents. As a result of performance, the individual attains certain outcomes. The model indicates this relationship by a dotted line, reflecting the fact that sometimes people perform but do not get outcomes. The process of rewarding performance influences an individual's perceptions (particularly the line of sight to rewards) and thus inspires motivation in the future. This is shown in the model by the line connecting the performance–outcome arrow with motivation.

In many ways, the expectancy model is a deceptively simple statement of the conditions that must exist if rewards are to motivate performance. It suggests that all an organization has to do is actually relate pay and other frequently valued rewards to obtainable levels of performance. This is insufficient and very difficult to accomplish.

For employees to believe that pay is performance-based, the organization must make a visible connection between performance and rewards and establish a climate of trust and credibility. The reason why visibility is necessary should be obvious; the importance of trust may be less so. The belief that performance will lead to rewards is essentially a prediction about the future. For individuals to make this kind of prediction they have

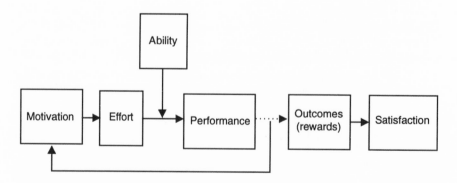

FIGURE 9.3. The expectancy theory model. A person's motivation is a function of (1) effort-to-performance expectancies, (2) performance-to-outcome expectancies, and (3) perceived attractiveness of outcomes.

to trust the system that is promising them the rewards. As discussed later, a high level of openness and the use of participation can contribute to trust in the pay system.

Skills and Knowledge

Reward systems can motivate not only performance but also learning and development. The same motivational principles apply. Individuals are motivated to learn those skills that are rewarded. Skill-based pay, discussed later, has been developed to capitalize on just this point. It allows an organization to target strategically what it wants employees to learn. Many job-based reward systems do this indirectly by tying increased pay and perquisites to obtaining higher-level jobs, thereby motivating individuals to learn managerial skills.

Culture

Depending upon how they are developed, administered, and managed, reward systems can cause the culture of an organization to vary widely. For example, they can influence the degree to which the culture is seen as entrepreneurial, innovative, competence based, fair, and participative. Reward systems have the ability to shape culture precisely because of their important influence on communication, motivation, satisfaction, and membership. The behaviors they cause to occur become the dominant patterns of behavior in the organization and lead to perceptions and beliefs about what an organization stands for, believes in, and values.

Perhaps the most obvious link between pay system practice and culture concerns performance-based pay. The absence or presence of this policy can have a dramatic impact on the culture of an organization because it so clearly communicates the organization's norms about performance. Many other features of reward systems also influence culture. For example, having relatively high pay levels can produce a culture in which people feel they are an elite group working for a top-flight company. Having employees participate in pay decisions can produce a participative culture in which employees are generally involved in business decisions and as a result are committed to the organization and its success.

Reinforcement and Definition of Structure

The reward system of an organization can reinforce and define the organization's structure (Lawler, 1990). Often, this is not fully considered in the design of reward systems, with the result that their impact on structure is unintentional. This does not mean, however, that the effect is usually minimal. The reward system can have a strong impact on how integrated and how differentiated the organization is (Lawrence & Lorsch, 1967). When people are rewarded the same way, it tends to unite them; when they are treated differently it can divide them.

In addition, the reward system can help define the status hierarchy, and it can strongly influence the kind of decision structure that exists. As will be discussed later, the key features here are the degree to which the reward system is hierarchical and the degree to which it allocates rewards on the basis of movements up the hierarchy.

Cost

Reward systems are often a significant cost factor. Indeed, pay alone may represent over 50% of an organization's operating costs. There are two strategic diagnostic questions concerning reward system cost objectives. How high should these costs be? How will they vary as a function of the organization's ability to pay? A reasonable outcome of a well-designed pay system might be, for example, an increase in costs when the organization has the money to spend and a decrease in costs when the organization does not have the money. An additional objective might be to have lower overall reward system costs than do business competitors.

How Does the Reward System Fit with Other Operating Systems?

Developing a reasonable outcome model for a reward system is complicated by the fact that other systems in the organization may influence the same behaviors. The practitioner must ask which individual and organizational behaviors are going to be primarily driven by the reward system and which are going to be driven by other factors, such as organization structure, work design, or information systems. Multiple systems driving the same behavior promote consistency. Alternatively, the reward system may balance the effects of other systems, providing the organization with a needed mixture of behaviors.

A good example of balance is between individual and organizational performance. Management may want individuals to focus on increasing their own performance regardless of the impact on others but to demonstrate cooperative behavior at critical times. In this situation, the reward system may acknowledge both individual and organizational performance or it may emphasize only one of these while work design or another feature is focused on the other goal. For example, if teams are created and their performance can be measured, this should lead individuals to emphasize team performance (Lawler & Cohen, 1992). But if the right mix of organizational behavior requires individual excellence, at least some of the reward system should recognize outstanding individual performance; the reward system will then end up contributing to a carefully designed balance between motivating team behavior and individual behavior.

How Is the Current Reward System Structured?

Once the decision has been made about the behaviors that the reward system is supposed to support and how it fits with the other operating systems in the organization, it is possible to assess the current reward system. Diagnosing how the reward system actually operates is basically a matter of reviewing organizational policies, practices, statements, and records to see not only what the organization indicates its reward systems are but how they operate in practice.

Often, there is a great difference between what the organization says it does and how it operates. For example, organizations often claim that they pay for performance but an analysis of raises frequently shows that they are not related to performance (Heneman, 1992). Similarly, organizations often indicate that they appraise performance on a regular basis but a check of the records shows that there are no written performance appraisals in the files of individual employees or that they are poorly and incompletely done. Perhaps the hardest feature of doing a diagnosis concerns identifying how well an organization executes its programs. To continue with the example of performance appraisals, there are really two issues here: first, whether appraisals get done and, second, whether they are done in a way that is effective in producing the behavior that the organization desires.

A useful dichotomy in thinking about options in the design of reward systems is the process/content one. As was mentioned earlier, the structural or content dimension of a reward system refers to the formal mechanisms, procedures, and practices (e.g., the salary structure, the performance appraisal forms), in short, the nuts and bolts of the system. Presented in the following pages are a number of diagnostic questions the practitioner can ask about the reward system. To put the answers in context, the discussion provides some of the advantages and disadvantages of alternative structures.

Are Rewards Based on the Job or on Skills?

Financial and some other rewards often are based on the types of jobs that people do. Indeed, with the exception of bonuses and merit salary increases, the standard policy in most organizations is to evaluate the job, not the person, and then to set the reward level. This approach is based on the assumptions that job worth can be determined and that the person doing the job is worth as much as the job itself is worth. These assumptions are in many respects valid, because through such techniques as job evaluation it is possible to determine what other organizations pay people to do the same or a similar job. This system assures an organization that its compensation costs are not dramatically out of line with those of its competitors, and it gives a somewhat objective basis to determining compensation levels.

An alternative to job-based pay, tried recently by a number of organizations, is to pay individuals for their skills (Lawler & Jenkins, 1992). In many cases this will not produce dramatically different pay rates than are produced by paying for the nature of the job: The skills people have usually match reasonably well the jobs they are doing (Jenkins, Ledford, Gupta, & Doty, 1992). This approach can, however, produce somewhat different results in cases where individuals are paid more because they are highly skilled. Also, in some cases individuals don't have the skills when they first enter a job and do not deserve the pay that goes with the job. These individuals must earn the right to be paid what the job-related skills are worth.

Perhaps the most important changes introduced by skill- or competence-based pay occur in the kind of culture and motivation it produces in an organization. Instead of being rewarded for moving up the hierarchy, people are rewarded for increasing their skills and developing themselves. This can create a culture of concern for personal growth and development—and a highly talented work force. In factories where this system has been used, it typically means that many people in the organization can perform multiple tasks; thus, the work force is highly knowledgeable and flexible (Walton, 1980).

Most often, skill-based pay produces somewhat higher pay levels for individuals, but this is usually offset by greater work force flexibility and higher performance (Jenkins et al., 1992). Flexibility often leads to lower staffing levels and fewer problems when absenteeism or turnover occurs. Indeed, it often causes lower absenteeism and turnover, because people like the opportunity to utilize and be paid for a wide range of skills. On the other hand, skill-based pay can be challenging to administer. It is not clear, for example, how to use the outside marketplace to determine how much a skill is worth. Skill assessment can also be difficult to accomplish. There are a number of well-developed systems for evaluating jobs and comparing them to the marketplace, but there are none that do this with respect to the skills an individual has.

A critical diagnostic question is whether the organization wants a flexible, relatively permanent work force that is oriented toward learning, growth, and development. If the answer is affirmative, skill-based pay may be quite appropriate. It has frequently been used in new plant start-ups and in plants that are moving toward more participative management

(Lawler, Mohrman & Ledford, 1992). It is being used more with professional and technical workers and with managers.

Are Rewards Based on Performance?

Perhaps the key diagnostic question concerning any reward system is whether or not it is based on performance. Once this question is answered, a number of reward system features tend to fall into place. The major alternative to basing rewards on performance is to base them on seniority. Many government agencies, for example, base their pay rates and some benefits on a person's job and tenure in that job. Likewise, in Japan seniority frequently determines pay, although individuals often receive bonuses based on corporate performance.

Most business organizations in the United States claim that they reward individual performance and call their pay and promotion practices merit systems (Milkovich & Wigdor, 1991). However, having a true merit pay or promotion system is often easier said than done. Indeed, it has been observed that many organizations would be better off if they didn't try to relate pay and promotion to performance and relied on other bases for motivating performance (Kerr, 1975). The logic for this statement stems from the difficulty of specifying what kind of performance is desired and then determining whether, in fact, it has been demonstrated (Heneman, 1992). There is ample evidence that a poorly designed and administered merit system can do more harm than good (see Lawler, 1971; Schuster & Zingheim, 1992; Whyte, 1955). On the other hand, when pay is effectively related to the desired performance, it can help to motivate, attract, and retain outstanding performers (Lawler & Jenkins, 1992).

How to relate pay to performance is one of the most important strategic decisions that organizations make (Blinder, 1990). The options open to organizations are enormous. The kind of pay reward can vary widely, including such things as stock and cash. In addition, the frequency of giving rewards can range from every few minutes to every few years. Rewards can be based on the performance of individuals, groups, or the total organization. Finally, many different kinds of performance can be rewarded. For example, managers can be rewarded for sales increases, production volume, their ability to develop their subordinates, their cost reduction ideas, and so on.

Rewarding some behaviors and not others has clear implications for performance; thus, decisions about what is to be rewarded need to be made carefully and with attention to the overall strategic plan of the business (see Galbraith & Nathanson, 1978). Consideration needs to be given to such issues as short- versus long-term performance, risk taking versus risk aversion, division performance versus total corporate performance, maximizing return on investment versus sales growth, and so on. Once the strategic plan reaches a definition of key performance objectives, the reward system needs to be designed to motivate the appropriate performance. Decisions about such issues as whether to use stock options (a long-term incentive), for example, should be made only after careful consideration of whether they are supportive of the kind of behavior that is desired. It is beyond the scope of this chapter to go into any great detail about the pros and cons of the many approaches to relating pay to performance. But a few general points do need to be made.

Bonus plans are generally better motivators than pay raise and salary increase plans. This is due to the fact that with bonus plans it is possible to substantially vary an individual's pay from time period to time period. With salary increase plans this is very difficult because past raises become an annuity (Heneman, 1992).

Group and organizational bonus plans are generally best at producing integration and teamwork. Under such plans it is generally to everyone's advantage that an individual work effectively, because all share in the financial results of higher performance. As a result, good performance is likely to be supported and encouraged by others when group and organizational plans are used. If people feel they can benefit from another's good performance, they are likely to encourage and help other workers to perform well. This is not true under individual plans. They tend to produce differentiation and competition.

Many organizations choose multiple or combination reward systems. For example, they may use a salary increase system that rewards individual performance while at the same time giving everybody in the division or plant a bonus based on divisional performance. Some plans measure group or company performance and then divide up the bonus pool based on individual performance. This rewards people for both individual and group performance in the hope that this will cause individuals to perform all needed behaviors.

Approaches that use objective measures of performance are better motivators than those that use subjective measures. In general, objective measures enjoy higher credibility; employees will often accept the validity of an objective measure, such as sales volume or units produced, when they will not accept a superior's rating. When pay is tied to objective measures, therefore, it is usually clearer to employees that pay is determined by performance. Objective measures are also often publicly measurable. When pay is tied to them, the relationship between performance and pay can be much more visible than when it is tied to a subjective, nonverifiable measure, such as a supervisor's rating.

A common error in the design of pay-for-performance systems is the tendency to depend on completely subjective performance appraisals for the allocation of pay rewards. Considerable evidence exists to show that these performance appraisals are often biased and invalid and that instead of contributing to positive motivation and a good work climate that improves superior–subordinate relationships they lead to just the opposite (see DeVries, Morrison, Shullman, & Gerlach, 1981; Latham & Wexley, 1981; Mohrman, Resnick-West, & Lawler, 1989).

A similarly grievous error can be the tendency to focus on measurable short-term operating results because they are quantifiable and regularly obtained anyway. Many organizations reward their top-level managers on the basis of annual profitability. This can have the obvious dysfunctional consequence of causing managers to be shortsighted in their behavior and to ignore strategic objectives that are important to the long-term profitability of the organization.

These are just some of the most common errors that can develop in the administration of performance-based reward systems. Other common errors include giving rewards that are too small, failing to clearly explain systems, and allowing poor administrative practices.

In conclusion, whether or not to relate rewards to performance is a crucial decision. Automatically assuming that they should be related can be a serious error. Admittedly, the advantages of doing it effectively are significant. What is often overlooked is that doing it poorly can have more negative consequences than positive ones.

How Do Rewards Relate to the Market?

The reward structure of an organization influences behavior partially as a function of how reward amounts compare to those of other companies. Organizations frequently have well-developed policies about their comparative pay levels. For example, some companies feel it is important to be a leading payer, and they consciously set their pay rates at a high level. Other companies are much less concerned about pay leadership and are content to target their pay levels at or below the market for the people they hire. This structural issue in the design of pay systems is a critical one, because it can strongly influence the kind of people that are attracted to and retained by an organization. It also influences the turnover rate and the selection ratio.

If many of the jobs in the organization are low-skilled and potential employees are readily available in the labor market, then a strategy of high pay may not be appropriate. It can increase labor costs and produce a minimum number of benefits. Of course, organizations don't have to be high or low payers for all their jobs. Indeed, some organizations adopt the stance of being a high payer for the key skills they need and an average or below average payer for other skills. This has the obvious business advantages of allowing organizations to attract the critical skills they need to succeed and at the same time to control costs.

The market position that a company adopts with respect to its reward systems can also have a noticeable impact on organization culture. For example, a policy that calls for above-market pay can contribute to the feeling that the organization is elite, that people must be competent to be there, and that they are indeed fortunate to be there. On the other hand, a policy that puts certain skill groups into a high pay position and leaves the rest of the organization at a lower pay level can contribute to a spirit of elite groups within the organization and cause divisive social tensions.

Some organizations try to be above average in noncash compensation as a way of competing for the talent they need. They stress hygiene factors (e.g., working conditions, administrative policies) as well as interesting and challenging work. This stance potentially can be a very effective strategy, giving organizations a competitive edge in attracting people who value these things.

Is Pay Geared Toward Internal or External Equity?

Organizations differ in the degree to which they strive toward internal equity in their reward systems. Those organizations that are oriented toward internal equity strive to ensure that individuals doing similar work will be paid the same even though they are in different locations and/or in different businesses. Some corporations set a national pay structure based on the highest pay that a job receives anywhere in the country. Those organizations that do not stress internal equity typically focus on the labor market as the key determinant of pay; although this does not necessarily produce different pay for people doing the same job, it may. For example, the same job in different industries, such as electronics and automobiles, may be paid quite differently.

There are a number of advantages and disadvantages associated with focusing on internal pay comparisons and paying all people in similar jobs the same. Transfers of people from one location to another are easier because there are no pay differences to compensate for. Internal equity can produce an organizational culture of homogeneity and the feeling that everyone working for the same company is treated well or fairly. It also can reduce or eliminate people's desire to move to a higher-paying division or location and the tendency for rivalry and dissatisfaction to develop within the organization because of "unfair" internal pay comparisons.

On the other hand, a focus on internal equity can be very expensive, particularly if the organization is diversified and, as usually happens, pay rates across the corporation are set at the highest level that the market demands anywhere in the corporation. The disadvantage of this practice is obvious. It causes organizations to pay a lot more money than is necessary to attract and retain good people. Indeed, in some situations it can get so severe that organizations become noncompetitive in certain businesses and find they have to limit themselves to those businesses where their pay structures make their labor costs competitive.

Is the Reward Strategy Centralized or Decentralized?

Closely related to the issue of internal versus external equity is the issue of a centralized versus decentralized reward system strategy. Those organizations that adopt a centralized strategy typically assign to corporate staff groups the responsibility for seeing that pay practices are similar throughout the organization. They typically develop standard pay grades and ranges, standardized job evaluation systems, and perhaps standardized promotion systems. In decentralized organizations, design and administration in the areas of pay, promotion, and other important rewards are left to local option. Sometimes decentralized corporations provide broad guidelines or principles, but the day-to-day administration and design of the system is left to the local entity. The decentralized strategy allows for local innovation and practices that fit particular businesses.

The advantages of a centralized structure rest primarily in the pay administration expertise that can be developed at the central level and the degree of homogeneity that is produced in the organization. This homogeneity can lead to a clear image of the corporate culture, feelings of internal equity, and the belief that the organization stands for something. It also eases the job of communicating and understanding what is going on in different parts of the organization.

As with all reward system strategic choices, there is no right choice between a centralized and decentralized approach to reward systems design. Generally, a decentralized system makes the most sense when the organization is involved in businesses that face different markets and perhaps are at different points in their maturity (Galbraith & Nathanson, 1978; Greiner, 1972). It allows unique practices which can give a competitive advantage to one part of the business but may prove to be a real hindrance or handicap to another. For example, such perquisites as cars are often standard operating procedure in one business but not in another. Similarly, extensive bonuses may be needed to attract one group of people, but make little sense for others.

How Much Hierarchy Is Reflected in the Reward System?

Closely related to the issue of job-based versus competence-based pay is the strategic decision concerning the hierarchical nature of the reward system. Often, no formal decision is ever made to have a hierarchical or an egalitarian approach to rewards in an organization. A hierarchical approach simply happens because it is so consistent with the general way organizations are run. Hierarchical systems usually reward people as they move higher up in the organization by giving them greater pay and more perquisites and symbols of office. This approach strongly reinforces the traditional hierarchical power relationships in the organization and creates a climate of different status and power levels. Steeply hierarchical reward systems usually have more levels than the formal organization chart and thus create additional status differences.

The alternative system dramatically downplays differences in rewards and perquisites that are based only on hierarchical level. For example, in those large corporations (e.g., Digital Equipment Corporation) that adopt an egalitarian stance, such things as private parking spaces, executive restrooms, and special entrances are eliminated. People from all levels in the organization eat together, work together, and travel together. This less hierarchical approach tends to encourage decision making by expertise rather than by hierarchical position and draws fewer status differences.

Once again, there is no right or wrong answer as to how hierarchical a system should be. In general, a steeply hierarchical system makes the most sense when an organization needs relatively rigid bureaucratic behavior, considerable top-down authority, and a strong motivation for people to move up the organizational hierarchy. A more egalitarian approach fits with a more participative management style and the desire to retain technical specialists and experts in nonmanagement or lower-level management roles. It is therefore not surprising that many of the organizations which emphasize egalitarian perquisites are in high technology and knowledge-based industries.

What Is the Mix of Rewards?

The kind of rewards that organizations give to individuals can vary widely. For example, money can come in many forms, from stock to medical insurance. Organizations can choose to reward people almost exclusively with cash, downplaying fringe benefits, perquisites, and status symbols. The reward mix can determine the type of people who work for an organization. Highly variable cash compensation programs and those with stable levels of cash compensation will attract different employees. Similarly, programs with high levels of benefits and those with cash compensation will attract different employees.

One major advantage of cash is that its value in the eyes of the recipient is universally high. When the cash is translated into fringe benefits, perquisites, and other trappings of office, it may lose its value for some people and, as a result, be a poor investment (see Lawler, 1971; Nealey,

1963). Certain benefits can best be obtained through mass purchase; these may be valued by some individuals beyond their actual dollar cost to the organization and thus represent good buys. Finally, as was mentioned earlier, there often are some cultural and organization structure reasons for paying people in the form of perquisites and status symbols.

Flexible or cafeteria-style benefit programs (see Lawler, 1981) allow individuals to create a reward package to fit their needs and desires. These programs have become increasingly popular in part because organizations get the best value for their money by giving people only those things they desire (Lawler, Mohrman, & Ledford, 1992). They also have the advantage of treating individuals as mature adults rather than as dependent people who need their welfare looked after in a structured way.

How Is the Current Reward System Administered?

Process issues come up frequently because organizations constantly have to make reward system management, implementation, and communication decisions. This discussion will focus on broad process themes that characterize the way reward systems are designed and administered.

How Much Is Communicated About the Reward System?

Organizations differ widely in how much information they communicate about their reward systems. Some organizations are extremely secretive, particularly with respect to pay. They forbid employees from talking about their pay, give minimal information to individuals about how rewards are decided upon and allocated, and have no publicly disseminated policies about such things as market position, the approach to gathering market data, and potential increases in rewards. At the other extreme, some organizations are so open that everyone's pay is a matter of public record, as is the overall organization pay philosophy. For example, many new high-involvement plants operate this way (see Lawler, 1978; Walton, 1980); in addition, all promotions are subject to open job postings, and in some instances peer groups discuss the eligibility of people for promotion.

The difference between an open and a closed communication policy regarding rewards is enormous. Here, too, there is no clear right or wrong approach. Rather, it is a matter of picking a position on the continuum from open to secret that is supportive of the overall culture and types of behavior needed for organizational effectiveness. An open system tends to encourage people to ask questions, share data, and ultimately be involved in decisions. On the other hand, a secret system tends to put people in more dependent positions and keep power concentrated at the top, allowing an organization to keep its options open.

There are some negative side effects of secret systems. They may lead to considerable distortion in views about the actual rewards people get and may create an environment of low trust in which people have trouble understanding the relationship between pay and performance (see Lawler, 1971). Thus, if strong secrecy policies are in place, a structurally sound pay system may end up being rather ineffective because it is misperceived.

Open systems put considerable pressure on organizations to do an effective job in administering rewards. To implement policies that are difficult to defend publicly, such as merit pay, the organization must invest considerable time and effort in pay administration. If such policies are administered poorly, strong pressures usually develop to eliminate them and pay everyone the same (see Burroughs, 1982). Ironically, therefore, if an organization wants to spend little time administrating rewards but still wants to base pay on merit, secrecy may be the best policy, although secrecy in turn may limit the effectiveness of the merit pay plan.

Who Makes Reward Decisions?

Closely related to the issue of communication is the issue of decision making. Open communication makes possible the involvement of a wide range of people in the pay decision-making process. Further, if individuals are to be actively involved in decisions concerning reward systems, they need to have information about policy and actual practice.

It is important to distinguish between decisions concerning the design of reward systems and decisions concerning their ongoing administration. It is possible to have different decision-making styles with respect to these two types of decisions.

Reward systems typically are designed by top management with staff support and administered by strict reliance on the chain of command. This presumably provides the proper checks and balances in the system and locates decision making where the expertise and accountability lie. In many cases these are valid assumptions, and the system certainly fits well with a management style that emphasizes hierarchy, bureaucracy, and control through the use of extrinsic rewards. It does not fit, however, with an organization that believes in open communication, high levels of employee involvement, and control through individual commitment to policies (Lawler, 1992). It also doesn't fit when expertise is broadly spread throughout the organization.

A number of organizations have experimented with involving employees in the design of pay systems (Lawler, 1981, 1990). For example, employees have helped design their own bonus system with generally favorable results. When employees are involved, they raise important issues and provide expertise that is not normally available to the designers of pay systems. Perhaps more importantly, once the system is designed, its level of acceptance and understanding tends to be very high. This often leads to a rapid start-up of the system and to a commitment to see it survive. In other cases systems have been designed by line managers rather than by staff support people. This can lead to greater effectiveness because the managers see the need to support, maintain, and be committed to them.

There also has been some experimentation with having peer groups and lower-level supervisors handle the day-to-day decision making about who should receive pay increases and how jobs should be evaluated and placed in pay structures. The most visible examples of this are in the new participative plants that use skill-based pay (Lawler, 1992; Walton, 1980). In such plants the work group typically reviews the performance of an individual and decides whether he or she has acquired the new skills. The limited evidence that exists suggests that this has gone very well (Jenkins et al., 1992). In many respects this is not surprising, because peers often have the best information about performance and are thus in a good position to make a performance assessment. The problem in traditional organizations is that many peers lack the motivation to give valid feedback and to respond responsibly; thus, their expertise is of no use. In more participative open systems this motivational problem is less severe, making involvement in decision making more effective. There have been isolated instances of executives assessing each other. This can work effectively if there is a history of open and productive communication.

Deciding on rewards is clearly not an easy task for groups. It should be attempted only when there is comfort with the confrontation skills of the group and trust in members' ability to talk openly and directly about each other's performance.

What Is the Actual Impact of Organizational Policies and Practices?

Once the practitioner has learned how the current reward system operates, the next step in organizational diagnosis is determining the actual impact of the organization's policies and practices. Some impact data can be obtained from looking at company records and analyzing individual behavior. For example, organizational performance can be analyzed, as can hiring, turnover, and other personnel data.

In assessing the impact of the current reward system it is also desirable to gather perceptual and attitudinal data from employees. Such data can be collected either by carefully structured interviews or by written attitude surveys. Both of these methods have distinct advantages, and often the best approach is a combination of the two. Interviews typically provide rich information about why the individual sees or doesn't see a relationship between pay and performance and how specific practices create this and other perceptions. Surveys, on the other hand, allow much better relative assessments of how satisfied employees are with their pay, the degree to which they see pay based on performance, how well they understand the pay system, and so on down the list of behaviors and attitudes that pay systems are supposed to influence.

How Does the Actual Impact of the Reward System Compare with the Desired Impact?

The final step in the organizational diagnosis is to compare the actual impact of the reward system with the desired impact. It is this step that combines the strategy-driven specification of what the reward system should do with the assessment of existing practices and attitude data. It typically shows significant gaps between what the reward system needs to do and what it actually does. For example, the reward system may motivate bureaucratic, empire- building behavior when the greatest need in the organization is for individuals to learn new skills, be increasingly flexible in their job behavior, and contribute to downsizing their particular work area.

The comparison between what the reward system should do and what it actually does should form the basis for redesigning the reward system. At this point the practitioner needs to lead the organization back to the basic design dimensions of the reward system and look at what can be done to close the gap between the desired and actual impact.

There are at least two obvious possibilities here. One is that the organization is simply positioned incorrectly on the reward system dimension in order to get the behavior that it wants. For example, there may be a stated desire for team behavior when, in fact, the system primarily rewards individual behavior. If this type of discrepancy appears, the reward system needs to be redesigned to produce the type of behavior that is needed.

A second alternative is that the reward system is positioned correctly but either poorly designed or poorly implemented. In this case the critical corrective action may be to involve a group of employees in redesigning the way the reward system is managed and implemented. In this way employees will better understand the policies and practices, be committed to them, and be more likely to produce the kinds of behaviors that are needed.

Reward system diagnosis and change should not stop with simply one diagnosis, a proposed set of changes, and implementation of those changes. Organizations are dynamic, as are the consequences of reward systems. Thus, it is important to continue to assess the impact of the reward system and its effectiveness relative to the business strategy and the behavioral objectives of the organization (Mohrman & Cummings, 1989).

Typically, either renewal or significant redesign of the reward system is needed when ongoing diagnoses are made. Often, no changes are needed in core principles nor in the basic policies and practices but improvement is needed in the way these policies are implemented and carried out. Frequently, new employees have not been trained in the policies and thus are not aware of how the reward system operates. Another common problem is that attention has not been focused on how well the policies are implemented, and the organization has become careless and wasteful.

EMPLOYEE INVOLVEMENT AND PAY SYSTEM DESIGN

The most prevalent approach to designing work organizations includes such features as hierarchical decision making, simple repetitive jobs at the lowest level, and rewards based on carefully measured individual jobs and job performance. This "control approach" appears to be losing favor (Lawler, Ledford, & Mohrman, 1989; Lawler, Mohrman, & Ledford, 1992). Numerous articles and books have recently argued that organizations need to move toward a more involvement- or commitment-oriented approach to management. The advantages of this approach are said to include higher quality products and services, less absenteeism, less turnover, better decision making, better problem solving, and lower overhead costs; in short, greater organizational effectiveness (Denison, 1990; Lawler, 1992).

Employee involvement approaches to organization design generally argue that three features of an organization other than rewards are critical:

1. *Information* about the performance of the organization and the ability to bring information about needed organizational changes to the attention of key decision makers.
2. *Knowledge* that enables employees to understand and contribute to organizational performance.
3. *Power* to make decisions that influence organizational practices, direction, and performance.

How information, knowledge, and power are positioned in an organization determines the core management style of the organization. When they are concentrated at the top, traditional, control-oriented management exists; when they are moved downward, some form of participative management is being practiced.

Organizations adopting employee involvement need to ensure that their pay system is aligned with this management approach. In designing a congruent pay system, practitioners must consider how it will affect core values, process, and structures. As might be expected, employee involvement calls for approaches in all three areas that are different from those used in command and control organizations.

Core Values

To support employee involvement, pay needs to be driven by a clearly articulated, well-accepted set of core values. These core values should not be a temporary commitment of the organization; rather, they should be fundamental beliefs that will be unchanged for decades.

Values should address the following core issues about reward systems:

1. Job security.
2. How pay levels will compare to those of other organizations.
3. The major determinants of an individual's pay (i.e., performance, seniority, etc.).
4. The individual's rights concerning access to information and involvement.
5. The relationship of pay levels to business success.
6. The degree to which the system will be egalitarian.
7. The degree of support for learning, personal growth, and involvement.

There are no "right" core values. Indeed, a part of the employee involvement process may be developing them. It is possible, however, to make some statements about the general orientation that are congruent with the major principles of the employee involvement approach to management. In particular, the core values need to emphasize the relationship of pay to the success of the business, individual rights, due process, open communication, egalitarian approaches, pay rates that are competitive with similar businesses, and rewards for individual growth and skill development. These core values are supportive of a management style in which the organization depends upon people to both think and do, a style that stresses a wide range of business involvement on the part of all employees.

Process Issues

Employee involvement suggests some specific process approaches to pay administration. In particular, it suggests greater openness of communication about pay practices and broader involvement on the part of all organizational members in the development and administration of pay and reward systems. Openness and participation are congruent with the emphasis on moving power downward and having individuals involved in both the thinking and doing sides of the business. For a reward system to be effective, it must be both understood and designed in ways that lead to individual acceptance. Participation in the design and administration process helps assure this. It also ensures that the system will fit the situation, because it allows the people who will be affected by the system to influence its design.

With openness and participation, widespread ownership of the reward system should develop, so that it is not the sole or primary responsibility of the compensation or personnel department. Instead, it becomes the responsibility of everyone in the organization to see that it operates effectively and fairly. All too often in traditional management structures the reward system becomes the property of the human resources department; as a result, it ends up being ineffectively and poorly supported by line management. It almost goes without saying that in the absence of broad support in the organization the reward system cannot reinforce particular business objectives and strategies.

System Structure

Some structural mechanisms fit particularly well with employee involvement. Many of them represent important changes in the way pay is currently administered in most organizations (O'Dell, 1987; Schuster & Zingheim, 1992). The following structural mechanisms are especially appropriate.

Decentralized Compensation Design and Administration

In a large corporation a centralized approach to compensation is incongruent with the idea of business involvement and with targeting structure and reward system practices to the business strategy. By their very nature, most large corporations are engaged in multiple businesses that have quite different needs and that compete with organizations that pay differently. Having a single approach to pay that emphasizes a corporate-wide approach to market position, merit pay, performance measurement, and so forth, makes it impossible for particular business units to participate in structuring their reward system effectively. Business units end up being forced to adopt a corporate structure that often is not congruent with what is needed to compete in their particular environment.

Smaller organizations tend not to have this problem because they often face a single external environment. Some large organizations that are in a single business may be in a similar position. In most cases, however, organizations that have multiple businesses need to decentralize compensation practice.

Rewards for Business Performance

If employees are to be concerned about the success of a business, their rewards must be driven by the success of the business (Lawler, 1990). This is not to say that individual pay for performance systems should be eliminated; they may still be appropriate if performance can be measured at the individual level (Mohrman, Resnick-West, & Lawler, 1989). Rather, organizations need systems that reward organization and business unit performance. Indeed, organizations need to be riddled with performance-based reward systems so that the pay of individuals is driven by their performance, the performance of their business, and total corporate performance.

At the plant level, for example, gain-sharing plans as well as corporate-wide stock ownership and profit-sharing plans could cover every employee. This combination can help push both power and information downward because it gives rewards for business performance to lower-level employees and legitimizes their getting information and power (Frost, Wakeley, & Ruh, 1974). It also can influence motivation and create a team culture.

At the management level emphasis needs to be placed upon long-term performance. This suggests replacing or supplementing many of the current short-term, profit-driven incentive plans for executives with 5- to 10-year incentive plans. It also argues for paying managers based on the performance of the organizational units they managed in the past as well as on the performance of their current units. This can help to ensure that when managers leave a position, they do not walk away from their past decisions.

Choice-Oriented Compensation

A fixed package of benefits, cash, and perquisites is inconsistent with the substantial individual differences that exist in the work force and with the idea that individuals can and should be able to make decisions concerning their own lives. Some organizations are already giving individuals greater choice. This was evident initially in the acceptance of flexible working hours, and it is evident in the more recent and growing popularity of flexible benefit systems (Lawler, Mohrman, & Ledford, 1992).

Individual choice does not need to be limited to fringe benefits and hours of work. Ultimately, organizations taking the employee involvement approach could allow individuals to have tremendous flexibility in determining their own total reward package. Flexibility could extend, for example, to the kind of perquisites and benefits offered and to the mixture of cash, stock, and bonuses. This has the potential of benefiting both the individual and the organization: It will help individuals get the rewards they value and assure the organization that its money is being spent in ways that produce the maximum impact.

Skill-Based Compensation

Employee involvement suggests paying individuals for their skills. Skill-based pay represents a major change in the nature of compensation practice. For example, an individual does not receive a pay raise for being promoted; he or she has to first demonstrate the skills associated with the new job. Once this is accomplished, however, a pay increase is awarded. Another possible change is that individuals at lower levels of the organizational hierarchy may be paid more than people at higher levels. With an emphasis on skills, it is quite possible that a highly skilled production worker or a highly skilled specialist may earn considerably more than a middle-level manager, particularly if the specialist and production worker are encouraged to learn managerial skills in order to become more self-managing. In this sense, pay becomes unhinged from the hierarchical nature of the organization.

Relatively little use has been made of skill-based pay in nonmanufacturing situations, and even within manufacturing it has been limited to lower-level employees. There is reason to believe, however, that the use of skill-based pay should be expanded. Skills are the key to effectiveness in the growing number of organizations that are emphasizing employee involvement. In addition, knowledge-based work organizations require that skills be spread throughout the organization. Skill-based pay can motivate skill acquisition and reinforce it, allowing knowledge-based and high-involvement organizations to build the kind of skill base they need to be effective.

The changing demographics of society also suggest that skill-based pay will be increasingly popular. The baby-boom cohort is rapidly approaching the expected age for reaching middle management. At the same time, employee involvement calls for flatter organizational structures and leaner staff groups. This means that the number of positions in middle management will be limited and that there will be fewer upward mobility opportunities for the large group of individuals in the age group that typically staffs middle management. In traditional organizations this would simply mean individuals staying on a plateau or in a dead-end position for a long period of time. If skill-based pay is put into place, people can be rewarded for making lateral moves and can thus continue to learn and develop. They may become more valuable to the organization by developing a better overall understanding of the business, and they will not be subject to the negative impact of topping out in pay.

Egalitarian Compensation

There are several respects in which the pay system can be made more egalitarian in order to match the emphasis in employee involvement on moving information, knowledge, and power downward. A number of organizations already call all their employees "salaried," have no time clocks, and put all individuals on the same benefit package. The egalitarian approach can be, and often is, extended to equalizing many of the perquisites that typically are allocated according to management level (e.g., parking spaces, offices). An egalitarian approach can be combined with flexible benefits such that individuals, though differing in total compensation levels, have access to all benefits and perquisites if they are willing to pay the price.

Also consistent with more egalitarian pay treatment is lowering the level at which such things as stock option and profit-sharing plans operate in organizations. The one thing that probably should vary as these plans move further down the organization is the amount of an individual's compensation that is dependent upon them. At the lower levels, individuals should participate only to a small degree in profit-sharing and stock option plans that are based on corporate performance whereas compensation should be heavily dependent upon these plans at the top level. As was mentioned earlier, long-term incentives may be the one type of plan that should be targeted only at top management.

The employee involvement approach also brings into question the wisdom of plans that pay senior executives much more than lower-level employees. Large differences can be justified under a traditional management system because the executives are expected to exercise considerable power and to control information. If employee involvement means that power, information, and knowledge are pushed downward, rewards like pay should be also.

Summarizing Employee Involvement and Pay

The management practices and strategies that are consistent with employee involvement require new pay practices. Because compensation is the fabric of any organization, it must be congruent with the overall management style and strategy of the business. It suggests new core values, new administrative processes, and, finally, some new pay structures.

As shown in Table 9.1, pay in the employee involvement approach needs to be characterized by egalitarianism, local control of decision mak-

TABLE 9.1. Pay and Management Style

	Traditional management	Employee involvement
Communication	Secret	Open
Decision making	Top-down	Wide involvement
Structure	Centralized	Decentralized
Pay for performance	Merit pay	Based on business sucess
Reward mix	Standardized	Individual choice
Base pay	Job based	Skill based
Degree of hierarchy	Hierarchical	Egalitarian

ing, individual choice, and, most importantly, a strong performance-based system that is tied to business success. Taken as a package, these new pay practices are congruent with employee involvement, and they promise to change the way work is done.

REFERENCES

Adams, J. S. (1965). Injustice in social exchange. In L. Berkowitz (Ed.), *Advances in experimental social psychology* (Vol. 2, pp. 267–299). New York: Academic Press.

Blinder, A. S. (1990). *Paying for productivity*. Washington, DC: Brookings.

Burroughs, J. D. (1982). Pay secrecy and performance: The psychological research. *Compensation Review, 14*(3), 44–54.

Denison, D. R. (1990). *Corporate culture and organizational effectiveness*. New York: Wiley.

DeVries, D. L., Morrison, A. M., Shullman, S. L., & Gerlach, M. L. (1981). *Performance appraisal on the line*. New York: Wiley-Interscience.

Frost, C. F., Wakeley, J. H., & Ruh, R. A. (1974). *The Scanlon Plan for organization and development: Identity, participation, and equity*. East Lansing, MI: Michigan State University Press.

Galbraith, J. R., & Nathanson, D. A. (1978). *Strategy implementation: The role of structure and process*. St. Paul, MN: West.

Gerhart, B., & Milkovich, G. T. (1992). Employee compensation: Research and practice. In M. D. Dunnette & L. M. Hough (Eds.), *Handbook of industrial and organizational psychology* (2nd ed., Vol. 3, pp. 475–569). Palo Alto, CA: Consulting Psychologists Press.

Greiner, L. (1972). Evolution and revolution as organizations grow. *Harvard Business Review, 50*(4), 37–46.

Heneman, R. L. (1992). *Merit pay*. Reading, MA: Addison-Wesley.

Jenkins, G. D., Ledford, G. E., Gupta, N., & Doty, D. H. (1992). *Skill based pay: Practices, payoffs, pitfalls and prescriptions*. Scottsdale, AZ: American Compensation Association.

Kerr, S. (1975). On the folly of rewarding A, while hoping for B. *Academy of Management Journal, 18*, 769.

Latham, G. P., & Wexley, K. N. (1981). *Increasing productivity through performance appraisal.* Reading, MA: Addison-Wesley.

Lawler, E. E. III. (1971). *Pay and organizational effectiveness: A psychological view.* New York: McGraw-Hill.

Lawler, E. E. III. (1973). *Motivation in work organizations.* Monterey, CA: Brooks/Cole.

Lawler, E. E. III. (1978). The new plant revolution. *Organizational Dynamics, 6*(3), 2–12.

Lawler, E. E. III. (1981). *Pay and organizational development.* Reading, MA: Addison-Wesley.

Lawler, E. E. III. (1990). *Strategic pay: Aligning organizational strategies and pay systems,* San Francisco: Jossey-Bass.

Lawler, E. E. III. (1992). *The ultimate advantage: Creating a high-involvement organization,* San Francisco: Jossey-Bass.

Lawler, E. E. III, & Cohen, S. G. (1992). Designing pay systems for teams.*ACA Journal, 1*(1), 6–19.

Lawler, E. E. III, & Jenkins, G. D. (1992). Strategic reward systems. In M. D. Dunnette & L. M. Hough (Eds.), *Handbook of industrial and organizational psychology* (2nd ed., Vol. 3, pp. 1009–1055). Palo Alto, CA: Consulting Psychologists Press.

Lawler, E. E. III, Ledford, G. E., & Mohrman, S. A. (1989). *Employee involvement in America.* Houston, TX: American Productivity and Quality Center.

Lawler, E. E. III, Mohrman, S. A., & Ledford, G. E. (1992). *Employee involvement and total quality management.* San Francisco: Jossey-Bass.

Lawrence, P. R., & Lorsch, J. W. (1967). *Organization and environment: Managing differentiation and integration.* Homewood, IL: Irwin.

Milkovich, G. T., & Wigdor, A. K. (Eds.). (1991). *Pay for performance: Evaluating performance appraisal and merit pay.* Washington, DC: National Academy Press.

Mobley, W. H. (1982). *Employee turnover: Causes, consequences, and control.* Reading, MA: Addison-Wesley.

Mohrman, A. M., Resnick-West, S. A., & Lawler, E. E. III. (1989). *Designing performance appraisal systems,* San Francisco: Jossey-Bass.

Mohrman, S. A., & Cummings, T. G. (1989). *Self-designing organizations.* Reading, MA: Addison-Wesley.

Nealey, S. (1963). Pay and benefit preferences. *Industrial Relations, 3*, 17–28.

O'Dell, C. (1987). *People, performance and pay.* Houston, TX: American Productivity Center.

Schuster, J. R., & Zingheim, P. K. (1992). *The new pay.* New York: Lexington.

Vroom, V. H. (1964). *Work and motivation.* New York: Wiley.

Walton, R. E. (1980). Establishing and maintaining high commitment work systems. In J. R. Kimberly, R. H. Miles, and Associates, *The organizational life cycle* (pp. 208–290). San Francisco: Jossey-Bass.

Whyte, W. F. (Ed.). (1955). *Money and motivation: An analysis of incentives in industry.* New York: Harper.

CHAPTER 10

Diagnostic Issues
for Work Teams

KIMBALL FISHER

As the work environment has changed, many classic bureaucratic organizations have proven too slow, too expensive, and too unresponsive to be competitive. Thus, many corporations have devolved into flatter and more flexible operations called work teams. This trend to create work teams has crossed into virtually every industry and has expanded into not-for-profit operations as well. Organizations such as Corning, Monsanto, Apple Computer, Aid Association for Lutherans, Shenandoah Life Insurance, Seattle Metro, and the San Diego Zoo have been using empowered teams in order to increase worker commitment and flexibility. In many cases they have been paid back with increased quality, productivity, and cost improvements while workers have seen commensurate gains in the quality of work life. It has become increasingly evident that these teams may well be replacing the traditional workplace management practices that have characterized organizations since the turn of the century. They are, to say the least, one of the most popular current organizational phenomena.

But the road to teams is not necessarily an easy one. This chapter reviews some of the important questions organizations must consider when determining the structures and strategies of their future: What are teams? How are they different from traditional operations? When are teams needed? What kind of teams are most appropriate in today's work environment? The chapter also examines the individual and organizational conditions under which teams are most likely to be effective, including the special issues associated with "greenfield" (start-up) and "brownfield" (established) applications. Methods for determining how well teams are functioning are examined. Finally, the chapter speculates on the place of self-directed work teams in the future.

THE NATURE AND PURPOSE OF TEAMS

Lack of a common language about teams makes a discussion about analyzing team effectiveness difficult. But there are some generally accepted working definitions that are helpful. The word *team* itself, for example, most commonly refers to a collection of individuals who share a common purpose (Katzenbach & Smith, 1993). This is what differentiates a team from a group, which is any collection of people. Thus, people with red hair are a group simply because they can be distinguished from other people, but they would not be a team unless they got together for some common purpose, say, to set up a foundation to study the historical contributions of people with red hair.

What Are Teams?

Using only this most simple definition of a team, it is already obvious that some organizations that call themselves teams are not teams at all. If a group doesn't have a clear purpose, it cannot by definition be a team. Moreover, if the participants in a group do not have a common understanding and commitment to that purpose, they are not a team. This is fairly easy to test. From time to time we gather "team members" from an organization and ask them individually to describe the primary purpose of their particular team. It is not unusual to have very different answers from participants.

In one such exercise with a group of engineers from a high tech company, some said that their primary purpose was to bring leading-edge technical products to the marketplace while others said that their purpose was to design more cost-effective products. These two factions were, of course, frequently at odds with each other because their purposes were often mutually exclusive. To muddy the water further, still other engineers in the group described their purpose in terms of a customer focus, such as creating state-of-the-art user-friendly products or solving customer problems. This engineering group had fundamental internal disagreements about their purpose that had created an underlying confusion that made it difficult for them to agree on product parameters. They were a team in name only.

Similarly, many so-called teams are actually employee or management groups with multiple or even contradictory agendas, which can make them incapable of productive action. Asking questions such as "What do you believe is the fundamental purpose of this team?" or "What is the most important reason for the existence of this team?" can identify disparate agendas or differing levels of commitment to the team purpose. Asking questions like "What gets rewarded here?" or "How do things get prioritized here?" or "What activities get the support of senior management [budget, personal attention, critical meeting agenda items, etc.]?" can determine whether support systems are in sync with the stated purpose of the teams.

In addition to these basic issues regarding a working definition of teams, however, there are other complexities for the organizational diagnostician to consider. What do contemporary managers mean when they say they want a team-based operation? Are they simply saying that they want people to have common goals? Usually not. Is there only one kind of team-based organization? Certainly not (Ketchum & Trist, 1993). So what do they mean when they say they want teams?

Unfortunately, they may mean several different things. People have used the team terminology in seemingly contradictory ways. For example, while some managers use the word *team* to describe a participative workplace (as in "Let's not make a unilateral management decision on this one; we'll take it to the team"), others use the same terminology to reinforce the traditional autocratic paradigm (as in "Don't rock the boat; we need you to be a team player"). It's no wonder that some people are confused when organizations say they want to create teams.

When managers in most contemporary organizations refer to teams, they are talking about something that is much more than a clearly purposeful organization. They are usually talking about a particular organizational structure that is commonly used as a vehicle for worker empowerment. Thus, while certain organizations could technically be called teams because they meet the first two criteria already discussed (clear purpose and common agreement to achieve the purpose), those characteristics alone do not distinguish classic bureaucracies from what are currently called team-based operations.

This chapter employs what is becoming the more common usage of the term in organizations: Teams are nonauthoritarian work structures with shared responsibility for decision making, problem solving, and organization design. More succinctly stated, the third criterion for the team operations reviewed here is that they are work structures based on the paradigm of commitment rather than control (Walton, 1985). That is, team operations are constructed and facilitated to elicit the commitment rather than the compliance of the work force (Fisher, 1989). Using these characteristics to define teams narrows the scope of this discussion from all so-called teams (such as some of the boot camp teams in the military or some of the sports teams managed by authoritarian coaching staffs) to only those teams built on a foundation of empowerment.

Teams are only a structural manifestation of an empowered work culture. To understand these kinds of contemporary teams, therefore, we need to better understand the emerging movement to empower employees.

Empowerment and Teams

Today it is estimated that virtually every major corporation in North America and Western Europe is using some form of empowerment somewhere in their organization. This workplace transformation has already been dubbed the "second industrial revolution" (Trist, 1981) because it challenges the fundamental assumptions and work structures of the first industrial revolution. Although it goes by a number of names, including sociotechnical systems, employee empowerment, and high-performance work teams, the workplace transformation in contemporary organizations is commonly known by the generic title of team-based organizations (Hoerr & Zellner, 1989). A number of these organizations are using a particular kind of team called a self-directed work team, which is a very advanced form of structured worker empowerment discussed later in this chapter.

Teams and Traditional Operations

These team-based workplaces are a departure from traditional operations. Said John Stepp (1987), while undersecretary of the U.S. Department of Labor, about traditional organizations:

> There are too many rigidities that have slowed us down and hampered our effectiveness. We see top-down decision making. We see overly prescribed tasks and narrow job definitions. We see long, drawn-out labor contracts and negotiations that more closely resemble cease-fire agreements among combatants than a rational agreement for organizing work and work relationships. Our industrial relations system is hampered by too many restrictions, too many inhibiting work practices, work rules, and personnel policies.

In stark contrast to these common operations of the past, many contemporary organizations have created work structures that are more democratic and flexible in nature. We see fewer levels of management. We see less authoritarian processes. We see organizations with dramatically improved labor relations and less restrictive contracts. These operations share a common underpinning, a philosophy of shared responsibility between management and individual contributors for results and decisions. Such organizations rely on employee empowerment rather than management direction.

Empowerment Continuum

Empowerment gives people more power to influence their own workplace. But there are obviously varying degrees of empowerment that are

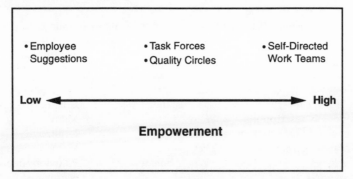

FIGURE 10.1. The empowerment continuum. Belgard·Fisher·Rayner (1989). Copyright 1989 by Belgard·Fisher·Rayner, Inc. Adapted by permission. Influenced by the work of John Sherwood.

possible even within a similar team structure. Teams can be dominated by management (lower empowerment) or they can be entirely self-directed (higher empowerment). One way to explain this is to visualize empowerment as a continuum of employee involvement (see Figure 10.1), with lower empowerment techniques like selected employee input on projects on one end, ongoing employee task forces and quality circles in the middle, and higher empowerment processes like self-directed work teams (SDWTs) on the other end (Fisher, 1993).

Self-Directed Work Teams (SDWTs)

What are self-directed teams? Let's use a slightly modified version of the definition offered by Development Dimensions International, the Association for Quality and Participation, and *Industry Week* for their study on the subject (Wellins, Wilson, Katz, Laughlin, Day & Price, 1990). Let's define a self-directed team as a group of employees who have day-to-day responsibility for managing themselves and the work they do with a minimum of direct supervision and who typically handle job assignments, plan and schedule work, make production and/or service-related decisions, and take action on problems.

Whereas traditional work groups typically are organized into separate specialized jobs with rather narrow responsibilities, SDWTs are made up of members who are jointly responsible for whole work processes, with each individual performing multiple tasks (Fisher, 1989). Whereas a traditional organization might be divided into groups of functional specialists, for example, SDWTs are usually responsible for delivery of an entire service or product, or they might be responsible for a geography or customer base. This is done to create (wherever possible) small self-sustaining businesses that can be jointly managed by the organizational membership.

TABLE 10.1. SDWTs versus Traditional Organizations

	Self-directed work teams	Traditional organizations
Driven by	Customers	Management
Nature of work force	Multiskilled	Isolated specialists
Number of job descriptions	Few	Many
Extent of shared information	Wide	Limited
Levels of management	Few	Many
Business focus	Whole business	Function/department
Nature of goals	Shared	Segregated
Atmosphere	Seemingly chaotic	Seemingly organized
Work emphasis	Goal achievement	Task achievement
Locus of high commitment	Workers	Management
Type of improvements	Continuous	Incremental
Source of control	Self	Management
Basis for decisions	Values/principles	Policies/procedures

When I was a team leader at Procter & Gamble, for example, we were divided into product organizations. The team members made decisions about who would perform which task rather than having individuals separated into jobs like operators, mechanics, and tradespeople. Everyone had the same title—technician—and everyone had a shared responsibility for the success of the team. These are common elements of SDWTs (Fisher, 1989). For other key differences between SDWTs and traditional organizations see Table 10.1.

A couple of caveats are in order when defining SDWTs. First, some people mistakenly believe that the teams are the end instead of the means to an end. SDWTs are a method of improving results, not a substitute for them. This all too common means–ends inversion has caused some organizations to lose sight of their organizational purpose and focus their time on the care and feeding of the structures instead ("Sorry, our poor customer service is caused by the fact that everyone is in a team meeting right now"). This is obviously a bad mistake. One way to determine if teams have become an end is to look at the measures operations use to determine whether the teams are successful. Operations using measures that focus on such key result areas as customer satisfaction or market share are more likely to be successful than those using measures such as number of teams, frequency of team meetings, or numbers of hours of team training.

Second, overemphasizing the self-directedness of the teams can lead people down the wrong path. In fact, the name *self-directed work team* itself can be misleading. Some believe that it connotes an absence of management personnel, which is inaccurate. SDWTs mean a change in the role of management, not an elimination of supervisors and managers. Those who use SDWTs as a means to downsize management staffs almost always harm the teams by stripping them of essential coaching and training resources. Others assume that the name implies that the team has complete latitude to do whatever it wants, which is equally inaccurate. All teams operate within certain boundary conditions appropriate to them. Perhaps a more accurate term would be one favored by my colleague Bill Belgard: *work-centered teams.* Simply stated, these are operations where skilled, well-informed people take direction from the work itself rather than from management.

Whatever you call them, if all else is equal, these work cultures are often credited with outperforming their traditional counterparts. At a conference about these unique workplaces Charles Eberle (1987), a former vice president of P&G, said:

> At P&G there are well over two decades of comparisons of results—side by side—between enlightened work systems and those I call traditional. It is absolutely clear that the new work systems work better—a lot better—for example, with 30 to 50% lower manufacturing costs. Not only are the tangible, measurable, bottom-line indicators such as cost, quality, customer service, and reliability better, but also the harder-to-measure attributes such as quickness, decisiveness, toughness, and just plain resourcefulness of these organizations. Importantly, the people in these organizations are far more self-reliant and less dependent upon hierarchy and control systems than in the traditional organization.

To better understand whether or not self-directed teams are here to stay let's briefly consider the history of these unique work cultures.

The Origin of Self-Directed Work Teams

Most attribute the origins of SDWT concepts to the early work of an Englishman named Eric Trist. In the 1950s Trist coauthored a paper in which the term *socio-technical system* first appeared (Trist, 1950). In this and other papers that were to follow, Trist challenged many of the fundamental assumptions of *scientific management,* an idea developed by Frederick Taylor at the turn of the century and perfected by Henry Ford in the U.S. automobile factories of the 1930s. At that time scientific management appeared to be the answer to the problems in rapidly growing industries caused by their dependence on a largely unskilled and ill-educated work force. Breaking down job responsibilities into small specialized increments enabled the workers to become proficient more rapidly and imposed a sense of order and predictability on the emerging chaos of industrialization. This, coupled with decision making and problem solving being the sole province of foremen and supervisors, facilitated the movement away from the little shops of independent craftsmen that characterized industry of the period and toward mass production and standardized factory work.

Scientific management brought with it a number of advantages, which current critics often fail to remember, including improvements in the quality and efficiency of work processes. It helped workers with little experience and education become fairly productive quickly. In fact, it often actually improved the work life of employees who had previously been subjected to deathtrap mining operations, exploitative sweatshops, and capricious shop owner management. But although it facilitated industrialization, scientific management also had some very serious negative side effects: It separated the worker from the consequence of his or her own work. It stripped the worker of the opportunity to understand the whole work process, participate in a variety of tasks, and do the planning, evaluating, and improving of work processes. Perhaps most detrimentally, it prevented an understanding of the customers who used the worker's products and services. These were all normal aspects of working in a small workshop or on the family farm. Consequently, workers became focused over time on their own jobs and job rights, which were often, ironically, counterproductive to both the good of the enterprise and the individual.

Sociotechnical Systems

After discovering a remarkably productive coal mining team in postwar England, Trist (1950) suggested an alternative to scientific management. He said that by forming work teams that had complete responsibility for an entire operation, the interface between people (the social system) and their tools (the technical system) could be more fully optimized. This, he further postulated, would lead to job performance that was more rewarding and productive for the increasingly experienced work force.

About a decade later, these ideas took root in the United States. In the 1960s and early 1970s experiments with what were called *semi-autonomous work teams* or *technician* operations started in P&G plants in Ohio and Georgia; a Cummins Engine facility in Jamestown, New York; and a General Foods plant in Topeka, Kansas. In these organizations academicians joined ranks with practitioners to create self-directed work teams that demonstrated remarkable competitive and social advantages over scientific management. Since that time numerous other organizations have followed suit by creating or redesigning workplaces where teams of employees get involved in operational decisions and in many of the traditional supervisory responsibilities of managing the day-to-day business. In these organizations the traditional barriers to maximum employee contribution—narrow job descriptions, restrictive functional distinctions, lack of ongoing business information, and hierarchically geared compensation and status systems—are minimized.

What started in a few manufacturing plants has also spread into the service sector in organizations like Shenandoah Life Insurance Company and American Transtech, a company broken off from the AT&T monolith during their 1984 divestiture. These teams have even spilled over into public organizations and utilities, like the financial arm of Seattle Metro; schools, like those in the Dade County, Florida, school-based management program; hospital and research organizations, like the Mayo clinic; and tourist and recreation facilities, like the San Diego Zoo.

Types of Teams

Although teams are not a new phenomenon, they currently are a popular way for organizations to provide a structure that facilitates empowerment. But there are several different kinds of teams used today that differ because of their tasks, membership, or scope. An average employee, for example, can be a member of multiple teams. He or she may be a member of his or her natural work team, safety team, new product development team, company team, equipment procurement team, vendor relations team, organization redesign team, and intraorganizational volleyball team all at the same time. This is fairly common and very confusing.

Generally speaking, teams can be separated into different categories depending on their duration and scope, as shown in Figure 10.2. There are

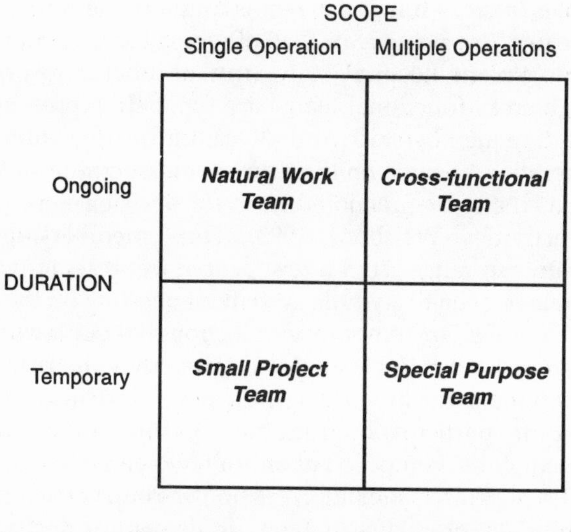

FIGURE 10.2. Types of teams.

teams that have ongoing responsibilities and others that will be disbanded after the team's task is accomplished. There are also teams that work within smaller organizational borders while still others cross multiple organizational boundaries. If we put these variables into a 2 × 2 matrix, we can divide teams into four general types: (1) natural work teams, (2) cross-functional teams, (3) small project teams, and (4) special purpose teams. Each of these deserves some elaboration.

Natural work teams are the collected individuals that form around normal work processes. They are a subsystem of an organization, such as a packing department might be to a manufacturing plant or a radiology unit might be to a hospital. They generally are composed of a small group of people (ideally, fewer than 10) who work together regularly in the same organizational unit. These are the teams represented on organization charts that have an ongoing operational responsibility to provide some products and/or services for customers. Also referred to as work teams, technician teams, or functional/department teams, these units are the most common target for becoming self-directed work teams because they have the most sustainable influence on organizational results and because they endure long enough to justify the inevitable investment in training and communication infrastructure.

Cross-functional teams are organization units with an ongoing purpose that crosses multiple organizational boundaries. Parts of P&G and Tektronix, for example, use teams with representatives from each natural work team for communication and administration. These teams meet on a regular basis (weekly and daily, respectively) to review systemwide issues and coordinate ongoing activities like project staffing and scheduling. Other examples of cross-functional teams might be safety teams, employee relations teams, or pricing teams, all of which have a standing task that affects the whole plant, hospital, store, firm, or other large organizational unit. Although cross-functional teams are typically representative in nature, with rotating membership to allow maximum opportunity for everyone in the operation to serve on the team, some operations use the whole organization as the cross-functional team for decision-making and problem-solving activities (Weisbord, 1993). Thus, membership of a cross-functional team can range from a few people (representative) to several hundred people or even to a whole system, depending on the task.

Small project teams are temporary collections of people formed to work on a particular task until it is completed. Then they disband. The task in this case is confined to the limits of a single natural work group and usually does not require participation from everyone on the natural work team; they are, consequently, composed of only a few people (ideally fewer than five). Examples of projects include creating personnel development plans, resolving equipment problems, making certain staffing decisions, evaluating equipment purchases, writing reports, developing proposals, and so forth. If these teams are properly focused and trained, they should be able to make and implement good decisions rapidly. People seldom work full-time on project teams; a single team member will often serve on several project teams concurrently, with these projects consuming only a few hours a week.

Special purpose teams are another kind of temporary organization that disbands upon the completion of the task. The scope of the tasks, however, is bigger than that of a small project team, with implications that cross multiple natural work groups. Vendor or customer problem-solving activities, for example, are normally conducted in special purpose teams. New product development, new technology investigation, future search conferences, organization redesign, and similar activities are typical projects. These teams require more time and support than small project teams. They often demand intense commitments from participants for several weeks or months, and it is difficult for a team member to be on more than one of them at any given time.

DIAGNOSING THE APPROPRIATENESS OF TEAMS FOR AN ORGANIZATION

Different types of teams may fit better in certain organizational situations than in others. But a few matters influence team-based operations broadly. This section discusses two issues affecting team effectiveness in virtually all applications: organizational readiness for change and team leadership. I also introduce some instrumentation we use as a vehicle for discussing these issues in a variety of client systems.

Assessing the Organization's Need for Change

An initial diagnostic step is to determine whether there is a genuine business need for changing to teams. Organizations that create teams simply because it is a current popular intervention will likely be disappointed with the results and naive about the extent of the effort required to change to a work culture that will sustain teams. Therefore, we often help organizations assess the appropriateness of using teams. For example, our experience indicates that unless leaders can articulate a clear and compelling case for changing to teams (especially if the operation is considering SDWTs), they are better off staying with traditional hierarchical structures.

The case for change depends essentially on the answers to three questions:

1. Why should we change?
2. What happens if we don't change?
3. What is in it for me?

Asking these questions couples the change to a team-based operation with organizational and personal needs and reduces the possibility of frivolous organizational change not grounded in operational realities. Our experience suggests that people who answer the first question with responses like "My boss wants me to do this" or "I don't think we need to do anything differently" generally will not invest the required effort to implement or sustain this change. This, of course, is also true for people who do not see any undesirable consequence to remaining in a traditional work system (Question 2), and it is especially true for people who believe that there is no personal benefit for them to go to a team-based system (Question 3).

In the most successful efforts we have seen, a critical mass of the leaders answer these questions with responses such as "We have to do this to improve our flexibility and employee commitment" or "We can no longer rely just on our technology if we are going to survive" or "I will enjoy coming to work more when we do this." Such replies indicate both a basic knowledge of team-based operations and a general willingness to invest time and energy in the implementation process. Where people do not believe that teams will provide organizational and personal benefits, the implementation will be more difficult even if teams are perfectly appropriate for that operation.

In addition to determining whether a compelling case for change exists, we have also found it useful during this evaluation process to have people assess their organization or business for potential fit with teams. We do this by providing descriptive statements of behavioral and structural characteristics of team-based organizations and having people assess the appropriateness of these statements for their operation over the next 3 to 5 years. The actual characteristics and format of our instrumentation is described in more detail later in this chapter. This readiness assessment uses a paper-and-pencil instrument developed by Belgard·Fisher·Rayner called Assessing the Organization Need for Change combined with focused interviews with a cross section of the organization.

When Teams Are Not Appropriate

As might be expected, some organizations are jumping on the team bandwagon regardless of whether it is appropriate for their operation. We have already discussed a number of criteria that characterize effective team-based operations, including purpose, shared agreement on purpose, and commitment paradigm foundation. But are all operations appropriate for team structures? The following key diagnostic questions can reveal where they are not:

• *Do people need to work together to get the task done effectively?* If there is no interdependency between people in an operation, then having a common purpose adds no appreciable value. One utility company, for example, wanted to put their line repair people into natural work teams. In this particular case, the repair technicians were spread geographically across the state and always worked independently on projects. Cost constraints limited the company's ability to get the technicians together, and the nature of their work offered few benefits from this collaboration, anyway. Was this a place for these teams? Probably not.

• *Is operational expertise limited to a few people because of technical or security constraints?* In such cases empowerment serves no purpose. I am reminded of an operation that wanted to create cross-functional teams between departments involved in the production of sophisticated weapon systems. Their customer had demanded (for security reasons) that each department not tell the other departments what it did. While this certainly caused significant communication and cooperation problems between departments, the customer was willing to trade these off to avoid the unthinkable consequences of a security breach. This environment was not one in which cross-functional teams were likely to be effective. Not surprisingly, they rapidly became frustrated with their efforts to create these teams when their customer would not abandon the requirement for the compartmentalization of duties and information.

It is important, however, to put these concerns about the inappropriate uses of teams into perspective. Many people argue that teams are also not useful in settings where

• Work is mundane and repetitious.
• Consistency is more important than innovation.
• Technologies are punishing.
• Single experts are best qualified to make independent decisions.
• Stability is more important than flexibility.

But even if we accept these arguments, there are fewer and fewer of these kinds of organizations around anymore. And although there is some merit to these arguments, I do know of successful examples of teams in each of the disputed categories. Lots of organizations, for example, use the teams to get rid of unnecessary mundane and repetitious work. By rotating from job to job each team member gets a chance to learn a number of skills and avoid the boredom that comes from performing the same task ad nauseam.

Nevertheless, it is also important to remember that teams are not a substitute for sound business basics. If you have a product or service no one wants to buy, teams won't necessarily help. Nor will they help if you are in the wrong business, or if you don't have the right technology.

"Greenfield" and "Brownfield" Applications

Once appropriateness of teams is determined, the organization must get down to the nuts and bolts of change. A frequently asked question at this stage is "Can you modify an existing organization, burdened with the habits and structures of its past, into these countertraditional teams?" Frankly, a number of practitioners have doubted the practicality of transforming existing organizations. Evidence of this was seen at companies like P&G, which, in spite of compelling evidence of the effectiveness of teams, resisted changing over existing organizations. For nearly 15 years the company used the "greenfield" approach almost exclusively to introduce team-based operations.

New plants came to be called "greenfields" because the typical start-up included building the whole operation from the ground up. Green fields were purchased from farmers, the fields were mowed, foundation holes were dug, and a brand-new organization was begun from scratch. This was the ideal time, of course, to introduce new work systems. New employees would be hired unencumbered by traditional work practices and jobs. Managers and supervisors would be brought in with the expectation of managing differently. New pay systems could be created from the start to support teamwork. Organizations could take the time to plan out an ideal work system without the constraints of keeping an existing operation running at the same time. Some operations (like Digital's Enfield, Connecticut, plant) invested up to 2 years just for the planning and preparation associated with the new team-based work system, a luxury unavailable in existing operations.

In spite of the compelling advantages of using the greenfield approach to create teams, however, a number of operations began experimenting with the "brownfield" implementation process in the 1980s. The reasons for this were pragmatic. During this time period very few operations had the capital to invest in starting up new units, such as manufacturing plants. Consequently, people who were becoming convinced that teams were important for them could no longer wait for the next start-up. There weren't any. They had to make it work in existing operations if they wanted to use teams at all.

To be sure, the brownfield approach is, in the words of one general manager, "like changing the tire on a bicycle while you're riding it." The momentum of long-standing control-oriented norms and relationships is difficult to redirect into teams. And it is hard to make major modifications to your social system while you are still required to produce products and/or services. But surprisingly, the early pioneers into brownfield applications found some advantages to this difficult process. Tektronix, for example, found that while a disadvantage of the brownfield approach is the length of employee experience in a particular operation (it's tough to break old habits), that same experience, conversely, provided an advantage to the redesign process. Let me explain.

Although a greenfield start-up provides fertile ground for alternative social systems, it also requires a tremendous investment in technical education as people learn their new businesses, customers, and equipment. In a brownfield you can focus more energy on the work system part of the change because you don't have to get the business and equipment up and running. Moreover, in a greenfield the team members can't really get fully involved in creating the team operation (at least the technical side of it) because they don't have enough knowledge to participate meaningfully. In the brownfield, however, people already know their operation and they can use this knowledge to redesign their organization.

Personal involvement in the process of actually creating the teams (from the beginning) creates a higher level of employee commitment to the change process and makes employees and managers more likely to view the organization itself as a tool for continuous improvement. In addition, if their involvement in a redesign process results in real improvements, employees are likely to remember the experience as they would a before-and-after weight reduction program: They often feel better about themselves and about the corporation when the process is completed, and they can see what they have accomplished. The flip side to this issue is especially problematic and worth noting: Involving people in a process to create teams can generate tremendous expectations for ongoing participation, expectations that, if unmet, can cause a degree of cynicism and distrust that organizations report as being much worse than if they had never started with teams in the first place.

Numerous companies have now used the brownfield approach to create teams. Although it does require considerable time to alter a culture rather than grow a new one (most organizations assume a 3- to 5-year transition time), successful brownfields in companies like Rohm and Haas and Corning show that it can be done. Particularly important in these transitions is the issue of effective process and leadership. The sociotechnical system analysis introduced by Trist and others in the Tavistock group in postwar England and two important derivatives—the P&G open system planning process (Hanna, 1988) and the search conference process (Weisbord, 1993)—have proven to be important guides to brownfield team implementation. While it is true that effective team implementations have been made without using the rigor of any of these processes, it appears essential that some redesign process be used.

It is particularly important that the emphasis of redesign not be to create teams. I know this is counterintuitive, but my experience is that people really must have the latitude of designing the organization that makes the most sense to them. If it appears to them that the end state of the design process is predetermined, then there is clearly no need to involve them in the process. Thus, what is most important is that the redesign *process* be team based, not that the outcome be a team-based organization. Moreover, it is becoming increasingly evident that perhaps the most essential part of the process is an intensive business education element for the design team. Absent this education about technologies, customers, and markets, the designers are unlikely to make any recommendations that are outside the box of their own past experience.

In addition to appropriate process considerations, effective leadership appears to be a key element of the brownfield approach. I can't think of a single successful transition to teams where the champion of the team implementation wasn't able to do both of the following: (1) create a compelling case for change and (2) create a vision of a better workplace than the current operation. While these leadership elements are extremely useful in the greenfield, they are critical in a brownfield.

Assessing Leader Readiness

One of the most critical dimensions for successful implementation of teams is leadership. Ironically, even in self-directed work team operations (elsewhere I have argued *especially* in SDWT operations; see Fisher, 1986, 1989, 1993), the effectiveness of the formal team leadership is most often the crucial difference between team success and failure. Although many team structures are initiated without strong team managers, I am aware of only a few teams that have sustained themselves over time without formal team leadership.

To be sure, the new management role is not the traditional one of planning, organizing, directing, and controlling (Fisher, 1993; Hirschhorn, 1991). It is a role of training, coaching, and leading instead. As already mentioned, rather than the pervasive control paradigm that has dominated traditional operations since the turn of the century, these leaders operate from the perspective of the commitment paradigm. That is, rather than believing that the primary role of management is to control people, these leaders believe that the primary role of leadership is to create a workplace that generates maximum commitment of employees. Thus, they are less interested in mandating policies and procedures than they are in providing information, support, and training.

To assess these inclinations and provide people the opportunity to discuss the new management role, we have been using a process developed at Belgard·Fisher·Rayner called Assessing Leader Readiness. In this process, leaders fill out an instrument that helps them identify their state of readiness to implement teams. They determine whether there is a genuine need for changing to teams and a willingness to make personal role modifications. It also helps them articulate their own fears about the change process.

In addition, the assessment checks three attributes of leaders that are especially important in initiating teams. These attributes are knowledge about team-based operations, contact with the operation, and ability to influence major change. If leaders are not aware, for example, that teams require much more than changing the titles and structures of the organization, they are unlikely to support the inevitable systemwide modifications in the cultural fabric of the operation, including things like policies, information systems, and pay systems which must change if the operation makes a serious effort at team empowerment. They will also be unlikely to willingly sponsor the training and other development activities necessary for both the implementation and sustaining of teams.

Similarly, our experience with companies like Martin Marietta, Rockwell, Apple Computer, and Weyerhaeuser suggests that effective leaders need to be in touch with the day-to-day operation and must also have the clout necessary to make changes, not just in the systems but in the culture of the organization. These two characteristics don't always go together. Often, people with the most knowledge about the operation have little power to change it while those with the power have lost touch with the operation. These readiness issues should be dealt with prior to a lot of implementation activity.

DIAGNOSING TEAM FUNCTIONING

How does one diagnose the effectiveness of teams once they are in place? In order to answer that question let's review the determinants of empowerment. After empowerment, we'll look at the specific success factors for teams.

Determinants of Empowerment

Empowerment is a function of four important variables: authority, resources, information, and accountability (Fisher, 1993). You might remember these variables by using the memory word *aria*, which is composed of the first letter of each variable. The beauty of the opera solo of the same name depends on whether the music is written, performed, and accompanied well. Similarly, the empowerment melody only works when all of the variables are in complete harmony. For people to feel empowered they need formal authority and all of the resources (budget, equipment, time, training, etc.) necessary to do something with the new authority. They also need timely, accurate information to make good decisions. And they need a personal sense of accountability for the work.

This definition of empowerment can be expressed as follows:

$$Empowerment = f\,(Authority, Resources, Information, Accountability)$$
$$Empowerment = 0 \text{ if } Authority \text{ or } Resources \text{ or}$$
$$Information \text{ or } Accountability = 0$$

This expression indicates that empowerment is a function of all four variables and that if any of the variables in the equation go to zero, there is no empowerment. This explains why some empowerment initiatives are a sham. Authority without information and resources, for example, is only permission. Telling people that they should go ahead and make decisions or solve problems without providing them access to accurate business information and without providing them the skills training, budget, and time to accomplish the task is a prescription for volatile failure. Not sharing accountability is paternalistic and condescending. It sends the message that the empowerment isn't real. It is only when all four elements are present that people will feel and act responsible.

Thus, we can diagnose the seriousness and effectiveness of an empowerment effort by asking about all elements of this formula. We have found it useful to ask a cross section of employees for specific examples of how the different variables are applied in the workplace. In one operation that claimed to use empowerment, for example, we could find no examples of an institutionalized information-passing infrastructure. Employees were completely reliant on management's discretion to share data with the "teams." Not surprisingly, the employees didn't feel very empowered, even though management had given them permission to get involved in management decisions and had provided them some training classes.

Critical Success Factors

In addition to understanding empowerment, diagnosing team effectiveness also requires a review of the critical success factors for teams. The instrumentation mentioned previously to help people determine the appropriateness of teams is also used later to determine the effectiveness of their teams. We ask participants to rate the organization's effectiveness on 10 factors that our experience and research have shown to be critical success factors for team-based organizations. They are customer orientation, technical excellence, shared values, performance commitment, environmental awareness, trust, reward systems, work autonomy/job flexibility, organization structure, and leadership. Generally speaking, this instrument checks observable organizational artifacts, such as systems, behaviors, and institutionalized processes, that affect team success.

In this process participants determine where the organization is now on a series of continua for each of the characteristics. They then identify where they believe the organization ideally ought to be in 3 to 5 years on each continuum. This allows people to do a simple gap analysis on the 10 characteristics and helps them determine whether they need to do anything different from what they are doing now.

For example, the environmental awareness continuum is shown in Figure 10.3. The statements at the left end of the continuum correspond to typical employee knowledge in a control-oriented organization while those at the right end represent typical knowledge in a team-based organization. This is one of the simple ways to observe the difference between a need-to-know organization and one where information is shared openly. Why is this important? In control organizations information is generally seen as a source of power. Hence, it is guarded jealously. These operations also seldom trust employees with strategic business information. Moreover, since most important decisions are made by management and not by employees, there is little need for the operation to go to the effort of collecting and disseminating data that are essentially useless to most employees. In operations where people see the kind of information at the right end of the continuum in Figure 10.3 as being unnecessary, of course, there is a small gap between the current state and the desired state and the two marks indicating these states are located on the left side of the continuum.

```
1  2  3  4  5  6  7  8  9  10
```

Everyone can state

- The name of the area they work for
- The name of their manager
- Their job in their area

Everyone can state

- Key business objectives
- Chief competitors and what differentiates their products
- Key cost data
- Main factors influencing product profitability
- Key customers
- How they, personally, impact business results

FIGURE 10.3. Environmental awareness continuum.

In operations where people believe that the information is important but unavailable, the marks have a large gap between them.

This self-analysis helps people understand the key characteristics that determine team effectiveness. More importantly, it generally leads to discussions about improvements because the analysis process is seen as congruent with teams. That is, because people determine how important each of the continua is in their operation, they tend to feel that the analysis process itself is participative in nature and a more appropriate approach for team-based operations. They are consequently more apt to believe the data and act on them.

When Self-Directed Work Teams Fail

SDWTs don't always, of course, produce sterling results. Although I am not aware of any studies to confirm this, SDWT consultants normally suggest that teams have about a 50% success rate. That is, for every 100 companies that begin this work, about half of them fail to get the desired improvements. Why? The single biggest reason is a lack of management commitment to the whole change process. Impatience or an unwillingness to make the personal management changes necessary to make it work have foiled many attempts to create sustainable SDWTs. Another typical reason for failure is organizational unwillingness to provide the necessary budget and time for training to help team leaders and team members get new skills.

But sometimes even when SDWT implementation and support are flawless, there can be failures. No organization design or management style can guarantee success. The airline People's Express, for example, was well publicized for using self-directed work teams effectively just prior to its failure. But caught between rapid growth and a questionable market, the airline went bust. Similarly, both Digital Equipment Corporation and P&G have shut down SDWT organizations. Although these operations in the eastern United States and Europe were more cost and quality effective than traditional facilities, they were not good enough to compensate for major declines in the market or for distribution advantages of other locations, respectively.

Diagnosing Reasons for Team Dysfunction

Obviously, some of the preparation and assessment work already discussed can first prevent and then later identify key concern areas relative to team dysfunction. But our experience suggests that after teams are started most team problems boil down to some combination of the following four maladies, some of which have already been covered earlier in the chapter: (1) inappropriate use of teams, (2) lack of management support, (3) lack of good information, and (4) lack of team member skills.

How do you determine whether these problems affect a particular team? Focused interviews with individuals and small groups can often highlight these problem areas. We will frequently open these interviews by asking people, "What is it that gets in the way of your team being as effective as possible?" Typical responses include the following: "We don't get time [or budget or training, etc.] to make this work"; or "We never find out what second shift [or management or the union, etc.] is doing"; or "We can't make a group decision [or solve problems or fix the equipment, etc.]."

Secondary questions or observations help focus the perceived obstacles. You can often suspect a lack of management support for teams when the teams are not provided with adequate resources to fulfill their new responsibilities. When people have resources but inadequate communication, suspect weaknesses in the information system infrastructure. If they have all the resources and data to operate effectively but don't know how to use them, the problem is normally a lack of skill training.

TEAMS AND THE FUTURE

Self-directed work teams have clearly not displaced traditional operations as the predominant organization type. But in the next few years we will see these teams replacing many of their more traditional counterparts.

An Idea Whose Time Has Come

There are several reasons why the practices of empowerment will accelerate dramatically over the next few years and consequently displace traditional supervisory practices. Empowerment is an idea whose time has come because the following are all statements of fact:

- Teams have demonstrated their ability to remain viable over time.
- New organizational environments require changing roles.
- New technology now makes empowerment practical.
- Worker expectations make participation inevitable.

Longevity of Teams

The first reason that SDWTs are not just another of the endless fads that have danced across the desks of modern corporations is that they have already been around for decades. Fads, on the other hand, tend to be popular for a few years and then fade away into obscurity. Multiple corporations have actively used these teams since at least the early 1960s and arguably earlier. Several companies have also reported that they originally used SDWTs at the start-up of their organization or new venture. As they grew, they often moved away from the self-directed work teams to the management philosophies and structures in vogue for organizations of their size and type. A lot of them are now trying to get back to their roots.

New Organization Realities

Empowerment tends to be most effective in precisely the kind of environments many organizations find themselves in today. Complex work assignments usually require the input and commitment of multiple people. The watchwords of responsiveness, quality, customer orientation, speed, productivity, and quality of work life have become more important than the previous, unspoken workplace mottoes of control and regulation. Many people who came from an organizational setting where empowered work teams may not have been very useful in the past are finding that changes caused by customer demands, employee expectations, competition, government intervention, public pressure, environmentalism, technology, or any other of a host of possible reasons have put them in a new world where empowered teams make a lot more sense now than they did before. These new realities require organizations to evolve and roles to change.

Technology

Another reason why these nontraditional work organizations and work roles will become more prominent in the future is team-facilitating technology. User-friendly personal computers, faxes, and telephone networking alternatives are cost-effective technological options that allow the increased utilization of meaningful work team involvement. A whole new information systems software genre dubbed "groupware" has emerged to facilitate team involvement as well. These packages include things like electronic messaging systems (e.g., electronic mail, teleconferencing), decision support systems (e.g., automated Delphi and nominal group techniques), systems to support collaboration (e.g., shared authoring processes, bulletin boards), and, most importantly, business information systems that make timely cost, quality, and project status information available to all team members. These technologies facilitate group decision making, problem solving, information gathering, and information assessing. Technology can also provide some substitutes for the information passing and coordination role of the traditional hierarchy. This allows teams to be directed by the work and information rather than by managers.

Worker Expectations

Worker participation is a manifestation of people's desires for democracy in the workplace. Legislated already in some Scandinavian countries, and discussed as a possible element of the European Economic Community initiatives, this trend will naturally follow the democratization of other political systems. SDWTs are typically the natural extension of this movement. Although they are not democracies in the strict sense of the term, they do allow worker influence on how the workplace is managed, which has normally been unavailable in traditional operations.

Success of Teams

Perhaps the most pragmatic reason that self-directed work teams are here to stay is that (all else being equal) they get better results than their traditional counterparts. In a review of organizations in seven countries that had made the transition from traditional work systems to SDWTs, Cotter (1983) found that (1) 93% reported improved productivity, (2) 88% reported decreased operating costs, (3) 86% reported improved quality, and (4) 70% reported better employee attitudes. Reports from organizations within American Transtech, DEC, Tektronix, Mead, TRW, James River, P&G, Martin Marietta, General Electric, Esso, Ford, and other corporations confirm these findings, indicating that SDWTs frequently outperform comparable traditional operations. Unlike a number of other corporate initiatives that have promised fire but delivered mostly smoke, SDWTs often improve many of the key organizational measures by 30 to 50%.

Many organizations in the consumer products, aerospace, and paper industries are actively using teams because they believe SDWTs provide significant competitive advantage. David Swanson, P&G senior vice president, confirmed this in a closed meeting at Harvard in 1984. He stated that the SDWT plants were "30–40% more productive than their traditional counterparts and significantly more able to adapt quickly to the changing needs of the business" (Hoerr & Pollock, 1986). Added Ted L. Marsten, Cummins Engine vice president, "This is the most cost-effective way to run plants . . . the people felt a lot better. . . and we got a much higher quality product" (Hoerr & Pollock, 1986). General Motors has actually used references to their teams in ads for the Saturn automobile, apparently because they assume that the advantages in quality, service, and/or cost-effectiveness will be obvious even to the consumer, who may be completely unfamiliar with organizational alternatives.

Teams aren't just for the megacorporations either: Johnsonville Foods, a sausage manufacturer in Sheboygan, Wisconsin, claimed that their productivity improved 50% since the company started using teams. Nor is the SDWT revolution limited to manufacturing companies: Federal

Express claimed that a team of clerks found and solved a billing problem that was costing the company $2.1 million per year (Dumaine, 1990). Insurance companies like Shenandoah Life Insurance have reduced cost and improved service through empowered teams (Hoerr & Pollock, 1986). And American Transtech office teams can process twice as many forms as they could under the traditional work system (Sherwood, 1988).

Growth of Teams

Will the SDWT become the predominant organization structure of tomorrow? A *Business Week* cover story suggested that it "appears to be the wave of the future" (Hoerr & Zellner, 1989) while a report in *Fortune* magazine boldly proclaimed that it *is* the wave of the future (Dumaine, 1990). But whether they completely displace traditional work systems or not, self-directed work teams are clearly growing. In a study by the Center for Effective Organizations at the University of Southern California, for example, researchers found that 67% of the surveyed organizations using empowerment techniques were also using SDWTs somewhere in their organization (Wright & Ledford, 1988). In a related study by Development Dimensions International, the Association for Quality and Participation, and *Industry Week*, a remarkable 83% of the companies experimenting with SDWTs in 1990 said they planned a considerable increase in their use by 1995 (Wellins et al., 1990). Similarly, a recent survey of 476 *Fortune* 1000 companies by the American Quality and Productivity Center showed that while only about 7% of the current workplace was organized into SDWTs, fully half of the companies questioned said they would rely much more on SDWTs in the years ahead.

As these numbers increase, there tends to be a ripple effect as companies see their competitors and collaborators using the approach. Everybody wants to keep up with the Joneses. Especially when the Joneses can deliver the same products and services that you do—only quicker, with higher quality, and at lower cost. After P&G used teams effectively on the soap side of the company, Colgate became interested and involved. Improvements on the pulp-and-paper side of the company were not unnoticed by competitors (and now SDWT devotees) James River, Crown Z, Champion, and others.

It is too early to tell whether the vast majority of management will be able to make the personal changes necessary for universal transformation from traditional to SDWT operations. These SDWT organizational practices are often in direct contradiction to the management philosophies and styles that catapulted powerful managers into their current positions of control and responsibility at every level of the corporation. Nor is it clear that other people will be able to change from the comfortable and pervasive work practices of the past. John Myers, human resources vice president for Shenandoah Life, suggests that "bureaucratic organizations become habit forming, just like cigarettes" (Hoerr & Pollock, 1986). Supervisors and supervisees alike often just can't bring themselves to change. And the majority of contemporary organizations are still on the fence watching the SDWT parade go by.

But SDWTs are clearly on the rise. Why? Not because they are more humane. Not because altruistic managements find SDWTs morally compelling. To paraphrase Winston Churchill, SDWTs are the worst form of organization except for all the others. They are frustrating and messy and chaotic. But they seem to get better results. Some organizations are excitedly leading the charge, others are moving cautiously, while still others are being dragged into a SDWT future by customers, competitors, or technologies. But they will go. Because as long as somebody can figure out how to improve results using SDWTs, others will have to figure out how to keep up with them.

REFERENCES

Belgard·Fisher·Rayner. (1989). *The empowerment continuum*. Beaverton, OR: Author.

Cotter, J. J. (1983). *Designing organizations that work: An open socio-technical systems perspective*. North Hollywood, CA: John J. Cotter & Associates.

Dumaine, B. (1990, May 7). Who needs a boss? *Fortune*, p. 52.

Eberle, C. (1987, June). *Competitiveness, commitment and leadership*. Paper presented at the Ecology of Work Conference, Washington, DC.

Fisher, K. (1986). Management roles in the implementation of participative management systems. *Human Resource Management*, 25(3), 459–479.

Fisher, K. (1989). Managing in the high commitment workplace. *Organizational Dynamics*, 17(3), 31–50.

Fisher, K. (1993). *Leading self-directed work teams: A guide to developing the new team leader skills*. New York: McGraw-Hill.

Hanna, D. (1988). *Designing organizations for high performance*. Reading, MA: Addison-Wesley.

Hirschhorn, L. (1991). *Managing in the new team environment: Skills, tools, and methods*. Reading, MA: Addison-Wesley.

Hoerr, J., & Pollock, M. (1986, September 29). Management discovers the human side of automation. *Business Week*, p. 74.

Hoerr, J., & Zellner, W. (1989, July 10). The payoff from teamwork. *Business Week*, pp. 56–62.

Katzenbach, J., & Smith, D. (1993). *The wisdom of teams: Creating the high-performance organization*. Cambridge, MA: Harvard Business School Press.

Ketchum, L., & Trist, E. L. (1993). *All teams are not created equal: How employee empowerment really works*. Newbury Park, CA: Sage.

Sherwood, J. (1988). Creating work cultures with competitive advantage. *Organizational Dynamics, 16*(3), 4–27.

Stepp, J. (1987, June). *Global competition: The role of industrial relations.* Speech presented at the Ecology of Work Conference, Washington, DC.

Trist, E. L. (1950, January). *The relations of social and technical systems in coal mining.* Paper presented at a meeting of the British Psychological Society.

Trist, E. L. (1981, June). The evolution of socio-technical systems: A conceptual framework and an action research program. *Issues in the Quality of Working Life* (Paper No. 2). Toronto: Ontario Ministry of Labour and Ontario Quality of Working Life Centre.

Walton, R. (1985, March–April). From control to commitment in the workplace. *Harvard Business Review*, pp. 77–84.

Weisbord, M. (1993). *Discovering common ground.* San Francisco: Berrett-Koehler.

Wellins, R. S., Wilson, J., Katz, A. J., Laughlin, P., Day, C. R. Jr., & Price, D. (1990). *Self-directed teams: A study of current practice.* Pittsburgh: Development Dimensions International, Association of Quality and Participation, and *Industry Week.*

Wright, R., & Ledford, G. (1988, November). *High involvement organization study.* Manuscript, University of Southern California, Graduate School of Business Administration, Center for Effective Organizations, Los Angeles.

CONCLUSION

CHAPTER 11

Toward Integrated
Organizational Diagnosis

ANN HOWARD
AND ASSOCIATES

Chapter 1 promised pursuit of three themes to advance the understanding and appreciation of organizational diagnosis. So far we have delivered only two: practice and scope. Figure 11.1 illustrates the ground we have covered: Against a background of organizational variables from the Burke–Litwin model (Figure 3.5), balloons bearing the names of chapter authors identify the focal point from which their chapter addressed organizational diagnosis.

Note that double-headed arrows interconnect all of the boxes in the open systems model of Figure 11.1. This brings us to the third primary theme of the book: the integration of organizational diagnosis. If the boxes are dynamically linked, then why not the balloons?

As discussed in Chapter 1, many organizations today, facing fast-paced global competition, are reengineering business processes and re-designing their organizations from top to bottom. No system functions independently, and no system remains unexamined. The time has come for organizational consultants to recognize that diagnosis and change efforts on one system do not function independently of other systems or the efforts of other practitioners. As Burke (1992) has stated, organizational consultation needs to evolve from implementing a set of standard tools that address small- to medium-sized organizational problems to enacting an emerging paradigm for the management of large-scale organization change.

The preceding chapters gave testimony to broadening concerns and more systems thinking. Ronald Zemke described in Chapter 6 how training needs analysis has expanded into the wider domain of human performance

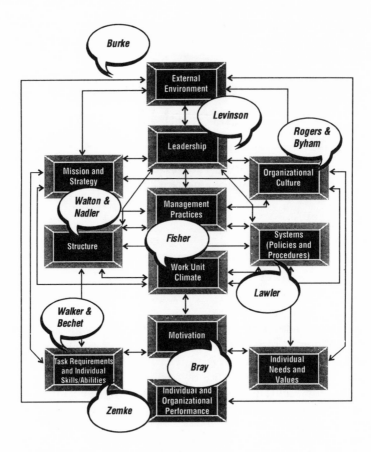

FIGURE 11.1. Authors' perspectives on organizational diagnosis.

technology. Elise Walton and David Nadler wrote of enlarging organization design into organization architecture (Chapter 4). James Walker and Thomas Bechet (Chapter 5) identified the evolution of manpower planning into strategic human resource planning. And Douglas Bray's personnel-centered organizational diagnosis (Chapter 7) used individual assessments to deduce organizational problems. In other words, the authors did not speak only to their nearby boxes in Figure 11.1. Their voices emanated from diverse focal points, but they echoed across the organizational systems.

This final chapter considers how to unite visions of organizational change into a coherent whole. That is, how can behavioral science practitioners advance toward integrated organizational diagnosis? To answer this question, we must pose others. For example: What do client organizations expect of practitioners, and what is their view of diagnosis? What are the barriers to integrated organizational diagnosis, and how might they be overcome? The previous chapters may give the impression that organizational diagnosis is an infinite regress of questions. This chapter moves to the other side of the interviewing table: Instead of asking questions, the authors will answer them.

INITIATING DIAGNOSIS

Smooth implementation of the diagnostic process is inevitably affected by the client's expectations about professional help.

What Do Clients Have in Mind When They Request Professional Services?

Clients typically seek out human resources practitioners to address a specific issue, often one they equate with "trouble." According to Harry Levinson, most clients request services "when they have some form of pain. Most often, people expect some form of relief."

Similarly, Edward Lawler says, "Clients normally have in mind a fix for their problem." Elise Walton and David Nadler add that the problem identified by the client is frequently not at the heart of the issue:

> Clients often have a clear presenting problem: strategy that hasn't been implemented, confusing and expensive business processes, a vague sense that the culture is "wrong." At issue is often the level of the problem; that is, there are problems underlying problems underlying problems. We often attempt to uncover root problems, or causes, which may differ from the presenting problem and the client-developed diagnosis and may generate a different set of solutions.

Warner Burke is often summoned to help with organization change or its aftermath:

> Clients have in mind either a specific project (e.g., facilitation of an offsite meeting; a workshop for managers on, say, performance management; a consulting skills program for human resources people) or a general assignment that involves organizational change of one form or another, such as culture change (helping to revamp the vision/mission and, perhaps, strategy) and/or structural change (modifying the organization chart, which these days usually means flattening the hierarchy). Organization development [OD] people are not always called on for organization redesign purposes, but they are usually asked for help in dealing with the *consequences* of a structural change.

While both problems and a need for change precipitate clarion calls for professional help, William Byham and Robert Rogers note that "very few clients call a consultant for diagnosis. They are attracted to a consultant by his or her reputation for conducting a training program, implementing organizational change, and so forth."

Do Clients Resist Diagnosis?

Clients seek help for problems and change, not for diagnosis. This answer to the previous question suggests that clients believe they already have their situations diagnosed when they request help. Does this mean that they resist the suggestion that further diagnosis is needed?

Not necessarily, say the authors, at least at first. Most clients do not find diagnosis unreasonable. "It makes logical sense to them," say William Byham and Robert Rogers. Adds Warner Burke, "They recognize the need for the consultant to get a 'feel for things,' to establish rapport with key people in the client organization, and to learn their particular business and ways of doing things." Kimball Fisher goes even further: "Experienced clients seldom balk at reasonable diagnostics. Some, in fact, demand it as a prerequisite to intervention."

Another reason diagnosis may be palatable is that, in Warner Burke's words, "All clients believe that their particular organization is unique, regardless of type and industry category. Thus, the consultant must learn—and appreciate—this uniqueness." Similarly, William Byham and Robert Rogers relate that "a good diagnosis before prescription makes clients feel, and rightly so, that the prescription is tailored to their particular needs."

This rosy view of client acceptance of diagnosis is tempered by certain restraints. Client sophistication can influence whether diagnosis will be accepted. Says Kimball Fisher, "For those who are less committed to a long-term change or less knowledgeable about the change process, resistance to the diagnostic process is common." There are also practical impediments. Edward Lawler reports that "clients generally are not enthusiastic about a diagnostic phase, particularly if it is going to be long and expensive." Similarly, Warner Burke remarks, "They do not want this phase to last forever, that's for sure."

Time pressures can be brutal in today's organizations. Says Kimball Fisher, "There is always pressure, of course, to get results as quickly as possible, and when clients view diagnosis as a way to delay results they become anxious." Ronald Zemke observes that managers get paid for solving problems and want help now, and that a trainer who tells a manager to slow down and analyze the problem first is exhibiting "behavior that can lead to involuntary retirement from the field of play. So it's easy to understand why many training people will simply hope against hope that management is right and the problem *can* be solved through training, all the while worrying over unseen sinkholes and snares, to mix a few metaphors."

Resistance to diagnosis grows with the size of the problem being attacked, according to William Byham and Robert Rogers:

> The difficult thing is getting customers to accept a more comprehensive diagnosis (the whole problem) rather than a specific diagnosis for a particular symptom. For example, none of our clients has ever resisted doing a job analysis ahead of the development of a selection system. However, they might resist the suggestion that the job analysis should not proceed until the effectiveness of the organization structure has been investigated, because this investigation will determine how empowered employees will be and will thus shape the employees' jobs. We still have found that many will go along with the higher-level diagnosis if it is thoroughly explained.

Perhaps a fair summary statement is that clients are willing to accept diagnosis as long as its value is thoroughly explained and it can survive a cost–benefit analysis. This may still sound discouraging, but it could be worse. "More difficult to sell, however, is an evaluation of the change effort," says Edward Lawler. Ronald Zemke adds, "The too often heard retort to the suggestion of an evaluation is, 'But *you're* the expert. Just do it right the first time.' "

DIAGNOSIS AND INTERVENTION

One of the risks of diagnosis is that the problems it uncovers may not be ones clients are prepared to tackle. This poses a new line of questioning to our authors: Does diagnosis always lead to intervention? If not, why not?

Why Diagnosis May Not Lead to Intervention

The diagnosis itself may sink prospects for intervention. Says Warner Burke, "Sometimes the diagnosis is done so poorly that the action to take as a consequence is anything but clear." Adds Edward Lawler, "Sometimes diagnosis does not lead to intervention because it fails to identify and produce consensus about what kinds of changes are needed or even what the problems are."

Producing consensus can be particularly vexing to a practitioner. William Byham and Robert Rogers offer an example:

> One of the more complex problems we face is the agreement with management that is not a true agreement. Over the last few years we have

encountered this especially in relation to the diagnosis of desired levels of empowerment. As noted in our chapter [Chapter 8], we believe that figuring out the level of empowerment desired by the organization is critical to the diagnosis of many other systems within the organization (selection, appraisal, training, and compensation, to name a few). In casual interviews with people within the organization, there often appears to be very great agreement on empowerment goals. But later, when asking executives to deal with specific issues, we find out that there is little agreement on general direction.

This is just one example of a diagnosis going beyond superficial vision to specifics. A consultant helps executives get down to reality and see how things are going to play out in terms of people affected, other parts of the organization, and impact on the bottom line. The consultant does this through asking questions, pointing out relationships, and so forth.

Clients may disallow interventions because the diagnosis reveals problems they have difficulty facing. According to Warner Burke, occasionally the "diagnosis generates such negative feelings that the client becomes immobilized or simply unwilling to deal with the data." Harry Levinson reports similar experiences:

> Sometimes the client doesn't want to proceed further out of fear or anxiety or reluctance to get at the root of the organization's problems. Sometimes there is internal resistance, as happened once when the top management of a police department was willing to undertake consultation but the middle management certainly wasn't. Their internal conflicts got in the way.

Ronald Zemke has found similar sensitivities: "Especially paralyzing to the progress of an intervention is the diagnosis that suggests that the sponsor is an integral part of the problem. 'I hired you to fix them, not blame me!' is often heard in one form or another."

Difficulty garnering political support for change is cited by Elise Walton and David Nadler as well as by Kimball Fisher. Similarly, Douglas Bray notes that issues such as "getting management on board" and concern about "upsetting employees" may affect whether intervention will take place. Bray and Fisher also mention practical hurdles, such as time and expense.

Linking Diagnosis and Intervention

William Byham and Robert Rogers admit that while the theoretical answer to the question, "Does diagnosis always lead to intervention?" is "No," in practice they have "never known an instance where diagnosis didn't lead to intervention. Why would management bring the consultant in if they didn't feel that something needed to be done?"

Kimball Fisher likewise reports, "The large majority of clients take at least some minimum steps after the diagnosis." He, in fact, tries to ensure that this will happen: "I believe it is the practitioner's responsibility to get the client to agree to some minimum level of intervention prior to the diagnosis as part of the initial contracting discussion." Fisher also reminds us that "diagnosis is an intervention. In my experience the act of diagnosis itself changes the client system being observed. Expectations are heightened, uncomfortable concerns are raised, and unresolved issues are surfaced publicly. If some additional intervention is not taken, there is a predictable increase in skepticism and a reduction in trust." Adds Ronald Zemke, "Diagnosis creates awareness and sets up expectations among people in the organization. To ignore or discount that is to dehumanize the process." Elise Walton and David Nadler make a similar point: "The question implies a clear line between diagnosis and intervention, not often found in practice. In fact, diagnosis *is* intervention, and the relationship between action and discovery is often iterative and interdependent."

SEQUENCING DIAGNOSIS AND CHANGE EFFORTS

Given that practitioners embark upon diagnosis from various corners of the organizational architecture, an integrated diagnosis must consider logical priorities. Is there a preferred sequence to diagnosis/change efforts? Does it matter what aspects of organizational functioning are addressed first?

Beginning Diagnosis at the System Level

Katz and Kahn (1980), strong proponents of the open systems model, recommend that diagnosis begin at the system rather than the individual level because this will account for the greatest amount of variance. In a like vein, Rummler (1988) has said, "Put a good performer in a bad system and the system will win every time—almost" (p. 8).

Several authors of this volume provide additional reasons for beginning at the system level. Warner Burke puts it this way:

> Unless one is consulting to a particular function (e.g., human resources) for particular purposes, it is best to begin at some general management level—a business sector head, for example—and to work at the outset with understanding goals, objectives, and business pur-

poses and how these fit with the external environment and with internal resources, capabilities, and needed changes. In other words, it is best to begin at a level where various organizational functions come together and require integration.

William Byham and Robert Rogers also emphasize initial goal setting:

The sequence should be to figure out where you're going before you figure out how you're going to get there. Compensation, training, and so forth, are systems within the organization that help it achieve certain goals. They should not be attacked before the organization has defined the goals they are trying to achieve.

Elise Walton and David Nadler believe that failure to work from strategy and goals is a common failure:

We tend to follow the old "structure follows strategy" principle or, more generically, the precept that direction/vision must precede all change, must *direct* all change. Otherwise, you get "ad hocracy" and lots of little changes that add up to very little result. The tendency to start up lots of little solutions to lots of little problems and never look at the systemic needs seems to be a common mistake in U.S. industry.

Beginning Diagnosis and Change Efforts Elsewhere

Although there are strong arguments for beginning diagnosis at the system level, this is not always feasible nor necessarily desirable. "Start with the pain the client expresses," says Harry Levinson. "Even though we know that the presenting problem is often not the real one or the basic one, that's where the client hurts and what the client wants you to at least start working on. In the beginning clients may not yet understand that forces other than those they are aware of may be operating."

Edward Lawler points out several ways in which the pay system can take the lead in organizational change efforts:

Perhaps most frequently discussed is the Scanlon plan or some other form of gain-sharing to improve plant productivity. In these situations the initial change effort is focused on the development and installation of a gain-sharing plan that pays bonuses based on improvements in productivity. The Scanlon Plan also emphasizes building participative problem-solving groups into the organization, but the clear emphasis is on the gain-sharing formula and the financial benefits of improved productivity. The participative management structure is put in to facilitate productivity improvement, which in turn will result in gains to be shared. Not surprisingly, once gain-sharing starts and inhibitors to productivity are identified, other changes result. Typical of these are improvements in the organization's structure, the design of jobs and work, and training programs. Often these are dealt with rather swiftly and effectively because the gain-sharing plan itself provides a strong motivation to do so.

There are other reward system changes that also can trigger broader organizational change efforts. For example, the introduction of skill-based pay can stimulate a broad movement to participation because, among other things, it provides people with the skills and knowledge they need to participate. In a somewhat different vein, a dramatic change in the pay-for-performance system can be very effective in altering the strategic directions that an organization takes. For example, installing bonus systems that pay off on previously unmeasured or overlooked performance indicators can dramatically shift the direction of an organization. Similarly, installing a long-term bonus plan for executives can cause them to change their time horizons and their decision-making practices in important ways.

Sequencing Subsystem Diagnosis and Change

Where diagnosis begins only partly answers the sequencing question. After the first step, what is the best order in which to approach the remaining organizational systems? Sometimes there is an urge to do everything at once. Elise Walton and David Nadler put it this way:

> We are looking at the interdependence of interventions and what that implies for our generic approaches to change. For example, a change in strategy may call for a new structure, which calls for new people with new skills. It turns out that you can't change the structure until you can change the people, and so on. The question is, How can you concurrently make all these changes?

Edward Lawler provides one example of simultaneous changes: "New participative plants represent an interesting example of participative reward systems changes being put in at the same time as other participative practices. Indeed, one reason for such plants' success is their ability to start with all their systems operating in a participative manner." Nevertheless, this type of organizational change is atypical, according to Lawler. "In a major organizational change it is difficult to alter all the systems in the organization simultaneously. Typically, one set of changes leads to another set of changes." Although reward systems change can be either a lead or a lag in the overall change process, he reports that it is most often a lag factor:

> This certainly is true in most efforts to change toward participative management. The initial thrust often is on team building, job redesign, quality circles, or some other area. It is only after these other practices

have been in place for a while that the organization tends to deal with the reward system changes needed to support these new practices. Often, there is surprise that these other important changes lead to a need for revision in the reward system. The connected nature of organizations makes it almost inevitable that when major changes are made in an organization's strategic direction or management style and practices, change will also have to be made in the reward system.

Kimball Fisher looks at the linkages between systems to determine an appropriate sequence:

Each phase of the diagnosis/change process should create a desire to complete the next phase of change. Reward system redesign, for example, is better done after (not before) organization redesign. This way it supports job structure changes and is seen as a natural extension of the previous redesign process. Similarly, communication infrastructure building should normally be changed prior to organization restructuring. If this type of sequencing is followed in creating team-based operations, for example, good information meetings normally generate interest and a desire to create teams. After team structures are in place, people are interested in creating pay and performance appraisal systems that support the new team structure. Done out of sequence, the various parts of the change effort are confusing and sometimes counterproductive.

William Byham and Robert Rogers keep their eyes on the ultimate outcome: "Regardless of where you start or the path you take, the resulting output should be as much alignment of systems with the vision and cultural goals as possible."

In summary, there are logical considerations, but no hard-and-fast rules about sequencing diagnosis and change efforts. Beginning at the system level offers some advantages, but different situations may favor other starting places and sequences. Says Edward Lawler, "It is hard to generalize about where you start a change process. I am asked this question frequently and usually resist answering it. I might add that organizations often see this resistance as a mark of a typical academic, if not an incompetent, because they think that there ought to be one way to proceed with the diagnosis/change effort."

BARRIERS TO INTEGRATED
ORGANIZATIONAL DIAGNOSIS

Some of the barriers to integrated organizational diagnosis recapitulate and exacerbate the obstacles to doing any diagnosis at all. Many practical problems fall into this category. But there are also barriers unique to an integrated organizational diagnosis, which derive from the segmentation of both organizations and professional practice.

Practical Barriers

A complete diagnosis could involve collecting a staggering amount of information. Douglas Bray offers this view:

> The variety and amount of information needed to gauge the human resources health of an organization is imposing. We must measure not only the knowledge, skills, and motivation of employees but also the effectiveness of organizational efforts to enhance these and employee performance, as guided by organizational values. The many things that must be known about employees and from them cannot be learned without the use of behavioral simulations, tests, focus groups, targeted interviews, and questionnaires. Because an organization's employees are in many jobs, at several levels, and in different divisions and departments, the total diagnostic job in even a moderate-sized company would be immense even if only management-level employees were included.

Bray's personnel-centered method uses sampling to bring the scope of the diagnostic effort under control.

The time required for an integrated diagnosis can be considerable, particularly management time. William Byham and Robert Rogers characterize this issue:

> Any time you try to deal with integrated organizational diagnosis, you're dealing with the top people in the organization, and they're hard to get hold of. You have to sell the value of the diagnosis to those people so they'll take the time off to participate. Most managers understand the value of diagnosis once it is explained, but there is also a constant push to do it quicker than it can really be accomplished.

Douglas Bray raises the issue of how much diagnosis the client will stand for or pay for. "This can be very elaborate or minimal. It is important for the practitioner to differentiate real needs from what would be 'good for you.' "

James Walker and Thomas Bechet describe other practical problems that are associated with data gathering:

> The work that people do may be examined from a variety of perspectives and purposes. In many organizations jobs are analyzed and described for compensation purposes, for organization planning, for

process and quality improvement, for identification of training and development needs, and for guiding future staffing and selection decisions. It makes eminent sense for a common analysis of work to serve all of these purposes.

However, these analyses are typically conducted at different times, by different people, and with somewhat different data being required. As a result, the incumbent employees and their managers are asked to provide information for different purposes at different times. And the responses change over time as work content changes.

Attempts have been made over the years to develop an integrated job analysis process, resulting in a data base that could serve multiple applications. However, it is difficult to anticipate information requirements for specific applications and to obtain credible information when there is no clear and pressing need for the information.

Because need for the information rests with those persons requesting it, the ownership of the information rests with them, not with the incumbent employees and their managers. It is preferable that employees and managers perceive the merit of a broad understanding of changing work activities and requirements, that they recognize that this information can enable them to continuously improve their performance, utilization, and development.

Organizational Silos

Organization structures can create barriers to integrated organizational diagnosis. For example, Joseph Harless, a human performance analyst, notes that there is no organizational entity identified as providing help with human performance. "Every door that we have is marked with a particular solution, like 'Training sold here,' 'Personnel selection sold here,' 'Work-process redesign sold here.' " (Froiland, 1993). Warner Burke calls such structural barriers "the chimney or smokestack phenomenon, overly 'sectorizing' business units. In other words, the lack of adequate horizontal processes."

Elise Walton and David Nadler describe how differences among organizational units can pose obstacles:

> Perspective probably encompasses the broadest range of differences, but clearly there are functional differences, one of the more notable ones being line/staff. In this case, the question of perspective is supplemented by the actor/observer differences; that is, line managers, as actors, and staff managers, who are often the observers, tend to have very different interpretations of an event.
>
> Another difference is in objectives, that is, in how organizational members answer the question, "How is the change likely to benefit or harm me?" To the extent that a certain diagnosis implicates their

weaknesses or suggests action that may be unfavorable, individual members may have a hard time integrating with the rest of the team. As always, the issue is how to build broad ownership of the diagnosis.

Professional Silos

One encouraging note about organizational silos is that current change efforts are successfully removing many of them. The same cannot be said for professional silos. As Warner Burke (1992) has put it, "As organizational and psychological consultants, we are becoming specialists instead of generalists, yet organizational conceptualization is moving more toward systemic and holistic thinking" (p. 6).

One problem created by professional specialization is a deviation in point of view. Elise Walton and David Nadler emphasize how differences in perspective can get in the way:

> Some consultants think the customers' interests must come first whereas others think the stockholders' interests come first, and, more important, those holding one perspective may know about the other and may discount ideas that emerge from that viewpoint as "biased." These would apply to diagnosis as well as interventions prescribed. To put it in industrial/organizational [I/O] psychologists' terms, some think rewards are important levers for change and others do not, some think change must follow a business imperative only and others do not, and so forth. We have created our own functional silos.

Harry Levinson views differences in perspective in terms of fundamental assumptions and beliefs:

> The greatest barrier to more integrated organizational diagnosis is the fact that different consultants make different assumptions about fundamentals of human motivation and behavior. If, for example, a consultant on salary structure doesn't understand the concept of ego ideal, Elliott Jaques's conceptions of cognitive capacity and mental processing, and the importance of unconscious motivation, that consultant and I will have a difficult time working together. A more common barrier is the lack of sufficient understanding of another consultant's area of expertise.

Warner Burke also considers silos of both perspective and knowledge as consequences of consultant specialization:

> Specialization means that consultants know a few things very well (e.g., compensation or training and development), but are not broadly based or sufficiently unbiased. Some push their own specific methods and forget everything else.

William Byham and Robert Rogers have similar concerns about the narrow focus of practitioners:

> The biggest barrier to integrated organizational diagnosis is in the mind of the practitioner. The consultant who is brought in to provide a service or product often tends to conduct a diagnosis only around that service or product rather than encouraging the client to "helicopter up" to consider the bigger picture before coming back down to the specific issues that need to be discussed.

Kimball Fisher adds that lack of common language and technique can make integrated diagnosis extremely difficult.

In summary, integrated organizational diagnosis faces practical obstacles such as time and expense, but these appear less intractable than the philosophical barriers. Kimball Fisher points to the mechanisms that act to keep these barriers in place:

> Reward and recognition systems in both business and academia make cooperative processes unattractive. Few consultants, internal or external, are willing to make the technical, administrative, marketing, and ego compromises to coordinate with a large group of diagnosticians and change agents.

PROFESSIONAL EXPERTISE

Given the problems it creates for integrated organizational diagnosis, professional specialization warrants further scrutiny. How much specialized expertise is required to diagnose and change various aspects of organizational functioning? Can one practitioner do it all?

Practitioners as Generalists

An argument can be made for generalist practitioners, but we must first define the term. Warner Burke makes the first cut:

> The operative term is *organizational*. We cannot claim expertise in diagnosing function problems, that is, in determining, for example, what is wrong with the company's marketing strategy, why the debt-to-equity ratio is out of whack, or what is wrong with a particular manufacturing process. The exception would, of course, be human resources.

What, then, does generalized organizational expertise include? In addition to the topics covered in this volume, Harry Levinson expects acquaintance with the psychology of economics, psychodynamics, professional ethics, decision making and cognitive complexity, succession planning and career management, and stages in organization development. Warner Burke offers the following sampler of the kinds of principles an organizational practitioner should understand:

- How an organization is a sociotechnical system and how strategy precedes structure.
- The folly of rewarding A when the organization wants B.
- The consequences of organizational change.
- What effective teamwork is and when teams are appropriate and when they are not.
- The importance of integration as well as differentiation.
- The importance of boss–subordinate relationships in the delivery of highly satisfactory customer service.
- When an issue implicates selection and placement rather than a lack of adequate training and development.
- That training and development are needed when people are being held accountable for responsibilities they are ill-equipped to perform.

Obviously, both kinds of lists could be quite extensive, which indicates the difficulty of becoming a generalist in organizational practice. William Byham and Robert Rogers support this view:

It takes a great deal of expertise to diagnose—much more than to prescribe or deliver. Diagnosis requires more understanding of the big picture, the various options available, and the interactions of different organizational systems, procedures, people, and so forth. One practitioner can do everything that is needed for a high-level diagnosis. But it might be quite appropriate to bring in additional specialists when the diagnosis gets down to specific areas, such as selection or training, or to subareas within those broader areas, such as assessment center methodology within selection methodology.

In contrast to intervention, diagnosis may require breadth more than depth of expertise. Says Warner Burke, "I believe strongly that the OD consultant and any I/O psychologist who works as an organizational consultant should first and foremost be a generalist when it comes to diagnosis." Douglas Bray also underlines that broad understanding is often important for diagnosis:

The personnel-centered approach would be demanding in terms of practitioner background and skills because it seeks to cover the waterfront. When it comes to interventions that might be stimulated by diagnosis, the story is different. Here specialization is required, whether that of personnel selection, training and development, or organization development.

Practitioners as Specialists

Although breadth aids diagnosis, it is still, in Warner Burke's words, "rare for one practitioner to be able to do it all." Edward Lawler agrees: "It is difficult for one practitioner to do a complicated organizational change process well. Not only is there an issue of required expertise, but there is an issue of finding a sounding board for ideas and issues and social support." Harry Levinson concurs:

> No practitioner can diagnose and change all aspects of an organization. A consultant needs to know what he or she doesn't know and therefore when to refer to others or to suggest to the client that other specialists should be consulted. For example, only yesterday I had to recommend to a client three consultants who could develop a compensation plan for executives.

He also raises ethical issues of trying to reach beyond one's area of expertise.

> One cannot be ethical without knowing the boundaries of one's knowledge, skill, and competence. Even if the practitioner has competence in more than one area, say, in both human resources and marketing, it is highly unlikely that he or she will have equal competence in the wide range of managerial issues that all organizations must deal with.

Ethical practice that also offers the broad coverage needed for a sound diagnosis implies supplementing one's skills with those of other practitioners. Elise Walton and David Nadler acknowledge increasing use of this approach:

> A fair amount of specialized expertise is required for our work, and we frequently find ourselves partnering with other firms that can provide specific expertise (e.g., market studies, financial assessments, in-depth survey capability). Particularly as change efforts get broader and more strategic, many different specialized skills are required.

In summary, the need for both generalized and specialized expertise makes divergent but complementary demands on different types of practitioners. In the world of I/O psychology, the "I" psychologists need to "helicopter up" (to borrow the phrase from Byham and Rogers) to the system level for a view of the forest while the "O" psychologists need to parachute down to examine the trees. Each group would benefit from reaching across the sky to the other.

Positioning Expertise in the Organization

Skills required for diagnosis and intervention may also vary depending on the level within the organization at which the consultation occurs. William Byham and Robert Rogers observe that "the skills required of diagnosticians at high levels of management are quite different from those required at lower levels. There is far less expert opinion required at higher levels and more facilitation—appropriately mixed with challenging people to really think through what they have decided." James Walker and Thomas Bechet believe this is because higher-level executives have an idea of what should be happening. "They have probably been through management training or had other exposure to organizational practitioners. Those at lower levels may never have worked with consultants before and need more content." Yet they admit that there may be a less flattering interpretation. "Senior executives look at three bullets, not the whole report. They put their trust in the consultant because they don't have time for the details."

Professional expertise may be positioned inside or outside organizational boundaries. There is accumulating evidence that the role of the internal consultant or human resources department is shifting. As one example, among members of the American Psychological Association's Division of Industrial and Organizational Psychology (the majority of SIOP members), the proportion who work in industry continues to decline, 24% in 1985 versus 19% in 1992, while those in the "other" category, primarily external consultants, shows a corresponding rise, 28% in 1985 versus 34% in 1993 (American Psychological Association, 1993; Howard, 1986).

James Walker and Thomas Bechet identify three emerging models of human resources practice: (1) internal practitioners perform routine administrative activities and consultants handle diagnosis and change efforts; (2) administrative activities are contracted out to service centers (e.g., compensation and benefits to financial departments) and internal practitioners handle many diagnosis and change efforts; and (3) both types of activities are contracted out, the hollow shell model. It is too early to determine if these waves of change will swell in one dominant course, and the model may vary by organizational size. But human resources activities do seem to be drifting away from corporate staffs and into business units, docking closer to internal customers.

Kimball Fisher warns that clients must not become detached from organizational diagnosis and change activities:

Specialized diagnostic and change expertise is certainly more helpful as organizations become increasingly complex. To the extent that practitioners use their expertise (intentionally or unintentionally) to make the client system dependent on the diagnostician, however, they do a great disservice to their customers. The only real expert in organizational diagnosis is the client. Even if one practitioner can't do it all (which is increasingly likely), a prime ethical directive for the practitioner team is to complete its work with the client system in such a way that the latter is better able to evaluate and maintain its own well-being.

Ronald Zemke adds this humbling thought about clients:

We're learning from reengineering, quality action teams, benchmarking task forces, self-directed teams, and the like, that our "expertise" isn't such a rare commodity. Good managers, focused on gaps—differences in desired and actual states of accomplishment—can do not only adequate but excellent diagnoses *and* intervention. It suggests to me that the advisor/support role we contemporarily hound managers to adopt may be a prescription we should consider for ourselves!

WORKING TOGETHER

We have concluded that diagnosis benefits from the breadth of a generalist but that few practitioners are able to execute grand change efforts alone. They typically need the assistance of specialists—for specialized diagnoses and for interventions. Achieving the goal of integrated diagnosis, then, entails collaboration, the subject of our last question. How can practitioners work together for more integrated organizational diagnosis?

Sharing and Learning

Given the extent of professional specialization, a first priority is to enhance knowledge and communication channels among practitioners. Elise Walton and David Nadler suggest that "practitioners themselves need to build a shared language system and a better way of dialoguing about diagnosis and intervention and that personal relationships (knowing your colleague well) seem to help integration." Similarly, Warner Burke advocates "being willing to listen to and learn from one another."

Harry Levinson suggests joint panels at professional meetings "to understand the range of each other's work and the areas in which we could complement each other." He recommends inviting specialists from outside of psychology to such conferences to further extend such learning. Kimball Fisher also notes the usefulness of sharing papers and presentations.

Students of industrial/organizational psychology, organizational behavior, human resources management, and related fields should also have the opportunity to learn integrated approaches. One model of a learning tool is the computerized simulation developed for teaching occupational psychology at Glasgow Caledonian University. Students adopt the role of an external consultant invited into a company for diagnosis and development of intervention plans. Using a hypercard navigation system, they can move through the organization and consult with personnel records, memos, transcripts of interviews, and the like, to help diagnose the organization's difficulties and dysfunctions (McQueen, Wrennall, & Tuohy, 1993).

Co-Consulting

A natural next step after sharing information is sharing consulting opportunities, or co-consulting. William Byham and Robert Rogers suggest a medical analogy:

> An appropriate model might be the internist-specialist, although the job requirements would be exactly the opposite in terms of difficulty. First, the organization gets a general examination dealing with critical success factors, vision, values, and so forth, which is then followed by more specific examinations by specialists.

Kimball Fisher suggests more direct sharing of responsibility.

> A major step toward integrated diagnosis is the sharing of practice and experience among diverse practitioners. This is best facilitated when people work together on real projects. Finding a way to demonstrate how the benefits of this integration are greater than the perceived personal and organizational costs would be useful.

There are various ways that integration can offer such benefits. Simply avoiding errors that derive from myopic views of organizational problems is one potential advantage. Keeping systems in reasonable alignment, so that the effects of one change don't negate another, is another advantage. In addition, consultants who work together, or at least have the benefit of studying each other's work, may be able to augment their own diagnoses. For example, Douglas Bray shows how two facets of his personnel-centered diagnosis—evaluation of incumbents and the job inventory—directly tie to organization culture and reward systems:

> One would want to know, for example, what values the organization espouses, what efforts have been made to inculcate these values in the incumbents, and what incumbent behaviors are desired as expressions

of these values before conducting the assessment process. In the individual assessment one would then seek to determine knowledge of these values, attitudes toward them, and their effect on incumbent behavior.

With respect to rewards, the job inventory would set forth all the facts about the financial rewards available to job incumbents, the salary plan, how increments are determined, the nature of commissions or bonuses and how team or division results are factored in, and so forth. Then in the assessment of incumbents, one would evaluate such things as their knowledge of these facts and their attitudes toward the plan and its administration, as well as how financial incentives affect their motivation and job behavior.

Edward Lawler offers another model for working together: "The kind of cross-functional teams that are often put together by large consulting firms are an example of how to work together to do a more integrated organizational diagnosis. I personally favor also involving individuals from within the organization in this kind of cross-functional diagnosis."

Just as change should be managed in an integrated way, so should the change agents. According to Beckhard and Pritchard (1992), many organizational leaders are, in fact, creating a process for managing organizational and management consultants. A liaison within the company may arrange consultants' meetings periodically to exchange ideas and interact with top management. For example, a change team at TRW Systems, composed of external consultants and internal human resource managers, was credited with generating considerable synergy, coordinating changes, and successfully coping with surprises.

An Assessment Center for Organizational Diagnosis

Integrated organizational diagnosis might be likened to an assessment center with the organization, not individuals, as the assessee. Various practitioners would serve as assessors and administer the exercises (their own techniques) to address the elements represented by the boxes in Figure 11.1. The assessors (practitioners) would meet at an integration session to pool the results of their exercises (diagnoses) and rate the organization on preestablished dimensions of individual and organizational performance. The organization's overall performance in the assessment center would be judged by how well it was achieving its critical success factors. Following the integration session, a feedback report and an integrated intervention plan could be based on the organization's diagnosed strengths and developmental needs.

Suppose, for example, that Translines, the transportation company introduced in Chapter 1, called upon all of the authors of this volume to deliver an integrated organizational diagnosis. We would meet first with the top executives to discuss the project and work together to pin down organizational strategy and critical success factors. Harry Levinson would launch his detective's investigation of various corners of the organization, paying particular attention to why the president was having so much difficulty setting a direction for the company and why the three vice presidents were unable to operate as a team. Warner Burke would collect data for the organizational variables (the various boxes) in the Burke–Litwin model and would develop a big-picture view of how the organization could be developed. Robert Rogers and William Byham would push the top executive group toward identifying a vision and values and deciding the extent to which they really were going to promote high involvement across the major divisions. The incongruencies and misalignments among the various organization systems would be identified. Elise Walton and David Nadler would discover the negative ramifications of the organization's centralized design and investigate new grouping and linking mechanisms.

Meanwhile, Edward Lawler would investigate the behaviors reinforced by Translines' reward system and consider better designs, and Kimball Fisher would identify barriers to the functioning of quality and safety teams. Ronald Zemke and Douglas Bray would take a look at problems in the performance not just of the area managers but of those who work with them and discern which problems could be best addressed by training or which by selection. Bray would also gather data from individual assessments on the impact of other organization systems, such as culture and rewards. James Walker and Thomas Bechet would incorporate the performance information into an investigation of systems to recruit, select, train, and decruit employees to meet the needs created by the staffing drivers that they would identify.

The assessors would meet in an integration session to evaluate the current situation in Translines and prepare an integrated diagnostic report. These integration sessions would continue at various stages of intervention. The company's progress would be measured periodically by rating its assessment dimensions, redefined to incorporate its new vision and values.

Is this scenario an unrealistic fantasy? Or does it herald the future? We hope we have convinced you that some kind of integrated organizational diagnosis is feasible and well worth pursuing. For now, just call it our vision of diagnosis for optimal organizational change.

REFERENCES

American Psychological Association. (1993). *Profile of Division 14 Members: 1993.* Prepared by the Office of Demographic, Employment, and Education Research, APA Education Directorate. Washington, DC: Author.

Beckhard, R., & Pritchard, W. (1992). *Changing the essence: The art of creating and leading fundamental change in organizations.* San Francisco: Jossey-Bass.

Burke, W. W. (1992, August). *The changing world of organization change.* Paper presented at the meeting of the American Psychological Association, Washington, DC.

Froiland, P. (1993, September). Reproducing star performers. *Training: The Human Side of Business,* pp. 33–37.

Howard, A. (1986, May). Characteristics of Society members. *The Industrial–Organizational Psychologist,* pp. 41–47.

Katz, D., & Kahn, R. L. (1980). Organizations as social systems. In E. E. Lawler III, D. A. Nadler, & C. Cammann (Eds.), *Organizational assessment: Perspectives on the measurement of organizational behavior and the quality of work life* (pp. 162–184). New York: Wiley.

McQueen, R. A., Wrennall, M. J., & Tuohy, A. P. (1993). *Occupational psychology and computer simulation.* Unpublished manuscript, Glasgow Caledonian University, Department of Psychology, Glasgow, Scotland.

Rummler, G. (1988). The 10 most important lessons I've learned about human performance systems. In G. Dixon (Ed.), *What works at work: Lessons from the masters* (pp. 5–9). Minneapolis, MN: Lakewood Books.

Index